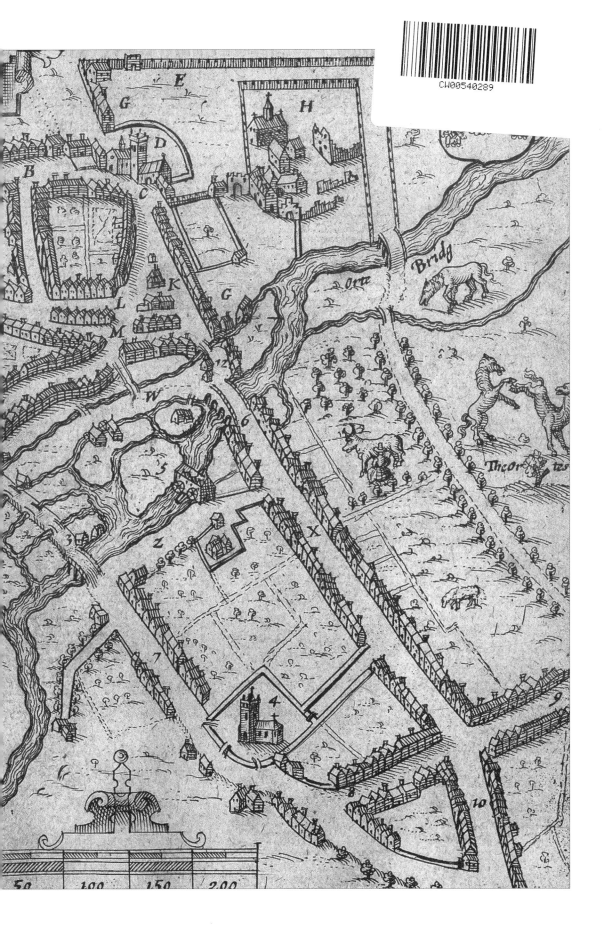

A HISTORY OF

READING

Balloons from the Royal Balloon Aero Club filling up with a highly inflammable cargo of gas at Reading gasworks in June 1906.

A HISTORY OF
READING

Stuart Hylton

Phillimore

2007

Published by
PHILLIMORE & CO. LTD
Chichester, West Sussex, England
www.phillimore.co.uk

© Stuart Hylton, 2007

ISBN 978-1-86077-458-4

Printed and bound in Great Britain

CONTENTS

List of Illustrations

ACKNOWLEDGEMENTS

When I wrote my first book about Reading, back in 1992, there was already a rich heritage of recorded history about the town, but relatively little of it still in print. I am indebted to the many people who, over the past thousand years or more, have documented the town's development and who have informed my work. These are listed in the bibliography. Much has appeared since then, and I hope my efforts here will encourage the reader to delve further into our town's past, and will be of some assistance to future historians. The local history section of Reading Central Library has been invaluable to me, both as a source of documentary history and for their fine collections of photographic and other visual history, which form the backbone of the illustrations to this book. I would like to put on record my gratitude for the kind support and expertise of David Cliffe and his colleagues. The conjectural picture of Reading Abbey is the copyright of Reading Museum Service and reproduced with their permission.

Errors and omissions are, of course, entirely my responsibility. I have tried to track down and seek the consent of any holders of copyright in the illustrations used in the book and have acknowledged them where possible. If any have slipped through the net, I would be grateful if you would contact me via the publisher, and I will try to ensure that any omissions are rectified in future editions.

INTRODUCTION

No town in the south of England hides its attractions more successfully from the visitor.

John Betjeman and John Piper (1949)

Betjeman was both rude about and fond of Reading. He described it as a much-maligned town, and one that at a superficial glance seemed hideous. He was right that the town hides its antiquity well. For the past two centuries and more, the pressures for growth and modernisation have swept away much of the evidence of the past that might have survived in a less dynamic environment. Many of the monuments to the town's history that do survive have been under threat – the abbey ruins and the abbey gateway, the old town hall, Prospect Park Mansion House and the structures of the Kennet and Avon Canal were all targets for demolition at one time or another. All the more important, therefore, that we celebrate and raise awareness of what survives, and remember those that did not, from their photographic and other records.

But, as Betjeman knew, there can be few towns of Reading's size that have such a long, rich and varied history, and that have played such a major role in the affairs of the nation. Twelve hundred years ago, King Alfred was fighting in the town for the control of his kingdom; one of the greatest religious institutions in the land dominated the life of the town for centuries, making it an international centre for pilgrimage and governance; Parliaments met here; kings and princes were regular visitors and were married and buried here; it has been sacked by Vikings and besieged in one of the key battles of the Civil War. Armies fought in the streets of the town in the so-called 'bloodless revolution' that overthrew King James II in 1688.

The modernisation process itself is an important part of that history. Reading's fortunes have been transformed by series of revolutions in transport, from waterways to stagecoaches, from railways to motor car and air travel, and the town serves as an illustration of the benefits – and the challenges – that these transformations have brought to the nation as a whole. Our history is also populated by an extraordinary range of characters – from St Thomas à Becket to one of the nation's most notorious murderesses; from notable martyrs and saints to the most controversial person ever to hold the post of Archbishop of Canterbury; from a man who effectively ran the country during the minority of the king, through one of our least competent Prime Ministers, to the inventor of modern photography. The town has also fostered businesses whose fame has spread worldwide – sometimes far beyond the normal reach of western civilisation itself.

When I wrote my first book about Reading, back in 1992, there was already a rich heritage of recorded history about the town, but relatively little of it still in print. I am indebted to the many people who, over the past thousand years or more, have documented the town's development and who have informed my work. These are listed in the bibliography. Much has appeared since then and I hope my efforts here will encourage the reader to delve further into our town's past. The local history section of Reading Central Library has been invaluable to me, both as a source of documentary history and for their fine collections of photographic and other visual history, which form the backbone of the illustrations to this book. I would like to put on record my gratitude for the kind support and expertise of David Cliffe and his colleagues.

Errors and omissions are, of course, entirely my responsibility. I have tried to track down and seek the consent of any holders of copyright in the illustrations used in the book and acknowledge them where appropriate. If any have slipped through the net, I would be grateful if you contact me via the publisher, and I will try to ensure that any omissions are rectified in future editions.

Chapter One

BEGINNINGS

Few towns are less prepossessing at first glance than Reading, seen from the windows of a Great Western train from London by that castellated gaol where Oscar Wilde languished. But few towns better repay exploration …

John Betjeman – English Counties (1948)

In the very beginning, the little river found its way to meet its bigger brother through the Sulham Gap, to the west of what we know as Tilehurst. But, somewhere in the mists of geological time, the freezing up of the springs between Theale and Pangbourne caused it to change its course. Turning east, it made for the Coley Gap, some four miles downstream. On its way it cut through a gravel terrace, where it broke into a number of shallow streams, across which a man could wade. Elsewhere along its banks, the ground was boggy and liable to flood, but the gravel terraces stood clear of flooding and their light soils were easy to work.

The lands around provided all the necessities of habitation. Cattle could graze in the water meadows, the higher ground would grow corn and pigs could root for food in the forests. There were reeds and timber for building and a constant supply of fresh water. There were also trade routes. The ford of the river stood on the crossing between an east-west route, linking what are now London and Bristol, and a north-south route between the Midlands and the South Coast.

Man has lived on these terraces for as long as he has had a settled existence and left traces of his occupation behind. With Paleolithic man it was his primitive stone tools, found not just between the Thames and Kennet but to the north, all over what is now Caversham; the Bronze and Iron-Ages left axe-heads, swords and spears. A horde of Bronze-Age axe-heads was found during the construction of a primary school in Emmer Green, and the largest Bronze Age settlement in the South of England, dating from around 1000 B.C., was unearthed during the building of the Reading Business Park in 1987. But the first group of settlers whose name we know were the Atrebates – a name which actually means 'settlers' or 'inhabitants'. They either originated from, or were closely related to, a tribe of the same name in what is modern-day France.

We know something about one of their leaders, a man called Commius. He was a Gaulish nobleman and a supporter of Julius Caesar, whom Caesar made

1 *Cattle grazing in the water meadows of the Thames. Although this picture dates from 1840, the view can have changed little since the earliest days of the town's settlement.*

the King of the French Atrebates. He was sent to England in 55 B.C. to win over his English counterparts, prior to Caesar's short-lived invasion of Britain that same year. His success may be judged from the fact that he was captured, and only released by Caesar's invading army. Three years later, Commius and Caesar fell out and Commius sided with Vercingetorix in his ill-fated rebellion against the Roman occupation of Gaul. After its defeat, Commius fled to England, this time successfully starting a new dynasty ruling over the English part of the Atrebates.

The territory of the Atrebates covered Berkshire, along with parts of Hampshire, Wiltshire and Surrey. It was centred on Calleva, about ten miles south of Reading, and our area near the Thames was their frontier, disputed with neighbouring tribes. After a period of hostility, the Atrebates made their peace with the Romans and their King Tincommius became one of the three client rulers for the Romans, defending their territory from neighbouring tribes. It was an appeal for help from the last of the Atrebatic kings, Verica, which provided the Roman Emperor Claudius with a pretext for invading Britain on a more permanent basis in AD 43.

The Romans adopted the Atrebates' settlement as their own, calling it Calleva Atrebatum (meaning 'the wooded place of the Atrebates'), or Silchester. It became a major town serving a wide area; by the third century AD its stone defences enclosed some 100 acres. A new series of Roman roads radiated out from it. They went to London, Bath, Winchester, Dorchester and Oxford, but none of them crossed the gravel terraces and went through Reading. A sizeable community remained in Silchester after the Romans left Britain in the fifth century, but the town did not flourish. Cunliffe's explanation for this is that the town, like the embryonic Reading itself, was in an area of conflict, first between the peoples of northern and southern Wessex, and then between Mercia and the West Saxons. Another possible reason was that the town was not on or near a river.

The first resident of Reading itself whose name we know is the man after whom the town is named. Reada, 'the red' – he was possibly red-haired – lived here some time around A.D. 600. His followers were known as the Readingas ('ingas' being Old English for 'descendants of'. In similar vein, their next door neighbours were the 'Sunningas' of Sonning). It is thought they came from what is today western Germany or the Low Countries. It was probably also around this time that Christianity was first brought to the area, after St Birinus set up his church at Dorchester-on-Thames in 634. Reading still found itself on the frontier between two kingdoms – Wessex and Mercia – and the area was fought over and controlled by both during the eighth century.

Come the ninth century and there were new threats to peace. Marauding Danes had overrun Mercia and East Anglia by the end of 869, and their two armies converged on Reading. One marched overland and the other sailed up the Thames, pillaging as it went. Their target was their most powerful remaining opposition – the kingdom of Wessex. At Reading, they occupied a former West Saxon fortress. The triangular site was naturally defended on two sides by the Thames and the Kennet, leaving them only to fortify the western side with earthworks. It is thought that the northern end of these might have been somewhere in the vicinity of where Caversham Bridge now stands. From there, the ditch would have run about 450 yards south to the Kennet. Cooper estimates that it would have needed a force of between 500 and 700 men to defend it, though Slade suggests the Danish army might have been much larger, numbering between three and five thousand.

Reading was an ideal centre of communications for them. The rivers gave them routes east, west and north. The ancient routes of the Icknield Way and the Ridgeway were within easy reach and, to the south-east, Roman roads penetrated right into the heartland of the kingdom of Wessex. Having established a base in the town in 871, part of the Danish force went out foraging. About six miles away, at Englefield, they met a West Saxon force led by Aethelwulf, who is thought to have led an earlier defeat of the Danes following the sack of Winchester. The Danes were driven back to their fortified position in Reading, and a larger Saxon army advanced on them from the west, led by their king, Ethelred, and his younger brother, Alfred. Local folklore has it that, as Alfred advanced up what is now the Bath road, he met and defeated a Danish force, leaving its leader hanging from a tree. Dark Lane in Tilehurst was once known as Dead Man's Lane, and was said to have been the scene of this deed. The Saxons were expecting a long siege but, as they were setting up camp, the Danes staged a ferocious counter-attack, driving the Saxons back in the general direction of Oxford (according to weapons dating from this time found in the Pangbourne area). Later in 871, the two sides met again at the Battle of Ashdown. This time

2   King Alfred, shown here on a statue in Wantage, fought a battle against invading Danes at Reading in AD 871.

the Saxons were victorious, but at the cost of their king, who was slain in the battle. Alfred succeeded him as King of Wessex. The Danes remained in Reading until the late summer or early autumn of 872, when they moved to new winter quarters in London. Further Danish raids on Reading took place in 1006, and by 1017 the entire nation was under the rule of a Danish king, Cnut. Reading passed into the hands of King Cnut's standard bearer, a man called Tovi the Proud. Shortly after that, the town was important enough to have its own mint, producing coins between 1044 and 1048.

The Origins of the Modern Town

St Mary's Church can lay claim to more than a thousand years of continuous use as a religious institution, and is a good place to begin looking for the earliest origins of the town we know today. It is a minster church, one that oversaw several smaller foundations covering a wide area, and would have been a magnet to the nearby population, drawing them in to live around it for both trade and protection. The survival of the name of nearby Minster Street from the earliest days of the town's history gives a strong indication that the original minster church was on or near the site of the present St Mary's, and its origins are generally held to lie in a 10th-century royal murder.

Queen Aelfthryth (the Latinised version of her name, Elfrida, is often used instead) was the second wife of King Edgar, the first man to be crowned king of all England. When he died in 975, he was succeeded by Edward, his 15-year-old son from his first marriage. His widow had a natural son, Aethelred, from their marriage and coveted the throne for him. Edward was invited to be Aelfthryth's guest at Corfe Castle in 978. While he was there, she had him stabbed to death and buried him in a hurried and distinctly unregal manner at Wareham in Dorset. His body was later reinterred with due ceremony at Shaftesbury Abbey, and he was known thereafter as Edward the Martyr. Aethelred is the king popularly referred to as 'the Unready', though the original term, 'unroed', translates more accurately as 'ill-advised'.

3   *St Mary's Church, seen here prior to its 1860s restoration, has seen more than a thousand years of worship on this site.*

Aelfthryth's part in the crime was discovered and, as part of her punishment, she was required to build a nunnery. It was thought to have been on the site of what is now St Mary's Church. It is also thought to have been largely destroyed in the Danish raids in 1006. If so it may have been restored, since we know that Leveva, the Abbess of Shaftesbury, possessed the church and lands at Reading at the time of Edward the Confessor (1042-1066). However, it was certainly defunct by the time William the Conqueror granted the church at Reading to Battle Abbey. No trace of it remains today, though there was speculation that some ancient brickwork, found in the cellars when the old vicarage was demolished in the 1960s, may have been from it.

There are three other intriguing pieces of speculation about these early years. The first is that traces of an earlier building were found beneath the foundations of Reading Abbey itself. Could this have been the nunnery? Or was it perhaps a church serving a different part of Reading, which was displaced by the coming of the abbey, and for which the present St Laurence's was a replacement? The second is an alternative hypothesis for the origins of St Mary's itself, which would make it even older. Asser, the biographer of King Alfred, speaks of a royal residence at Reading. Normally there would have been a church attached to such a building, and this early settlement is thought to have been in the vicinity of modern St Mary's (ninth-century Saxon silver coins have been found in the graveyard). Could this have been the true origin of St Mary's, and could Aelfthryth's nunnery simply have been attached to it? If so, given that Alfred ruled from A.D. 871–99 and Asser himself died in A.D. 908, this could put the date of St Mary's foundation back a further hundred years before the commonly accepted one of 979. The third concerns the possibility of there having been a Reading Abbey before the one founded in 1121. The abbey's foundation charter, dating from 1125, makes an obscure reference to an earlier Reading Abbey, which had been 'destroyed for their sins, their possessions alienated and their lands seized upon by laymen'. Was this a reference to Aelfthryth's building, or to some other institution entirely?

St Mary's would emerge from under the shadow of the abbey's dominance of the town with the dissolution of the monasteries in 1539 and was extensively restored, using materials salvaged from the abbey, during 1551 to 1555. We know the Elizabethan building had a steeple, because in 1593 or 1594 it blew down during an exceptional storm. Early photographic evidence of it exists from the 1840s, thanks to pioneer photographer Fox-Talbot's period of residence in the town. This shows it as it was, prior to its restorations of 1863 and 1872.

Central Reading's other major church, St Laurence's, has origins that potentially go back almost as far as those of St Mary's. (Laurence can also be found spelt Lawrence. I have standardised on the version that appears outside the modern church.) It is possible that a church existed on or near the site of the present St Laurence's before Reading Abbey was even built. One reason for believing this was that, up until 1557, St Laurence's did not have a churchyard attached to it. Instead, their parishioners were buried in a former Saxon churchyard to the north of the abbey church, within the abbey precincts. It seems unlikely that they would have been given permission to do so after the abbey had been founded, suggesting that the right may have existed for a church that predated the abbey.

4   *St Laurence's Church was first built at about the same time as Reading Abbey, in the 12th century, though much altered over the following centuries.*

The current St Laurence's was probably first built at about the same time as the abbey, and parts of the original Norman church (such as a small round-headed window high in the south wall) remain. It was enlarged to its present size in 1196 by Abbot Hugh II, at about the same time as the hospitium of the abbey was being built nearby. The north aisle, St John's Chapel and the arcade between the chapel and the chancel date from about 1210 and the tower in its present form is from 1458. The story goes that the architect of St Laurence's was an apprentice of the man who designed St Mary's Church. When he saw that his apprentice's work was much superior to his own, the architect of St Mary's is said to have thrown himself from his own church tower.

At one time, one of the gateways into the abbey was attached to the south wall of the church. Above this were three small rooms, known as the Compter, which were originally used for the incarceration of monks convicted of ecclesiastical offences. After the dissolution of the abbey, it was used for debtors and other lay prisoners until its demolition around the start of the 19th century. At the eastern end of the southern wall once stood another cell. This one was known as 'the Hole', and was used as an overnight lock-up for prisoners. Its alternative name, 'the Churchwarden's Pew', commemorates a drunken and disorderly 18th-century church official, who spent a night in there. Another of its architectural features for many years, the Blagrave Piazza, is discussed in chapter four.

Life in Saxon Reading

What might life in the Saxon town of Reading have been like? As we have seen, according to Asser there was a 'royal vill' somewhere in or near the town, which was at that time centred around the area occupied today by St Mary's Butts. On the basis of a similar one, excavated at Cheddar, the centrepiece of the vill is likely to have been a great hall, measuring some 80ft by 20ft, with a thatched or shingled roof, supported on timber pillars and surrounded by a range of other buildings and a palisade. The ordinary people – numbering no more than 100 or 150, or less after the plague had visited them – would have lived in huts, measuring about 20 feet by 15ft. The town would have had a timber church and at least one mill. They would have grown barley, for bread and for brewing unhopped beer, kept small black cattle, semi-wild pigs and sheep that provided both wool and milk. This diet would have been supplemented by anything that hunting or fishing could provide. Less than half the children would have survived to their teens and anyone aged over 50 counted as old. Most of them would have been free men or 'ceorls' but there would have been a number who were slaves (often criminals, debtors or prisoners of war).

> Life would seem to us to have been nasty, brutish and short, with a monotonous diet, periodic food shortages, primitive medical care, scratchy clothing (which was normally also rather dirty and flea-infested) and great dependence on the weather. Houses were built of wood or wattle and daub,

5 *St Mary's Butts was the centre of the town prior to the building of the abbey. The market was held here and medieval archers honed their skills in the street for Agincourt and other great battles. This view from the north, dated 1886, shows the additional housing that stood in the street at that time.*

with thatched roofs and earth floors. They would have had just one main room and perhaps some subsidiary accommodations for animals.

Cecil Slade in *Petyt*

Some of Reading's place names that survive to this day may also give us clues to the early life of the town. The name 'Portmanbrook' was given to the fields to the north-west of the medieval town, which the burgesses later rented from the abbot, a name that continues today in Portman Road. The name suggests that the Anglo-Saxon town was a significant trading centre, or 'port', and that some of its inhabitants were therefore 'portmen', a distinct step up from the average peasant. The area on the south bank of the Thames near the eventual site of Caversham Bridge was known as the Vastern (as in Vastern Road – from the Old English 'foest-oern', or fortified house). As we saw, it is thought that this might have been the northern end of the Danish fortifications in 870. In support of this the graves of a man and a horse were found in this area, the man carrying a ninth century Viking sword, during the construction of the Great Western Railway in 1840.

Castle Street and Castle Hill are more of a mystery. The name Castle Street is found as early as about 1250, but no trace of any castle remains and no-one even knows where it stood. Some time around 1150 King Stephen is thought to have erected a castle somewhere within the precincts of the abbey, during the war with his cousin Matilda following Henry I's death. But, by 1152, he had surrendered it to Henry, Duke of Normandy, who immediately had it destroyed. Its exact location is not known today, though one suggestion is that the mound in the Forbury Gardens – generally thought of as originating from the Civil War – could be connected with it. In any event, modern Castle Street is some distance from the abbey precincts, suggesting that the one might not be a reference to the other. An alternative site for the castle might have been at the west end of Castle Street, on the high land overlooking the town.

Reading in Domesday Book

In 1086, William the Conqueror commissioned a survey of England to establish the wealth of his new kingdom. His main interests were in the size of his own holdings and those of his vassal barons, who held their estates on condition of their allegiance to the king. The term 'burgus', used to describe Reading in Domesday Book, does not necessarily mean that it was a borough in the Anglo-Saxon sense of a fortified town. It may simply mean that Reading was an important town, though not necessarily fortified. It was by this time owned by the King, as it had previously been by King Edward. It had a total of 59 plots listed, sufficient for 40 plough teams, though 56 teams were recorded as living there. There were 55 villeins (peasants in a state of serfdom – obliged to work for a lord and being generally subject to his control over their lives) and 30 bordars (an even lower class of peasant, ranking just above slaves). Battle Abbey at this time held extensive lands and property, granted to them by William himself: 29 dwellings on the western side of the town, yielding a total rent of £1 8s. 8d. per year; 12 acres of meadows; woodland sufficient to feed five pigs; two mills and two-and-a-half fisheries. An unnamed church (presumably St Mary's) stood somewhere within their land-holding and paid Battle Abbey a sum of £3 a year. The Battle Abbey lands were recovered by means of a property swap in 1122, to enable the King to present them in turn to the newly established Reading Abbey.

The other main estate in Reading not in the King's hands in 1086 was that of Henry de Ferrers, whose descendants would become the earls of Derby and who was already one of the country's biggest landowners, with estates in 15 counties. It consisted of several acres of land and two houses, including the largest one in the town, in which de Ferrers used to entertain important visitors. These estates had previously been held by an Englishman called Godric, who had been the old king's representative in Berkshire but who died at the Battle of Hastings. This estate also came back into royal ownership, in 1156–7.

Estates that would form part of the modern built-up area of Reading at that time lay well outside the town's boundaries. Another Englishman named Brictward had previously held estates at Calcot (which had passed to the Count of Evreux) and Southcote (now owned by Walter de Braose). Much of Caversham was held by an important Norman figure, Walter Giffard, and another Giffard, Osbern, had an estate at Herlei (Earley). Inglefelle (modern Englefield) was owned by William, son of Ansculf, while Henry de Ferrers had land in Borgefelle (Burghfield) and Roger, son of Seifrid, held an estate at Purley.

Chapter Two

'For the salvation of my soul': Reading Abbey

The salvation of my soul, and of King William my father, and of King William my brother, and of William my son, and Queen Matilda my mother, and Queen Matilda my wife, and of all my ancestors and successors.

(The object of the abbey, as set out by Henry I in the charter of 1125)

To understand life in the medieval town of Reading, we need to look first at the great institution that sprang up in its midst and which was to dominate the life of the town for centuries – Reading Abbey.

Henry I endowed Reading Abbey shortly after the death of his son in the White Ship disaster off the Normandy coast in 1120. Henry himself laid the foundation stone in 1121. The choice of Reading as its site may be down to a number of factors. The King owned extensive lands there; it was on some important trade routes and it was conveniently located in relation to the royal residences in both London and Windsor – an important consideration for a royal household that was almost permanently on the move and that would have looked to the abbey for hospitality from its earliest days.

Within two years, building work was far enough advanced for them to appoint the first abbot. Their choice was Hugh de Bores, a descendant of the Counts of Amiens. He was regarded as one of the leading theologians of his day and was previously Prior of St Pancras in Lewes, the headquarters of the Cluniac order in England. Many of the monks who founded Reading Abbey came from St Pancras's parent church, the great Benedictine Abbey at Cluny, near Macon in France. It was founded by St Benedict in the sixth century and at its zenith was one of the most important centres of the Christian world. De Bores's reputation attracted many novices and in Rouen, on 29 March 1125, the King signed the foundation charter for the abbey.

The abbey was founded for the salvation of King Henry's soul, and prayers for it could begin in earnest after 1135. He died that year in France and his body was sewn into a bull's hide for the journey back to Reading, where it was interred in front of the high altar. He has been regularly 'disinterred' ever since. In 1819, a stone sarcophagus found in the abbey was claimed to be his, and generations of treasure hunters have searched for the silver coffin in which he was alleged

6 *Modern speculation about what Reading Abbey might have looked like, just prior to its dissolution.* *(Copyright Reading Museum Service (Reading Borough Council). All rights reserved.)*

to have been buried. Also buried there were his widow from a second marriage, Adela, William, a young son of Henry II and Reginald, one of Henry I's sons.

Set in the midst of the primitive settlement that was 12th-century Reading, the abbey was a massive undertaking that must have left the local people open-mouthed in wonder. Longer than Westminster Abbey or Winchester Cathedral and with a floor area of 35,400 square feet, it was built in a late Norman style; large Norman churches such as Durham or Gloucester are the nearest surviving examples of its likely architectural style. Its royal patrons spared no expense on its lavish decoration and ornament. Among the gifts that the King presented to them was: '… a special shrine, weighing 20 pounds 9 ounces and adorned with sapphires, rubies, pearls and other precious stones … [it] probably enclosed the most prized of all relics, the reputed hand of St James …' (Hurry).

St James was martyred in about A.D. 44, and his hand was said to have been cut off, along with his head. The rest of him is preserved in the Church of Santiago de Compostella. According to Harper the hand had come to England in 1125 courtesy of King Henry's daughter, Matilda, who was by then the widow of King Henry IV of Germany. He further tells us that, many centuries later, while digging the foundations of the new gaol in the ruined abbey precincts in 1786, a boxed and embalmed hand was unearthed. It was presented to a local museum, where it was exhibited as the former property of the saint until 1855, when it was sold for £30 to a Mr Lewis Mackenzie, who took it to Scotland. The hand eventually found its way into the safe–keeping of the Roman Catholic church in Marlow. An alternative hypothesis from Guilding is that the 'actual' hand of James was taken by the authorities at the dissolution of the abbey, and that what they dug up was the hand of Queen Adela of Louvain, the second wife of Henry I (though why her hand might have been preserved in this unusual manner is not clear).

The immense undertaking of the abbey took centuries to complete. The great church itself was consecrated by Thomas à Becket on 19 April 1164, in the presence of Henry II, just six years before Becket perished at Canterbury at the hands of Henry's knights. At about this time, another royal knight actually became a monk at the abbey, under rather unusual circumstances. Henry de Essex had been accused by Robert de Montfort of cowardice and treachery during a battle in Wales, and it was ruled by the King that a judicial trial by combat between them would be used to settle the matter. This was to take place on an island in the Thames at Reading in 1163, under the supervision of the King himself. During the course of the combat, Essex received what was thought to be a fatal wound, and was thus judged to have lost and to be guilty. He forfeited all his estates and was outlawed for what was thought to be the very short period he had left to live. Monks from the abbey carried Essex back there to prepare him for burial, but he made a miraculous recovery and lived the rest of his days within the confines of the abbey. De Montfort had the island on which they fought named after him.

Life in the Abbey

Life for these early monks was austere. They were roused at three o' clock in the morning to attend the first of the day's eight church services, some of which could last up to two hours in the unheated church. As we have seen, an important part of these was to pray for the souls of their founder and his family. In between the services, some of the monks engaged in private prayer, reading and meditation. Others worked in the abbey gardens, or had jobs that contributed in some other way to the upkeep of the community. However, the abbey also employed at least as many servants as it had monks – everything from lawyers and accountants, through building craftsmen, to people to cook and do the laundry.

There were also artistic and literary pursuits. Books were laboriously copied in the days before printing, and music was composed there. One of those pieces – *summer is icumen in* – holds an important place in the development of music. The piece, also known as *The Reading Rota* or *Round*, was thought to have been written between 1280 and 1310 by John of Fornsete, the Keeper of Records at the abbey, but is described by the *Oxford Companion to Music* as having a complexity that was not paralleled elsewhere until the 15th century.

Singing aside, much of the monks' lives was spent in silence – their two meals a day were punctuated only by one of their number reading from the scriptures. Before them would be a plate containing mostly bread and vegetables, sometimes augmented by eggs, cheese, oysters, fish or poultry. No red meat was eaten, but they were allowed beer and wine. The monks, often recruited in their teens, had no possessions other than the few items the abbey gave them, and lived a life of poverty, chastity and obedience.

But the church was only part of the story. It sat at the centre of an entire community that, by the time of its dissolution, extended to some 30 acres, half as big as the town itself. The boundaries of the abbey lands are marked today by Forbury Road, Kings Road, Blagrave Street and the railway. It included a mill, a bakehouse, stables, an infirmary and its own graveyard. But hospitality and charitable works were central to the purpose of the abbey. Part of its foundation charter provided that: 'Whoever shall … be made Abbot, let him not misuse or bestow the alms of the monastery on his lay kindred, or on other persons, but use them for the entertainment of the poor, of pilgrims and of guests'.

Two of the first buildings to be built as part of the abbey were therefore a leper house and a hospitium. The leper house was dedicated to St Mary Magdalene and opened in 1134. It housed not only lepers but also sufferers from cancer and a variety of skin diseases. Whilst being cared for, the inmates were also ostracised – made to wear special uniforms, and to carry a clapper with which to warn others of their approach. They were forbidden to enter the church, mill or bakehouse, or to dine with the unafflicted.

The abbey had one, or possibly two, sources of water supply. One was the Holy Brook, which ran through the site, powering the abbey mill and flushing their lavatories (*domus necessariae*). The other (a rather more speculative one) was a supply said to have been brought in by lead pipes from a spring in Whitley, in a pasture at the end of Silver Street, known as the 'Conduyte Close'. This latter supply of water was claimed to have some sort of miraculous healing qualities (which would no doubt have helped with its sale to gullible pilgrims).

One of the secular activities authorised under the terms of the foundation charter was education, and it has been suggested that the year of the abbey's foundation also marked the origins of Reading School. Were this so, it would make the school the 10th oldest in England, but evidence of early schooling activity in the abbey is sketchy. A member of the King's household, one Radulfo de Gorges, was said to have been sent there for his education in 1246, and the abbey accounts for 1345–6 show a payment of the modest sum of 3s. 4d. to a schoolmaster. Neither is evidence of a flourishing, continuous educational institution.

Reading's place in the communications of the nation, and the abbey's prominence in its spiritual life, meant that the abbey attracted many visitors. A hospitium, or guest house, was provided as part of the original buildings, but it was soon overwhelmed by the volume of guests. A new and larger hospitium, dedicated to St John, was commissioned between 1189 and 1193. It included an almshouse, a refectory and a dormitory. The almshouse provided accommodation for 26 poor men and women of Reading, and to give an indication of the scale of hospitality provided by the abbey, the refectory or dining area measured some 40 metres by between six and nine metres, and the dormitory was over sixty metres long – only part of the last of these survives. Guests were allowed to stay for a maximum of two days and nights. Its running was entrusted to the 13 sisters 'such as had been the wives of Persons who had borne some office in the town' (which presumably means the widows of burgesses). The hospitium

7 Part of the abbey's hospitium survives to this day, albeit much restored. It is pictured here c.1899.

was rebuilt again in about 1438 but, soon after (in about 1445), the almshouse for poor sisters was closed and the hospitium itself was closed down by 1480, its finances siphoned off by the abbey. Local people complained to Edward IV during a visit to the town in 1481 that: 'The charitable work of the hospitium for the poor and sick had ceased and that th'abbott take the profytt therof, and doth no such almes nor good deeds ther with'. (Hurry)

Among the many other complaints made to the King was that there was also apparently no sign of a grammar school that Abbot Thorne had promised to provide for the town. It was not until 1485 that the abbot finally set this up, receiving an endowment of rents worth £10 a year from Henry VII. This offers an alternative foundation date for Reading School, but this, too, appears to be backed up by scant documentary evidence.

The building work continued over the years. An inner gateway to the abbey was added in about 1250; work on an eastern 'Lady Chapel' started in 1314 and St Laurence's Church was much altered in 1438. There were also building initiatives within the town itself. In 1476–7, a man variously known as John Leech, John Leche and John a Larder (the latter from his post as the larderer in the abbey kitchen, maintaining stocks of food for the community and their guests) was responsible for building almshouses for eight poor people in front of the church in St Mary's Butts.

The Abbey in its Wider Context

The abbot was much more than just a churchman. He was a peer in the House of Lords and was closely involved in the affairs of state as an advisor to the King. Between about 1127 and 1345, the abbey even had the right to mint its own money. The abbey was fabulously wealthy by the standards of the day, holding a long list of benefices. In (the old) Berkshire alone, they owned Beenham, Bucklebury, Cholsey, Englefield, Pangbourne, the three Reading parishes, Sulhampstead, Thatcham, Tilehurst, Warfield and Wargrave, along with numerous manors and other property, some as far away as Warwickshire. The abbot himself had the use of a country house at Bere Court near Pangbourne and a deer park at Whitley.

The abbey received not just land, but also many powers and rights: freedom from performing service to others; unhindered passage for all its representatives throughout the land; freedom from tolls and the power to run local courts in the Yield Hall, with all the powers previously available to the King (though in practice the King retained some checks and balances over the legal powers exercised by the abbot). The abbot also ran the town gaol and appointed bailiffs from among members of the guild to maintain law and order, as well as appointing the warden or head of the guild itself.

The abbey gave Reading an important place in the governance of the nation. Henry II met there with the patriarch of Jerusalem in 1185, and in 1240 the nation's prelates and peers of the realm assembled to discuss demands being made by the Pope; Parliament met there in 1263 and 1453 and in 1264 a Council of Bishops was held in Reading. John of Gaunt, the third son of Edward III, celebrated his marriage in the abbey in 1359 and Edward IV himself announced his secret marriage there in 1464. His bride was an English woman, Elizabeth Woodville, rather than the French princess he was supposed to marry for reasons of international diplomacy.

By the time of its dissolution, Reading was the sixth wealthiest monastic establishment in England. However, the finances had not always been in such good condition. In 1275, King Edward I had taken over the running of the abbey's finances himself, since they were loaded with debts. Things went from bad to worse in 1290, when two men named Jonas de Newbury and Isaac de Pulet counterfeited the seal of the Abbot in an attempt to defraud the abbey of large sums of money. The pair of them ended up in the Tower of London. By 1305, the abbey's debts had reached the substantial sum for the day of £1,227 7s. 8d.

Reading, with both its abbey and its friary (discussed later), became an ecclesiastical centre of nationwide note. In the mid-12th century the town had no equal in England as a place of pilgrimage. Pilgrimage was a mixture of religious devotion and holiday and the pilgrims themselves were a mixed bunch. Most welcome were the great and the good, who would be able to pay for hospitality in the abbey and who would farm their retinues out to accommodation in the town. Then there were professional pilgrims, who travelled from shrine to shrine. Some, called the palmers, had travelled as far as Jerusalem. A more mixed blessing were the poor and needy, who came seeking the abbey's charity, and the sick, who came in hope of a miraculous cure. The abbey boasted enough relics of saints for the abbot to assemble his very own composite version. Among more than two hundred relics were the aforementioned hand of St James, bones of Mary Magdalene, St Stephen and St Andrew, the skull of St Philip and a fragment of that of St Ursula, one of St Luke's teeth, blood and part of the skull of St Thomas à Becket, the jawbone of St Ethelwold, some hair and a belt from the Virgin Mary, not to mention pieces of the true cross, part of the rods of Moses and Aaron and manna from Mount Sinai. Small wonder that a string of more than thirty miracles began to be reported by the visitors. A woman called Ysembela had the withered left side of her body restored and a blind man called Gilbert wept tears of blood as his sight was restored. In another reported case:

> William, a small boy born in Reading with wizened legs 'no thicker than a human thumb' was carried into the Abbey church one Christmas Eve. Lying prostrate before the altar of St James 'the withered and shrunken sinews began to slacken and become moist, and his bones began to grow and harden'. Within twenty-four hours his lameness had gone.
>
> (Rixon)

A visit to Reading Abbey could also earn the pious pilgrim an indulgence (a reduction of the time to be spent after death in purgatory as a punishment for sin) of up to 386 days for visiting St James's hand on his saint's day, and souvenirs of one's pilgrimage to Reading, such as an ampulla of holy water, could also be bought. The scallop shell, which is generally associated with both pilgrimage and St James, appears on the abbey's coat of arms and no doubt also featured on many of the objects the visitors took home with them.

The Abbey and Town

A serious riot broke out in the town in 1253, possibly in reaction to the abbey trying to increase local taxes in an attempt to reduce its debts. Whatever the cause, the guild was summoned to appear before the King and explain: 'Why, armed, they repelled the abbot's bailiffs in Reading … and why by day and night in the said town they have lain in wait for the abbot's bailiffs and servants and preventing them from carrying out their functions'. (Slade)

The guild argued, but was unable to prove, that they were simply trying to uphold rights granted to them by Edward the Confessor before the existence of the abbey. The King therefore sent in the Sheriff of Berkshire to ensure that the abbey officials were allowed to carry out their duties. However, the following year, the King sided with the guild against the abbot, ordering that he must not try to move the market from its traditional site in St Mary's Butts, or demand services beyond those the guild previously had to perform for the King, or to force them to attend a court other than the one in the Yield Hall, or to deprive the guild of its possessions. He also 'granted' the guild (albeit at a cost of £100) the right to buy and sell throughout England without being liable for tolls or other taxes.

The following year a more comprehensive settlement of the relations between the town and the abbey was reached at the King's Court in Westminster. This was known as the final concord and provided, among other things, that the corn market would not be moved, and that the guild retained its rights forever, along with its Yield Hall and various properties and land it held. The abbot also benefited in a variety of ways; the land he rented to the guild – the Portmanbrook – had its rent increased from an old penny to half a mark (6s. 8d.); he got to keep all the fines levied at the local court, and chepyngavel, the trading tax the guild members paid to the abbey, was also increased. The abbot's right to appoint a warden to head the guild was confirmed and the warden was required to swear an oath of allegiance, not just to the guild, but also to the abbot. Much of this was no more than the formalisation of long-established practice, but it governed relations between town and abbey for many years to come.

For much of their 400-year relationship, town and abbey managed to resolve their differences through diplomacy, and the times when the monarch had to intervene tended to be the exception rather than the rule. Another exception was in 1481, when the guild took the opportunity of Edward IV passing through the town to present him with a long list of grievances about the abbot's various derelictions of duty. In addition to the school problem, mentioned earlier, these included the state of Caversham Bridge, High Bridge and others in the town, St Edmund's Chapel (where there had been complaints about the lack of a chaplain as long ago as 1376, and which had now been converted into a barn), problems with the Chapel of the Holy Ghost on Caversham Bridge, St James's almshouses at the western end of the abbey being closed since 1465, and the leper hospital of St Mary Magdalen having been demolished and its income appropriated by the abbot – not to mention the closure of the hospitium, also discussed earlier. The King delegated responsibility for sorting out this can of worms to Richard Beauchamp, the Archbishop of Salisbury, who died before getting to the bottom of it. It was left to a new king, Henry VII, to grant the town an important new charter in 1487, which bypassed some of the abbot's traditional controls over trade and gave new rights to the guild. Further disputes followed in the 1490s, when the failure of the abbot to appoint a warden of the guild led to them appointing their own and rejecting the abbot's choice of constables.

Even more protracted was the argument between guild and abbey over the 'foreign' (i.e. non-Reading) butchers who used stalls in the out-butchery in Broad Street. The guild had become accustomed to taking their rents until Abbot Thomas Henley decided they rightfully belonged to the abbey. Years of dispute and litigation followed, culminating in a judgement in favour of the abbot in 1452.

In at least one case, the monarch himself was responsible for a dispute. Henry VI, during a visit to Reading some time before 1458, granted the warden of the guild the right to have a mace borne before him, always providing: 'That it be not prejudiciall unto oure church and monasterie of Redyng'. (Slade)

The guild duly invested the grand sum of 16½ pence in having a mace made, but the abbot clearly thought that this would be prejudicial to his status in the town, and made furious complaints to the King. These led to the King decreeing that the mayor had used the mace 'otherwise than was or is according to our entent'. The mayor lost his mace and, for good measure, also had his right to call himself 'mayor' removed for the next thirty years or so.

Dissolution

The abbey evidently enjoyed a degree of self-government, electing their own abbot, subject to his ratification by the monarch. In 1305, for example, 65 monks took part in the election, though two were disqualified – one on the grounds that he had been excommunicated, and the other because he was 'an idiot'. The last one to be elected, in 1520, was Hugh Cook, though he took his chosen surname from the place where he was born, Faringdon. He had no difficulty securing the ratification of the monarch to his appointment, and he and Henry VIII became good friends.

However, the tempting financial prize that the monasteries represented and the King's continuing attacks on the church establishment left them deeply vulnerable. Henry was not the first monarch to pursue their wealth. Edward I for one had confiscated money from the abbey in 1295. Henry commissioned the *Valor ecclesiasticus* of 1535, a form of judgemental Domesday Book, identifying the wealth of the monasteries, which concluded that: 'With honourable exceptions, most of them have waxed fat and lazy on the offerings of the credulous as they gaped on winking images, rotten animal bones and filthy rags exhibited as holy relics of the saints, and enough pieces of the true cross to build a galleon'.

In 1536, all monasteries with an income of less than £200 a year were suppressed. The larger institutions followed in the period to 1539. In most cases, evidence of scandal and corruption could be conveniently proven (or manufactured) against them, as a pretext for the dissolution, but such evidence was apparently harder to come by in the case of Reading.

Hugh Faringdon's execution was thus an act of judicial murder, born more out of the King's financial necessities than any wrongdoing on Faringdon's part. An act of treason needed to be proven against him to enable Henry to close the abbey and seize its considerable wealth, but Faringdon, as a mitred bishop, had a right to be tried before Parliament. There was doubt as to whether Henry would secure his conviction by legitimate means. So Thomas Cromwell seized upon Faringdon's difficulty with the idea of having the King as spiritual head of the church (despite his having supported the King in all the measures needed to secure his divorce), and imprisoned him under the 1534 Treasons Act. He then overrode the legal processes and issued written instructions to his kangaroo court that left them in no doubt as to the expected outcome. 'The Abbot of Reading to be sent down to be tried and executed at Reading with his accomplices … counsellors to give evidence against the Abbot of Reading … See that the evidence be well sorted and the indictments well drawn.'

Just in case there was any possibility that the hearsay evidence against him would be challenged, Faringdon was not allowed to offer any defence.

So, on 14 November 1539, Faringdon died a barbarous traitor's death in the Forbury; dragged through the streets on a hurdle, part-hanged, mutilated and his limbs torn asunder and flung into a cauldron of boiling pitch. With him

8 *Martyrdom of Julines Palmer, Master of Reading School, at Newbury in 1555.*

died John Enyon, the priest to St Giles, and John Rugg, a monk from the abbey. Faringdon's worst crime was said to be that: 'He wolde pray for the Pope's holynes as long as he lived and wolde ons a weke say masse for hym.' (Victoria History)

Faringdon was eventually canonised as a saint in 1895. But, well before even his execution, the abbey had already been suppressed and many of its treasures legally looted by the King's servants. As for the monks who had lived there, some of the older ones were given pensions, but the majority were left to fend for themselves as best they could. The abbey and its lands reverted back to the Crown.

One survivor of the dissolution was the master of the grammar school, Leonard Cockes. Despite having been a close friend of Faringdon, with strong Catholic leanings, Henry VIII awarded him the job of schoolmaster for life in 1541. Less fortunate was one of his successors, Julines (or Julius or Joceline) Palmer. Despite also being a devout Catholic, he had first been employed as a tutor to the sons of Sir Francis Knollys, who was well known as a persecutor of papists. When the Catholic Mary ascended to the throne, Knollys left the country rather swiftly and Palmer was appointed master of the grammar school. He witnessed the martyrdom of the Protestants Latimer and Ridley and, despite having no religious affiliation with them, was sufficiently moved by it to write a paper, which was seized upon by his enemies. Palmer initially fled, but made the mistake of returning to collect some of his belongings. He was arrested and suspended in a cage above the doorway of St Laurence's Church, before being taken to Newbury and tried for heresy. Palmer was burnt at the stake in July 1555, aged just twenty-four.

Local man Sir Thomas Vachell, from 1529 one of the town's Members of Parliament, was one of the assistants to Thomas Cromwell, Henry VIII's leading advisor during the dissolution of the monasteries. In early 1540, Cromwell was made High Steward of the Borough of Reading, with Vachell, whose other titles were Overseer of Abbey Property and Bailiff of Reading, as his deputy high steward.

Vachell was not popular with the guild. They protested to Cromwell that Vachell was 'not their friend' and did not have their confidence. When Cromwell fell from grace, he was succeeded as high steward by Sir William Penyson (or Penizon) who also pocketed the income from the town's fairs. But Vachell retained his place, selecting the town's mayor in 1541. Thereafter, under the charter granted the town by Henry VIII in 1542, the burgesses themselves were able to choose their own mayor. For the first time, Reading became a borough; the mayor and burgesses were now a corporate entity, able to own property in their own right. Meanwhile, both Vachell and Penyson got some valuable grants and leases of abbey property, but the biggest prize, that of Lord of the Manor of Reading, went to another Reading man, William Gray, a close associate of the Duke of Somerset (who would later be executed alongside him).

There continued to be royal accommodation in Reading, using the former abbot's residence, right up to the time of the Civil War. Possibly the last time it was used was in 1625, when an outbreak of plague drove Charles I from London. Royal stables were established in the former dormitory of the hospitium. The free school, established at the time of Henry VII, went into the hospitium's former refectory. The abbey mill turned from supplying the monks to become a commercial enterprise in its own right, one that survived into the 20th century.

But for the great abbey church itself, there was no reprieve. Its period of most rapid decline started in 1547 with the death of Henry VIII and the boy-king Edward VI ascending the throne. His protector was the rapacious Edward Seymour, Duke of Somerset (after whom Reading's Duke Street is said to be named). Among the titles he acquired within months of Edward's accession were the manor and lordship of Reading, which brought with it the income from the town's fairs.

Spriggs dangles the fascinating prospect that the people of Reading could have bought the abbey church from the King, and had perhaps the finest parish church in the country. But it was not to be. Within a year of Henry's death, Somerset had begun stripping the 450 tons of lead with which the abbey roof was covered. Every other possible building material followed and by 1549 the church was largely gutted and roofless. Even the gravestones were recycled. The materials went to London, to Windsor, for the construction of poor knights' lodgings at the castle, and elsewhere. One local beneficiary was Reading's St Mary's Church, which got stone, tiles and timber for its own restoration, as well as the monks' stalls from the abbey choir. St Laurence's also eventually benefited from the abbey's downfall. Prior to 1556, it had no graveyard of its own, but in that year it acquired the former abbey land to the rear of the church for its own use. When Somerset finally got his come-uppance in 1549, one of the charges for which he was tried and eventually beheaded was the felony of converting the 'lead, stone and stuff' of Reading Abbey to his own use'.

The abbey was valued in 1650. The abbey house, that was still more or less intact, was said to have a rental value of £15 a year; but the old hall and the other buildings which occupied the site were held to be fit only for demolition, and were valued at £200 for the building materials in them. The eight-and-a-half acre site on which the ruins stood was put at £8 2s. Come the Restoration and Charles II rented the site to a courtier, Thomas Clarges, in return for a mews house in London and a payment of just 40s. a year. Such was the downfall of one of the nation's greatest and richest religious institutions.

The town's economy had been in a bad state well before the dissolution. The 1440s had been particularly disastrous, with civil war, plague and feuding among continental merchants that disrupted the town's cloth industry. There was a recovery in the last quarter of the 15th century and, by the 1520s, tax receipts put Reading as the 10th wealthiest provincial town in the country. But by the time Dr John London came to Reading to oversee the dissolution, he reported back to Thomas Cromwell that Reading was 'a town of much poor people'. The dissolution made a bad situation worse. The abbey had been the town's largest employer and purchaser of goods and services. It had attracted many visitors to the town and also provided much of what passed for social services to the poor and needy of Reading. As we have seen, much of its income, which might otherwise have been recycled within the town, now went to the king or to other outside parties. By 1546, the guild, ill-resourced to carry out its new responsibilities, was insolvent and had to take a £6 loan from the churchwardens of St Laurence's. Just to add to the town's woes, it suffered a further outbreak of the plague in 1543–4 and one of influenza in 1558–9.

The Competition

> They cared for naught save the gospel of Christ.
> (The grey friars of Reading, as described in the 1947 Official Town Guide)

A group of nine Franciscan monks landed in Dover in October 1224. They were known from the robes they wore as grey friars, and were sworn to a vow of poverty. Despite this unpromising marketing proposition, they set about recruiting others to their order and within ten years their numbers within Britain had reached a thousand. In 1234 a group of them arrived in Reading, bearing a letter from Pope Gregory I that instructed the Abbot of Reading to give them some land on which to build their friary. The abbot was none too pleased to see a rival institution setting up on his doorstep, but the Pope could not be disobeyed. So he gave them the most unpromising piece of land in his possession, an area near the south side of Caversham Bridge, which in winter flooded so badly that it could be entirely cut off from the town.

The grey friars struggled to eke a living from this situation but fought a losing battle, apparently building a fine church on a hopeless site. But by 1285, a fellow Franciscan had been appointed Archbishop of Canterbury. Armed with a letter from him, they went back to the abbot and by 1288 were given the site at what was then known as Town's End, on which Greyfriars Church now

9 *Greyfriars Church, seen here in its ruinous state prior to its 1863 restoration, was seen by the abbot as a rival to Reading Abbey.*

stands. Mindful of any threat to the abbey's income, the abbot gave them the land on condition that they strictly observed their code of poverty and did not infringe any of the abbey's rights or income sources. Their church was completed in 1311 and, despite its chequered history, large elements of it survive to this day as the country's most complete example of Franciscan architecture. The grey friars remained there until they, too, were caught up in the dissolution of the monasteries in 1538. This time, before state theft could strip it bare, private enterprise stepped in. As Dr London, the King's commissioner for the dissolution, reported, local people: 'Fell to stealing so fast in every corner of the house that I have been fain to tarry a whole week here to set everything in due order.'(Dils, in Petyt)

At that time, most of the land and buildings were sold to a Robert Stanshawe, a groom of the king's chamber. Thomas Vachell became custodian of such valuables as the church possessed, and he helped the town's guild secure the building (or what remained of it, after Government and private looting) as their new guildhall, in 1543. It continued in that use until about 1570, when it became a hospital and workhouse, and thereafter the town bridewell or gaol. Its sorry state in this use by the early 19th century is described later. The bridewell fell into disuse in 1844, when the new county gaol opened. Attempts were first made to buy the church for restoration as a Catholic place of worship, which were rejected (leading to the building of St James's Church amid the abbey ruins), and it was almost two decades later (1863) that the roofless remains of

Greyfriars were acquired and restored as a church.

As if Reading Abbey's importance as a centre of pilgrimage were not enough, Caversham also possessed a shrine that attracted people from the length and breadth of the land, and possibly even predated the abbey. The Shrine of Our Lady of Caversham first appears in a document of 1199 from King John, referring to 'the Church of Kaversham together with the Chapel of the Blessed Virgin Mary and all things pertaining to them'. However, it is thought that it may have existed at the start of the 12th century, since Agnes Giffard, widow of the first Earl of Buckingham, is said to have donated an important relic to it as early as 1106. The shrine was the property of Notley Abbey, some of whose monks lived in Caversham to look after it, and to minister to the local population.

Its centrepiece was a life-sized wooden carving of the Virgin Mary, later silver-plated and decorated with a jewel-encrusted golden crown. It boasted its own collection of donated holy relics:

10 *St Peter's Church, Caversham, seen here prior to its 1878 restoration, was once the home to the Shrine of Our Lady, a famous place of pilgrimage.*

part of the rope with which Judas hanged himself, the dagger that killed Edward the martyr in 979 and its principal relic, part of the spear that pierced Jesus's side during the crucifixion. It, too, boasted its share of miraculous recoveries from illness. Those cured would leave behind a wax model of the part of the body that had been afflicted, cast-off crutches or some other symbol of their cures. The shrine may originally have had a home of its own, but was later housed in St Peter's Church in Caversham. But all trace of it was lost during the suppression of the monasteries in 1538.

Caversham Bridge itself also had a chapel near its northern end, dedicated to St Anne, the mother of the Virgin Mary. This was itself a relatively more minor place of pilgrimage, though it doubled with the secular function of collecting the tolls from those using the northern end of the bridge for the Lord of the Manor of Caversham. St Anne's Well, near the northern end of the bridge, was deemed to have healing properties. A chapel at the Reading side of the bridge, dedicated to the Holy Ghost, performed the similar roles of toll booth and shrine on behalf of the Abbot of Reading.

Chapter Three

Corn, Cloth and Catering: The Medieval Town

All burgesses of Radinges who are in the merchant gild in Rading be for ever free of Shires and hundreds and all pleas complaints tolls passages and cartage-tolls and may buy or sell wheresoever they wish throughout England without tolls and that no one molest them under penalty to us of ten pounds.

Part of the charter granted to the town by Henry III in 1253.

The Growth of the Medieval Town

The abbot of Reading, like his counterparts in some other abbey towns, turned out to be a species of medieval town planner. His guiding principle was to promote the financial interests of the abbey, and a number of the town's principal streets were built to this end, and date from the abbey early days. New Street (known today as Friar Street) ran from the abbey entrance to Towns End (roughly where the modern Friar Street crosses the Inner Distribution Road). The first mention of it appears in about 1170, and rents in the street were initially set lower than in the established centre, around St Mary's Church, to encourage take-up. At the abbey end of Friar Street, New Street opened out into a new marketplace. This was thought to have been laid out in around 1130–5 by one Ralph Gray, again with the active involvement of abbot Anscher. At about the same time, High Street (the modern Broad Street) came into existence, linking the southern end of the new marketplace to the northern end of the old market in St Mary's Butts. Interconnecting lanes, in particular Gutter Lane (Cross Street) completed the grid.

The construction of London Street after 1254 committed the town to expansion beyond the south bank of the Kennet, though some development had already taken place there. In wet weather, the Kennet used to flood and cut worshippers off from services in St Mary's. So, from 1191, the pastoral needs of this new suburb were served by St Giles's Church. The area became known for the sale of woodland products and hence what we now know as Southampton Street was therefore known as Wood Street before 1294. As we will see later, this is just one of many Reading streets where particular crafts came together during this period. Silver Street, for example, was formerly Sievier Street,

11 *Market Place, originally created by a 12th-century abbot to draw trade away from St Mary's Butts. This view dates from the Second World War.*

12 *Broad Street, another 12th-century creation to link the town's old and new markets. This was how the south side looked, 1895.*

13 *A seedy-looking Cross Street in 1887, another important part of the medieval street pattern.*

14 *St Giles's Church, built at the end of the 12th century to serve the growing population south of the Kennet, and seen here in 1802.*

where sieve makers used to live. This arrangement had advantages for everyone. It made industries easier to inspect and regulate for the authorities, it was more convenient for customers to find the product they wanted and, in the case of noxious industries, it became easier to contain the nuisance.

Reading soon became one of Berkshire's leading market towns. While its population is estimated to have more than doubled between about 1100 and 1348, there was relatively little increase in the town's size. Plots were subdivided, storeys added to houses and backland developed, in a mixture of planned and ad-hoc growth. At the time of Domesday Book and before the abbey, Rixon estimates Reading's population at between four and five hundred. By applying a good deal of guesswork, he puts the lay population by 1297 at around eight hundred and thirty-five. Add in the abbey population and it gives a total of around one thousand two hundred and fifty. The 14th century was a disastrous time for the nation. There were crop failures and large-scale deaths of livestock over the period 1315 to 1322, followed by the Black Death of 1348–9 (discussed later). It says much for the strength of the town's economy that its population was thought to have recovered to roughly its 1297 size of 1,250 by 1381. By 1525, Rixon suggests Reading was up to 1,900, as big as Southampton and larger than a city such as Cardiff.

Reading also became an important centre for the transhipment of goods travelling to or from London by water. Goods travelling along the Kennet beyond Reading either had to be transhipped to flat-bottomed craft called showtes, or go by road. The passage through Reading on the Kennet was controlled by the abbey, by means of a lock at Brokenburghlok. Boatmen passing in either direction had to summon the lock-keeper from the abbey, who would open the gate within two hours (less, if advance notice had been given). Burgesses were charged 5d. for a boat and 1d. for a showte; for strangers, passage through the lock cost 5d. and 2d. A new wharf was also built in the 12th century, just south

15 *London Street, built in the 13th century to link the abbey to the main road to London.*

16 *Silver Street, the medieval Sievier Street, was long the site of some of the town's worst slum housing. This view was taken in 1927, shortly before these houses were demolished.*

of where the Holy Brook joins the Kennet. This consisted of an area where showtes and shallow-drafted boats could be run aground and moored to a series of posts. Horse-drawn carts would then come down into the shallows and help with the unloading. A two-storey warehouse was built nearby and, by the 14th century, a communal docking area had been provided, available to anyone for a fee. In 1405 an agreement was reached between guild and abbey for the passage of boats up the Kennet to Town Wharf. One of the conditions was that no one on the boats should: '… make any play, riot or noise that might turne to the prejudice, damage or dis-ease of the said abbot and convent'. (Slade)

One point of conflict on the river was between shipping interests and fishermen and mill-owners, whose lines, nets and weirs proved such a hazard to shipping. The problem festered for centuries: Richard I ordered the removal of all weirs from the Thames in 1197, Magna Carta includes complaints from the nobles about navigation along it and Henry III imposed fines for the erection of illegal weirs along the river in 1227. These illegal weirs were not an absolute barrier to navigation, but they added to the time and cost of the journey, since the owners did not open them for nothing. There was even a suggestion that, for part of the 14th century, Henley was the upper limit of navigation on the Thames, isolating Reading and causing great harm to its economy.

On a lighter note, there was another conflict involving the river and communications. Clothes-washing in these days was done in the River Kennet, the favoured spot being outside the guildhall. The women used to beat the clothes with wooden implements called battledores to get the dirt out. The noise of this, combined with the animated conversations of the women, was such that the burgesses in the guildhall could not make themselves heard to conduct their business: 'Ther ys such betyng with batildores as noe man can nott here another'.(Rixon)

Although the Roman road network had bypassed Reading, the medieval town once again became an important centre of communications. An early map of principal roads, dating from around 1360 (known as Gough's map) shows the route between London and Bristol passing through the town and another road going from it to Oxford. Typically, there were disputes about the responsibility for the upkeep of the town's roads. The abbot was hauled up before the King in 1401 because of their ruinous state, but he was able to persuade the monarch and a jury that they were not his responsibility. In the second half of the 14th century the roads had suffered a decline, not because of wear and tear, but because the disastrous decline in population resulting from the Black Death was resulting in the roads reverting to nature. The state of the town's bridges was also a recurring and fruitful subject for litigation between the abbot and the guild over the years.

The Management of the Town

Before the abbey, the king's influence was exercised by a series of peripatetic royal officials. Once it was under the control of the abbey, the town was subject to a much closer, hands-on control from a resident management. The main official for the abbey was the steward. He was the head of the abbot's urban administration – his representative on earth, as it were. He presided over the meetings of the town's courts and was the champion of the abbot's authority. The abbey guarded this authority fiercely. Not even crown officials were allowed within the town, to collect debts owing to the King. Reading, as a monastic borough, became an island of immunity from royal influence. Below the Steward were the reeves (until the end of the 13th century, when their role began to be taken over by the bailiffs).

If they were resistant to the King's authority, the abbey was equally opposed to any suggestion of self-government by the guild. From the mid-13th century onwards, monastic boroughs across the country began to encounter a spirit of organised resistance to monastic lordship from local people.

Reading's merchant guild is first mentioned in 1253. Their existence coincides with – and may result from – a serious clash between the abbot and local people, discussed in the previous chapter. Some historians characterise relations between the abbey and the townspeople as one of constant conflict, with the abbey being 'imperious and unbending' and the burgesses 'estranged and embittered'. But Rixon argues that, generally, the relationship was one of 'courteous pragmatism'. For the most part, the guild managed to conduct its disputes with the abbey by means of words, rather than violence.

But there was a serious outbreak of violence in 1244, which left several dead and the abbot facing a £100 fine for 'the homicides and other transgressions committed by his men'. As we saw, violence in the streets in 1253 led to the citizens of Reading being told by the King to stop using violence against the abbot's officials. Other monastic boroughs suffered even more severe violence, but Reading was under somewhat of a less restrictive regime than some boroughs. They were not, for example, forced to use the abbey's mills to grind their corn or their ovens to bake their bread. Nonetheless, the guild learned from this early reverse and concentrated thereafter on diplomacy, rather than confrontation.

The guild started life with the purpose of regulating commerce, but its functions soon expanded into 'a friendly society, dining club, religious confraternity and, most imposingly, a prototype corporation'. By the mid-1300s the guild was, in effect, the corporation, with the guild's warden also serving as the town's mayor. By the early 13th century, the town was divided into five wards, each named after a street – there were High, New, London, Old and Minster or Castle wards. Each had appointed two street-keepers or wardmen, whose job was to 'make a true presentement of all manner of felonyes, pety anoysances and defaultes'. They also assessed and levied some of the local taxes.

From 1368, the town also shared two constables, whose duty was 'to make true presentement of all maner of bloodshedynge, entryes, assalts, affrays and of arrests broken'. They kept the peace, repaired the stocks and prevented 'ryottes, routes … and unlawful assemblies'. The non-representative nature of the guild was sometimes exploited by the abbot, for example when he decreed that half of the town's constables and wardmen should be appointed from outside the ranks of the guild. Over the years there were several occasions when the right to nominate constables was disputed between the abbot and the guild, in 1390 ending up before the courts.

As we saw, the title of mayor was also a matter of controversy. It emerged in 1301, when the King attached it to the warden of the guild. The abbot objected to what he saw as an increase in the status of the guild, but his objections were overruled. The guild nonetheless chose not to use the provocative term in sensitive dealings with the abbey. The mayor had a variety of functions. He was the champion of the guild in its dealings with the king, the abbot and others, he defended the liberties of the borough and sought to extend them by securing new privileges and concessions, he was responsible for the day to day running of the guild and liased with the abbot's steward, he oversaw the election of Reading's Members of Parliament and organised parts of the tax collection.

The guild became something of a self-appointed oligarchy – there was no question of having to be elected onto it – but this was as much as anything to

17 *The original guildhall or yeld hall, a view taken from the* Victoria History of Berkshire.

do with the difficulty of recruiting new members, to take on roles that meant giving up, or seriously reducing, their other breadwinning activities. By the 14th century, the guild was responsible for many of the town's utilities – the guildhall (a large building, seating over seventy-five people), the shambles (the meat and fish market), the wharf house, the stocks, the weighbeam, the town's clock (installed some time before 1414 in defiance of the churches' monopoly on telling the time) and the communal lavatory (built near the guildhall in about 1350). The guild had to remove dung periodically from the Cornmarket, sluice down the fish market and impound stray pigs. These latter were a notable nuisance in medieval towns; there were by-laws with fines for allowing your pig to stray, and from time to time pig catchers were employed on a profit-sharing basis. There were also toll booths and gates to be manned, to collect payments from those entering the town to trade, and taxes to be collected, to meet the MPs' expenses and the other costs of running the town.

On the expenditure side, the guild offered gratuities (we would call them bribes) to people whose influence might serve their interests. In 1430–1, shortly after the start of the out-butchery dispute (referred to in the previous chapter), the judge was sent two capons, seven hens and two gallons of wine by the guild, in anticipation of a satisfactory outcome to the case.

A number of responsibilities were shared between the guild and the abbey, such as running the market and generally keeping the town in what then passed as a clean state. Some were disputed – like the responsibility for keeping the town's roads and stocks in good repair. Others were entirely the responsibility of the abbot. He dealt (not always satisfactorily) with the upkeep of the town's water supply, its bridges and ran the courts. There were two of these – the portmoot met every two or three weeks, at which the abbot's steward dealt with cases such as trespass, debt and breach of contract, the conveyance of property and the binding of apprentices. The Court Leet met about twice a year, to deal with rather more serious cases. The role of a Court Leet has been described elsewhere as 'an uphill struggle to keep the town sanitary and moral'. The proceeds from any fines went into the abbey's coffers.

The guild long held ambitions to be independent of the abbey – to be incorporated – and their wish was granted by the dissolution of the abbey and the new charter granted by Henry VIII in 1542. The guild now had sole responsibility for running the market, the town gaol and courts to hear minor offences. They could now appoint all the borough's officials. As we saw, they were also given what remained of Greyfriars Church as a new guildhall, and the old one was leased out in the same year. However, they were not properly resourced for their new responsibilities, with many of the taxes formerly payable to the abbot now going to the king or his officials, rather than to the guild.

Life in Medieval Reading

What kind of a settlement would the Reading of the 12th century have been? One historian paints this picture:

> … a little hamlet of some thirty one-storied chimneyless hovels, composed of wattles banked up with mud, covered with a thatch of straw and surrounded by arable fields, pastures and woodland. The humble villains and bordars, clad in coarse woollen homespun, and wearing the same clothes by night as by day, lived on barley meal or on a mixture of rye, oats and beans, varied with pig's flesh and washed down with copious draughts of ale or mead. At night they slept on a pallet of straw. A little Saxon Church provided Christian fellowship.
>
> The tenants in villenage spent their time in cultivating the land of the King's demesne, and also their own holdings, which in the form of scattered strips lay in the open fields round the village. Fishing and milling were also practiced, while the swineherd found mast for his numerous pigs in the adjacent woodland.
>
> (Hurry)

They led lives that were laborious and without variety and would have been:

> Removed equally from excessive poverty and from the prospect of much wealth. They could and did make their savings add strip to strip, accumulate the wages of the harvest and, there being little to tempt them to expenditure, constantly invest their earnings in plots of land.
>
> (Pearman)

The ordinary peasant would have rented his land and cottage from the Lord of the Manor, repaying him in cash or in labour. A cottage might cost as much as 3s. 6d. or as little as 6d. a year. One William de Ruledge held a lease on land in Caversham valued at 10s. per year and the accounts show how he repaid it in kind. For example:

> Weeding the Lord's corn for three days: valued at 1½ d.
> Mowing hay for three days: 4d.
> Reaping five acres of corn in autumn: 20d.
> Carry corn for three days: 9d.

In total, these days of work would have paid off about a third of the debt from William's land-holding. In times of labour surplus the Lord of the Manor would prefer to take the money, since labour could be bought for less than the sums allowable to the villein for work against their rental debts.

The only safety nets for the poor and needy of medieval Reading were the churches, or acts of individual charity. The abbey provided for some of the sick in its leper house, built almshouses for the elderly and distributed surplus food at its eastern gate, near modern-day Orts Road. This was not universally welcomed, since it was said to attract professional beggars from outside the town.

Many wealthy individuals would make provision in their wills for a range of charitable works, from the supply of clothes, through the distribution of money to the building of almshouses. The condition was often attached that the beneficiaries would be expected to pray for the souls of the departed and thereby ease their passage into heaven. The rate of exchange, between prayer and cash, was something of an inexact science. One Richard Bedowe bequeathed £6 13s. 4d. for a priest to sing and pray for his soul for a year, 'the said preest to synge longer for me if my goodes … will further extend'. Apparently, one way of making the prayers go further was to sub-contract them out to a smaller religious institution with lower overheads.

The opportunities for recreation would have been limited for the residents of medieval Reading, but we have a record of some of the organised celebrations. May Day would be the occasion for singing and dancing round a maypole outside St Laurence's Church (a pagan custom that the church was happy to embrace). These might be accompanied by plays re-enacting the adventures of Robin Hood. Easter was the time for a cycle of mystery plays and there would be other religious-themed dramas at Whitsun and on Corpus Christi day. In 1506–7 the Forbury was cleared and scaffolding erected, it is thought as a platform for the dramatic recreation of the Garden of Eden, and St Giles in 1526–7 staged historical pageants and processions around the parish. But possibly the biggest events of the year were the town's fairs.

Fairs were an important event in both the social and economic life of the town, and an important source of income for the abbey. Three fairs had been granted to the abbey by the start of the 13th century. The first, granted by Henry I in 1130, ran for four days from the Feast of St Laurence (10–14 August). This one died out some time before 1307, due to an over-supply of

18   *The Forbury, originally the forecourt to the abbey and the scene of the medieval town's markets and fairs, seen here c.1820.*

fairs, as more and more were granted to new religious foundations; a second, granted by Henry II in 1164, ran from the Feast of St James (25–28 July) and the third, from King John in 1205, ran from the Feast of St Philip and St James (30 April–3 May). The centre of activities for them was in the Forbury. Given that they were held around these important saints' days, they were a mixture of the sacred and secular (sometimes very secular), with pilgrims swelling the ranks of those who had come to buy, sell, be entertained or to engage in some of the many opportunities fairs presented for criminal activity. Holy relics would be carried in procession through the streets of the town; traders, some from as far away as East Anglia and continental Europe, added to the variety of goods on sale. Stalls would sell all sorts of food and drink, and there would be entertainers – jugglers, minstrels, gleemen (musicians) and buffoons (clowns). There were performing animals – dogs, monkeys and bears – and violent sports, such as wrestling and cudgel play for those who were so inclined. Last, and certainly least, were a rich variety of confidence artists, thieves and pickpockets to beware of. If all this were not enough, there was always the possibility of a visit to the stocks or a public execution to enliven the day.

The Black Death

In the summer of 1348, ships in the port of Bristol offloaded a cargo that would dramatically change the course of the nation's history. The cargo was not goods but rats, and they brought with them the epidemic that was known at the time as the Great Mortality, but which we call the Black Death. In little more than a year, the population of England was reduced by a third, and further outbreaks in 1360–2, 1369 and 1375 meant that the national population level in 1300 was not reached again until the 17th century. Entire communities were wiped out in some areas. It is not known how badly Reading was hit, but we do know that the abbot of Reading, Henry of Appleford, was one of its victims in 1361, and that nearby Henley lost 60 per cent of its population. A similar rate of loss in Reading would have meant between 500 and 750 deaths in 1348–9, with more in the succeeding epidemics. The Black Death prompted a widespread economic collapse, as well as personal tragedy for the victims and their families but, for those who survived, it brought great opportunities in the longer term. Labour shortages pushed wages up and the cost of living was reduced. There was more land to rent and buy and many peasants enjoyed unprecedented prosperity.

Reading's Economy

Medieval Reading grew from a small market town to one that had a specialised and increasingly major role in the economic life of the whole region as a supplier of grain, cloth and services. The town's growing importance is reflected in its progress through the ranks of provincial towns in terms of their taxable wealth. In 1200, Reading was below 50th; by 1334 it was 38th, ranking alongside places like Derby, Northampton, Leicester and Plymouth and, as we have seen, by 1525 it was as high as 10th.

It was a diverse economy, and many of its industries congregated together; shoemakers located in Market Place tanners around Old Street (St Mary's Butts) near the waters of the Kennet bakers in Bread Lane, off London Street and butchers and fishmongers in the rows that bore their names at the eastern end of what is now Broad Street. There were vineyards within the town itself in the 14th century, though these disappeared as the climate grew colder. More specialised trades – cutlery, metal-working, goldsmiths, bell-foundries, spice dealers – hinted at the wider catchment the town increasingly served. Part of this market came from the hordes of visitors drawn to the town by the abbey.

19   *Mill Lane took its name from the mill that stood there from medieval times until the beginning of the 20th century. The mill is seen here c.1880.*

These in turn created their own business niches; lawyers served the litigious visitor, lodging houses provided accommodation for the retinues of the distinguished and stables, grooms and wheelwrights cared for their horses and carriages. There were barbers, cooks, taverns and hatters to minister to the visitors' every other need. But the largest single occupational group in the medieval town was victualling. If 19th century Reading was characterised by beer, biscuits and bulbs, then medieval Reading was, Rixon suggests, identified with corn, cloth and catering. Table 3.1 shows the relative importance of different occupations in Reading, on either side of the great divide of the Black Death of 1348–9:

Table 3.1 Occupational structure of Reading 1150– 542 (from Rixon)

Occupation	1150-1349	1350-1542
Victualling	28 %	19
Clothing	9	16
Textiles	3	14
Metalworking	9	8
Building	6	6
Mercantile	6	7
Leather	7	14
Misc. manufacturing & Agriculture	32	16

Business was closely regulated – in different ways – by the Crown, the abbey and the guild. The Crown's main interest was in enforcing a uniform national set of weights and measures. At first, a crown official called the Clerk of the Market did this in conjunction with the abbey, but from the early 14th century this responsibility passed entirely to the abbey. The abbey's prime concern was the collection of tolls and fines from businesses – as we have seen, one of their staple sources of income was an annual 5d. a head trading tax, called chepyngavel. The guild was mainly interested in the maintenance of quality control and proper trading standards – not just in the interests of the customer, but also (and possibly primarily) to make life more difficult for any outside trader who was not a guild member. These rules were codified in the 14th century in the *Puncta Gilde*. Among its provisions were the setting of times and places for trade to take place, the prevention of what we would call gazumping or the creation of artificial shortages, price controls, notably over beer, and some rudimentary quality control measures – such as forbidding the sale of meat from animals that had died suddenly without explanation or that had gone mad. The standards for outside traders were naturally set higher than for locals.

Successive abbots sought to manipulate the trade of the town to their advantage, often in the face of opposition from the town's business interests. London Road was laid out with the aim of diverting trade from the old market. Its purpose was to draw traffic from the Winchester road and across the High

Bridge over the Kennet into the new market. The High Bridge itself predates these works, appearing in a document of around 1175 as the 'novum pontem' (new bridge). In the agreement of 1254, the abbot was forced to agree that the corn market should stay in its customary position and that no other changes to established patterns of trading should be made in the town, no doubt to stop the abbot further manipulating the market.

Despite this setback, the abbot's strategy worked. By the 14th century the area between the north bank of the Kennet near High Bridge, and the marketplace had become the economic epicentre of the town, according to contemporary rent records. It contained the guildhall, the town and abbey wharves, the woolbeam (where wool bales were weighed) and a labyrinth of craft workshops. Even so, the area around the crossroads at St Mary's, the original heart of the town, remained buoyant into the late 12th century.

The weekly market would have been the main focus for business. There is no reference in Domesday Book to the town having a market – only Cookham and Wallingford were mentioned as having them – but it is thought to have started some time in the late 11th century (though the first written reference to it was not until 1186). A second market, the one promoted by the abbot in Market Place, ran from the 1130s and the two operated in parallel for many years.

Heresy

By the late 15th century, the Roman Catholic church in Reading was over-stretched and its grip on the people correspondingly weaker. The vicars of St Mary's and St Laurence's both had a wide range of responsibilities and were largely absentees, and Reading's trading links with London made the town fertile ground for heretical views imported from the capital. Some were brought over by continental non-conformists but others, like the Lollards (followers of John Wycliffe, who opposed much of the fancy ritual and some of the doctrine of the Catholic church) were home-grown.

In 1412, one Thomas Punche of St Giles parish was arraigned before the Bishop of Salisbury to answer charges of heresy. There were 17 such cases involving Reading people between 1485 and 1493, 25 in just three years between 1493 and 1496 and an average of three a year over the period 1502 to 1524. Thomas Cromwell was warned by the Bishop of Lincoln as early as 1528 about the infiltration of dangerous literature into Reading Abbey and, in 1536, copies of the rebel manifesto of the Pilgrimage of Grace (seeking the restoration of Catholicism and curbs on the king's power) were being printed and circulated in the town.

Chapter Four

FAIR STREETS AND GOODLY HOUSES:
FROM DISSOLUTION TO CIVIL WAR

Reading excelleth at this day all other townes of this shire in fair streets, and goodly houses; for wealth of the townsmen, and their name in making cloth.
William Camden – *Britannia* (1586)

C amden's view of Reading's fair streets is not shared by other contemporary observers. In 1586, and for centuries on either side, walking through Reading could be a hazardous and unpleasant experience. The streets were often dark and narrow, with the overhanging jettied upper storeys of the houses further reducing the light. The traveller's way was also strewn with obstacles: in 1593, Mr Deane had constructed a sawpit in the street 'to the annoyance of the passengers that way', and was also storing his timber in the street. Widow Gosling had her dungheap outside the Katherine Wheel, opposite St Laurence's Church, while others encroached onto the streets with their unauthorised house or shop extensions, ovens or other obstacles, often gambling on being able to pay the Corporation a fee to allow them to keep their extension. Few frontagers, including the Corporation itself, bothered with their responsibility to maintain the part of the street outside their houses, with the result that few streets were even paved, and even these were rough affairs of flints and pebbles. The area around the marketplace was cleaned out once a week by the town's scavenger but, for the rest, the responsibility for cleaning the street was also supposed to rest with householder adjoining it. In practice, this generally meant the street became an open sewer.

Pigs were kept in most backyards and hog sties could be rented at the old Yield Hall. These animals frequently escaped, wandered the streets and rooted among the piles of refuse (to the annoyance of local residents and passers-by). They generally ended up being impounded by the town hogherd (to the annoyance of their owners, who would sometimes try illegally to liberate their captured animals – one Walter Hawkes' wife was fined sixpence for attempting to do so). 'Mastive dogges' were kept by many householders, not always securely, and these might leap out on the unwary. The problem of dogs was so serious that, in 1646, the authorities appointed a man specifically to kill strays. The problem was not

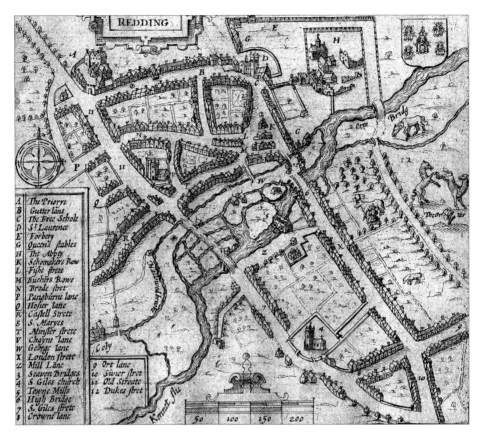

Legend on map:

REDDING

A The Prioyre
B Gutter lane
C The Free Schole
D S.ᵗ Laurence
E Forbery
G Queens stables
H The Abbey
K Schomakers Row
L Fyshe strete
M Buchers Rowe
N Brode stret
P Pangbirne lane
Q Hoser lane
R Castell Strete
S S. Maryes
T Minster strete
V Chayne lane
W George lane
X London strete
Z Mill Lane
3 Seaven Bridges
4 S Giles church
5 Towne Mills
6 High Bridge
7 S. Giles strete
8 Crowne lane

9 Ort lane
10 Siuier stret
11 Old Streate
12 Dukes stret

20   *The earliest surviving map of Reading, by John Speed, dated 1611.*

just limited to the streets. One of the tasks assigned to the sexton and clerk of St Mary's in 1573 was driving stray dogs out of the church. Other factors also impeded movement around the town, such as the fact that all 19 of the town's bridges were in a ruinous state.

By night, the only street lights were the candles or oil lamps that each householder was supposed to display in his doorway, and it was a brave or desperate man who travelled through the centre of Reading after dark – or one up to no good.

Rules to maintain a pure supply of drinking water were as widely ignored as the regulations to keep the streets clean and clear from obstruction. A Commission of Sewers was set up in 1576, but everyone, from the Corporation who failed to clean the gratings that were supposed to prevent refuse from the streets going into the Holy Brook, to the individuals who polluted the water courses with industrial effluent or clothes washing, seemed to ignore them. Many would draw their water from the Holy Brook, while others would have had their own private well or used the communal wells outside Greyfriars Church or in the marketplace.

The earliest surviving map of Reading was made by John Speed and dates from 1611. It shows a town of about five thousand people, most of whom lived within a triangle with Friar Street as its base and its apex in Whitley, where Sievier Stret (modern day Silver Street and its extension, Mount Pleasant) met St Giles Strete (now Southampton Street). Within the town centre, the eastern end of Broad Street was divided in two, into Fishe Strete and Buchers Rowe, whose functions in the town's economy will be self-evident. What is now King Street was similarly divided into Sun Lane and Back Lane.

The marketplace is also shown on the Speed map as having buildings in its centre. These were removed under a 1611 bequest from the eminent Reading mathematician John Blagrave, who left £200 to enlarge the marketplace by removing 'the middle row of houses between the pump and the cage'. By 1619, additional money from Blagrave had also added a 'very faire walk, under the south side of St Lawrence's Church, 10 foot broad at the least and in length from the church porch to the west end of the belfry'. This was the Blagrave Piazza, which can be seen on early photographs and engravings of the church. It was originally intended to give shelter to market traders, and to provide a home for the oatmeal market, though it came to have other uses, such as containing the town's stocks, pillory and tumbrel or cucking stool (a chair in which scolds, disorderly women or fraudulent traders were strapped and exposed to the abuse of the public, or ducked in a convenient pond). John Man, whose 1810 book *A Stranger in Reading* provided a highly critical view of the town at that time, had a very different view of the piazza, describing it as 'a most clumsy and ill-formed arcade … erected in defiance of every rule of architecture; a recepticle for idleness and vice, and where, I am told, midnight orgies are held, unbecoming to the sacredness of the place, and impeaching the vigilance of the magistrates'. Its reputation for sordid goings-on continued until it was eventually demolished in around 1868. The other features that drew people to the 17th-century marketplace were the 'Plumpe' and Well, leased by the Corporation for four pence a year, from which many townspeople got their water.

The market was the centre of the town's economic and much of its social life, and Childs uses contemporary records to paint a picture of the exotic mixture of people gathered there:

> The market was 'full' about eleven o'clock. Curious figures, intent on business, lawful or otherwise, mingled in the crowd. The stranger, 'lycenced to practise chirurgerye' seeking 'to show his quality', but confounded by abuse and blows; 'the black, shaghaired and spare fellowe' caught cutting a purse from a woman's girdle; the footpad with false passport and unconvincing tale of a journey 'to London to pursue a Turke about cutting out his tongue'; the town sergeants in 'new clokes', about to cry a proclamation; servants of the Warden of the Fleet Prison, watching sentence done in the pillory on a victim of the Star Chamber; a company of players holding the licence of the Master of the Revels, and 'servants of her Highness the Lady Elizabeth, turned away from the Town Hall and told 'to forbear'; boys of the Free School, watching cudgel players, and a crowd which called the constable 'coxcom', tried to 'stare him out', and thrust at him with the 'hiltes of the cudgills'; Vincent

Lancellus, 'Arrabian by nation and Doctor of Fisicke', permitted to practice
in Reading under licence of the Archbishop of Canterbury; a wild-eyed
group discussing the last story of witchcraft; Robert Hatt 'of the Burmoodes
alias the Sommer Ilandes, on his way to the Town Hall to ask for 'some
poore children, having £5 or £6 a piece, to pay their passage and to apparel
them', whom he will surely bring to prosperous estate; constables flogging a
wife-deserter tied to the tail of a moving cart; sailors from the western ports;
'stronge and able men fitt for the warres', billeted on the town; fugitives
from justice; Dutchmen; 'poore travellers and Irishe'; workmen without
work; thieves and honest folk.

The cloth market was held in a place called Tothill, just opposite the gatehouse
to the *George Inn*, and the wool market was near to Fisher Row. The south side
of Broad Street, at its western end, was reserved for the sheep market and hog
pens, next door to which lived Sir Edward Clerke, who was for many years
steward to the Corporation. Minster Street at this time was very narrow and
so often blocked by wagons that, in 1648, the Corporation closed it off with
the chains, from which modern-day Chain Street derives its name. Archery was
still practised by the local people and the town had two archery butts. One, in
modern day St Mary's Butts, served the parishes of St Mary's and St Laurence's.
The other, beside the road near St Giles's Church, served that parish.

To the east of London Strete were only fields, known as the Ortes (from the
medieval latin word *ortus*, for garden). They had been given to the townspeople
by Queen Elizabeth's charter, and were rented out as smallholdings. The remains
of the abbey, which stood a little way back from the rest of the town, were
surrounded on three sides by fields. There was no development along Caversham
Road, north of the former Greyfriars Priory, nor was there any along Pangburne
Lane (what we now call Oxford Road). Castel Strete marked the start of the route
to Bath, but was only built-up for a short distance west of Old Streate (as St
Mary's Butts was then called). St Giles's Church is shown surrounded by fields or
gardens, and with only sporadic development along the frontage of what is now
Southampton Street. Cattle grazed in the churchyard of St Laurence, and there
were gardens, too, near to the Compter Gateway into the abbey, from where boys
would steal flowers on a Sunday and sell them for 'halfe penne a piece'.

The Kennet, in the heart of the town, divided into a number of islands, which
were more or less adequately bridged. Movement between the north and the
south of the town could be difficult in winter, when the area became muddy or
flooded, and the responsibility for the upkeep of the town's 19 bridges, which
had been such an issue between the town's burgesses and the abbot, remained a
matter of dispute long after the dissolution.

Among the other recognisable features of the town shown on the map were
the already ruined abbey and the High Bridge across the Kennet. Three mills,
two of them in the town centre, used the waters of the Kennet for grinding
corn and fulling cloth, and a further mill was powered by the Holy Brook. The
town was not yet particularly urbanised. Most of the buildings were two or, at

21 *High Bridge, from where this 1802 view of Duke Street was drawn, was originally built in the 12th century.*

the most, three storeys and between the rows of houses were extensive orchards and garden plots. William Elkins's house in Castle Street had a cherry orchard behind it and William Laud's family grew peas and beans in the garden of his house in Broad Street. Hops were grown near Caversham Bridge.

There is no accurate estimate for the population of Elizabethan Reading but, based on the numbers attending church in the chantry certificates for 1547, the total is probably around three thousand five hundred. What is also clear is that it was a growing population, with a surplus of births over deaths of about two thousand in the century to 1640.

In one respect it was surprising that the population was growing so rapidly, since there was no shortage of things to die of in pre-Civil War Reading. Commonly reported causes of accidental death included slipping under the wheels of heavily laden carts in the muddy and crowded streets, or falling into the Kennet from its unprotected banks. Many conditions that would not even be serious today could be life-threatening with the primitive healthcare of four centuries ago. Influenza trebled the town's normal death rate in 1558–9. Childbirth and infancy was a particularly dangerous time for both mother and child. Midwives were registered, but only by the bishop as a guarantee that they were orthodox in their religion. Their only training was the number of confinements (including their own) that they had attended. Even if the child survived the birth (and one study of Elizabethan Reading found that seven per cent of children were stillborn) childhood still carried grave risks – in St Mary's Parish between 1600 and 1640 13 per cent of all infants died in their first year and more than a third of all burials in the parish were of children.

Epidemics of the plague continued to be a major cause of death, hitting the town on average every 10 years or so; 1564, 1596, 1608, 1624–5, 1634 and 1638 were particularly serious outbreaks. The outbreak of 1608 took 104 lives in St Giles's Parish alone in just three months, and the one in 1638 took about one in 17 of the town's population. In the 1608 outbreak, one in seven of the victims were children and a third of the deaths occurred in just eight families. In an earlier case in St Mary's Parish, a clothier named Edmund Spier lost his wife Amy and four children in the space of a few weeks.

People and goods from towns with reported plague were banned from entering Reading. Corpses were checked for evidence of the plague and, if any was found, the house was closed up, along with any live occupants. They were provided with food but guarded in order to prevent their escape until the period of quarantine was over. The ultimate precaution was to isolate the victim and their family for five or six weeks in specially built plague cabins at Conduit Close, Whitley.

Medical treatment for other ailments was equally rudimentary, even assuming the patient could afford what was available. There was a clear hierarchy of medical men in the town, with physicians, or doctors of physic, at the top of the ladder. They at least had a university degree and a licence to practice from the Archbishop (though, as with midwives, this had rather more to do with their spiritual rectitude than their professional competence). Next to them came the apothecaries, the rough equivalents of our pharmacists, who counted as craftsmen rather than professionals, though many of them were citizens of some substance. Last and most certainly least were the barber-surgeons, who performed services such as blood-letting, then regarded as a cure for all sorts of diseases. Some of the latter may also have operated as a primitive dentist, and several supplemented their incomes with a second job.

The Governance of the Town

By the time of the Civil War, Reading was by far the leading town in Berkshire, as was demonstrated by the assessments for the payment of ship money in 1636. Reading had to pay £220, compared with £120 for Newbury, £100 each for Windsor and Abingdon and just £20 for Wallingford.

As we have seen, Henry VIII's 1542 charter, which created a corporate borough after the dissolution of the abbey, was relatively ineffective, since it denied the town the money it needed to provide essential services. It was only when Elizabeth I granted a new charter in 1560 that the town gained at least the potential to administer its own affairs properly. Under this, a group of 21 burgesses elected a mayor and other officials, and the mayor, as a Justice of the Peace, was able to conduct preliminary hearings of criminal offences and deal with petty crime. Most of the town's burgesses appear to have been tradesmen of one kind or another (and those few listed as gentlemen probably acquired that status by accumulating wealth through trade, and thus, as somebody else put it, were able to 'live idly and without manual labour'). To fund its activities, the

Corporation could now draw upon the income from court fines, from tolls at fairs and markets and the income from 270 properties, given to them in return for the Crown being relieved of responsibility for maintaining the bridges and running the free school. The charter also gave the town 50 timber oaks from Whitley and Binfield and 200 loads of stone from the abbey to repair the bridges.

There was a primitive version of social services, funded by the community. The Poor Law of 1601 required each parish to appoint Overseers of the Poor, whose job was to support the poor at home. Their first source of funding was voluntary contributions, but they also had powers, when necessary, to levy a poor rate. This latter became an increasingly important source of funding. Records survive of the collection and spending of this money for St Giles Parish in 1634–5. A total of £71 was raised from 126 ratepayers, two-thirds of whom paid a penny or a halfpenny a week. The seven richest men in the parish contributed almost a fifth of the total.

About fifty individuals or households benefited from the money, mostly at a rate of three or four pence a week. The money went to families with sick members, to those caring for orphans, for funeral costs (someone called Old Sheldine, a long-term recipient of parish aid, finally got 2s. 4d. for his shroud and burial) and to apprentice youngsters from impoverished families. Things apparently got worse after the privations of the Civil War, discussed later. Figures for St Laurence's and St Giles's from the 1660s suggest that some 13.8 per cent of householders were regularly in receipt of poor relief, and that this was just the tip of an iceberg of poverty.

But this charity was complemented by ferocious sanctions against those seen as undeserving. Elizabethans, in Reading as elsewhere, made a clear distinction between the 'deserving' or 'impotent poor' – those who could not support themselves due to old age, illness, disability, or who were below working age – and 'sturdy beggars', whom they defined as able-bodied but work-shy. They missed the point that a series of recessions in the cloth industry, European wars and a rising population left many people genuinely unemployed. In 1590, the town council decided that 'their house, commonly called the Hospital, shall be converted to a house of correction, as well as for setting the poor people to work, being able to work for their reliefs, and for the setting of idle persons to work there'. This was the former Greyfriars Church, which after the dissolution of the monasteries had first been used as a town hall.

The beadles were sent out to collect all the able-bodied beggars off the streets, having first whipped them in the marketplace. The overseers were then faced with the task of clothing, feeding and housing them, their only source of income being whatever money they could generate from the inmates' labours. They received public funding only for children too young to work. The poor became a real threat to law and order in 1637, when a group of them tried to steal corn from the marketplace and it took two hours to disperse them.

This was a period of extremes of poverty and wealth. In 1524–5, 1 per cent of the town's population owned one-third of the town's movable goods, while over half of its citizens were living at the bare minimum needed for survival. If anything (and the records are not conclusive on this) the gap between rich and poor grew greater after 1600. Status was minutely observed in the town, and was even reflected in the seating arrangements in church. The gentry, civic dignitaries and local nobility like Sir Francis Knollys and his family would occupy the front rows and the prestige (and thus the rent payable for a pew) fell steadily from there on back, from 12 pence for the front rows to a penny for those nearest the door.

At the bottom end of the labour market, the poor seemed to be getting poorer. Many craftsmen seemed to die in considerable debt to their employees, since there was apparently no regular arrangement for paying them, apart from when some immediate cashflow problem arose for the employee – for example, his needing to buy new clothes. There was also the problem of substantial inflation: local prices are not generally well documented but, in the century to 1640, the price of foodstuffs appears to have increased five-fold and that of manufactured goods by not much less. Rents appear to have increased even more dramatically. Between 1560 and the end of the century, records show the rents on some properties in the town going up between five- and six-fold.

Complaints about the lack of work seem to be particularly common from the early 17th century, particularly among cloth workers. This may help to explain the hostile attitude to strangers or outsiders. The town was a very closed community with considerable suspicion of outsiders, who were variously accused of breaches of the trading laws, of taking work from local people and of becoming a burden on the parish. 'Outsiders', for this purpose, would have included people from as nearby as Caversham and Shinfield. By the 1630s, each parish employed two overseers to track down outsiders in the town and report them to the authorities, and the power of the authorities to act against them was enshrined in the charter granted to the town in 1638. In a few cases, outsiders whose skills were in short supply locally might be allowed to stay, provided they promised not to become a burden on the parish. Others might end up in the house of correction, making low-grade cloth or dressing hemp. But in most cases they would be whipped and expelled, and those who harboured them would also be punished. One exception to the ban on foreign tradesmen were the annual fair days, when most normal restrictions on trade seemed to be relaxed.

One other feature of the 1638 charter, which seems to run counter to the apparent shortage of housing at this time (and its consequences for house prices), was a ban on building cottages, or sub-dividing them into 'obscure receptacles of poor people' (or, as we might put it, affordable housing). But this may again be designed to protect the interests of local people against an influx of foreigners, moving into sub-standard accommodation to take up low-paid employment in the town.

Given the limited help available to the poor from the public purse, individual acts of charity took on a particular importance. One trend over this period was for bequests to the church to decline, with a corresponding rise in charitable donations to the poor, helping to substitute for the loss of the charitable

22 *St Mary's Butts.
The almshouses in front
of the church were finally
demolished in 1886.*

23 *The almshouses
provided by Sir Thomas
Vachell on Castle Street
in 1635 survived until
this photograph was
taken c.1890. Their
replacements remain
there to this day.*

functions of the abbey. These donations took a variety of forms; Thomas Deane
gave an investment yielding £3 per year to fund 'good, wholesome, well-sized
bread' to be distributed to the poor of St Giles on Christmas Eve, Good Friday
and Ascension Day. Others paid for fuel or clothing, or for young boys to be
apprenticed – Archbishop Laud's 1640 bequest paid for 10 Reading apprentices
each year.

There was also an increase in the provision of almshouses. Those provided by
John a Larder in St Mary's Butts (discussed earlier) dated back as far as 1476.
Bernard Harrison in 1617 provided four tenements in St Giles's 'provided
no man be put in who has a wife under fifty years of age'. William Kendrick
accompanied his 1634 gift of five tenements in Silver Street (four to be let to
men, one to a woman) with the rather unusual requirement that the woman
tenant be paid a shilling a quarter for washing the men. Sir Thomas Vachell's
1635 gift of a tenement off Castle Street for six 'aged and impotent widowers'
was rebuilt in the 19th century and is still there today.

24 *John Kendrick, whose bequest to Reading in the form of the Oracle led to much dispute over the centuries.*

Perhaps the most important initiative to alleviate poverty during this period came not as the result of any communal initiative but from an individual act of charity. John Kendrick was a Reading-born man. It is thought he went to Reading School and known that he graduated from St John's College, Oxford in 1589. He went on to make a vast fortune in the clothing industry and, on his death in 1624, left a number of bequests to the town. The most important of these was the sum of £7,500, with which the Corporation was to 'purchase unto them and their successors for ever, a faire plot of ground' on which they 'shall erect and build a strong house of bricke, fit and commodious for setting the poore to work therein'. The idea was that they would be engaged in the clothing industry that had bought Kendrick his fortune.

Right from the start, this bequest was ill-conceived. As we have seen, the clothing industry was by then already in decline, and the Civil War that was looming would deal it a series of body blows from which it would never recover – hardly the ideal basis for a job-creation programme. In fairness to the Corporation, it should be noted that a similar, smaller bequest by Kendrick, entrusted to the authorities in Newbury, was equally unsuccessful. Nonetheless, a site was bought at the junction of Minster Street and Gun Street, the workhouse was completed and stocked and began operating in 1628. The chosen site was formerly the business premises of John Kendrick's brother, William, and it is worth noting that William himself was dubious about the nature of his brother's bequest. His view was that 'we are not sure the trade of clothing will continue'.

The workhouse, known as the Oracle building soon came under criticism, on the grounds that a small clique of the town's clothiers – members of the Corporation or their friends – had acquired some of the stocks of materials bought with the Kendrick bequest, and were using them to undercut their local competition. Thus, far from creating jobs, the money was having the effect of putting people out of work. A petition from some of the local clothiers to the Corporation not surprisingly fell on deaf ears, and one William Treacher was heard in 1631 to express the wish that the money used to build the workhouse had been thrown in the river. He was in turn thrown into the town lock-up for his impertinence.

By 1639, the complaints had reached as far as the Attorney General, at which point the Reading-born Archbishop of Canterbury, William Laud, intervened and forced the Corporation to buy land with part of the bequest. They were required to use the income from this land for charitable purposes. Repeated unsuccessful attempts were made during the 17th century to wrest control of the Kendrick bequest from the Corporation. After the Civil War, the building was used to house the poor, rent-free and provided with subsistence by parish alms; unsuccessful attempts were also made after 1660 to breathe life into the local clothing industry.

By 1726 this burden on the parish had become intolerable. There were complaints that there was, among the recipients of the charity: 'a want of industry in the poor and that their children were being brought up in idleness … all which evils and inconveniences arose from the custom of relieving them with money'. The Corporation re-equipped the Oracle and set the residents to work, spinning flax for sailcloth and cotton for candlewicks. They also provided a school for their children. This decision was not popular in the town. A scurrilous verse, opposing it, was sold on the streets of the town and its author, a Mr Hinde, was thrown into gaol while the Corporation considered whether it was actually libellous. Hinde claimed that the Corporation were effectively locking the inmates into the Oracle 'to prevent the poor from begging about the streets and being disordered in liquor'.

The next onslaught came from a member of the Corporation itself. Alderman Watts claimed in 1749 that the Oracle had fallen into a ruinous state and was being misused. Most of it was apparently being leased out by two or three other aldermen to outsiders, contrary to Kendrick's wishes. A series of other abuses were laid at the door of the Corporation, including one that they could not account for some £18,439 10s., this being the balance of the Kendrick bequest and the interest that should have been accumulated on it. Somehow, the Corporation once again managed to survive this attack on their stewardship.

But in 1849 the governors of Christ's Hospital finally came forward with a successful claim against the Corporation, and the bulk of Kendrick's bequest passed to them. By then the building was semi-derelict and home to a number of petty criminals. That part of the bequest that was deemed not to have been misapplied was used in Reading to found the Kendrick Schools. The Oracle building survived just long enough to be photographed by the inventor of modern photography, William Henry Fox-Talbot, before its demolition in 1850. The Corporation bought the site back from Christ's Hospital two years later, when it was learned that they planned to build large numbers of sub-standard houses on it, and it would be a century and a half before the name, at least, of the Oracle would re-emerge.

25   *The entrance to the Oracle workhouse, from a very early (c.1845) picture by photographic pioneer William Henry Fox-Talbot.*

The Town's Economy

Five guilds controlled the business life of Reading – the clothiers and clothworkers, the cutlers and bellfounders, the tanners and leathersellers, the mercers and drapers, and the victuallers. Between them, these guilds encompassed the full range of business activity in Elizabethan Reading. Anyone wishing to trade in the town was expected to have served an apprenticeship there; if not, they had to pay a hefty admission fee. The length of an apprenticeship and the age at which it started could vary enormously; records show apprenticeships of between seven and 12 years, beginning at between 10 and 13 years of age. There were financial obligations on both sides; the apprentice (in practice, his parents or some local charities set up for the purpose) had to pay four or five pounds to be taken on, and had to pay an additional 3s. 4d. to the corporation at the end of his apprenticeship, before moving up to become a journeyman (the next step towards being a fully-fledged craftsman). For his part, at the end of the apprenticeship the master had to supply his pupil with a new set of clothes and the tools of his trade. The guilds regulated the system and dealt with any case of inadequate training or cruelty.

Beyond the journeyman stage, it was something of a lottery as to whether a particular tradesman moved on to become a craftsman. Some inherited their families' businesses; others were able to buy into it through the generosity of their masters, or with the help of charitable foundations like that of Sir Thomas White, who from 1566 gave interest-free loans to would-be craftsmen. Others (rich widows were apparently prominent among them) made loans to would-be craftsmen on a purely business basis. From these, the craftsman would have to provide a home for themselves and their families, along with a workshop and a retail outlet. The working day is likely to have been a long one. One employer, not thought to be untypical, had his staff working from 6 a.m. to 8 p.m. in the summer and 7 a.m. to 7 p.m. in the winter, with one hour for dinner.

Woollen cloth was at this time still the main product of the town. As the King's antiquary John Leland observed, the Kennet was 'commodious for dyers, well occupied there; for the town chiefly standeth by clothing'. Up to 1579, around thirty per cent of the town's male employment was in clothmaking or related businesses – 40 per cent if you include its distribution. Much of the spinning of the wool would be put out to women with spinning wheels, working at home, with the balance being done centrally by the clothiers. The cloth came in the form of broadcloth and a narrower version called kerseys, probably using wool from the Berkshire Downs. There was also something called Reading cloth, a product highly prized by both the home and overseas markets. For a time, it brought the town prosperity. Reading in the 1520s had been 16th in the national rank of towns in terms of size, but 10th in terms of its taxable wealth, and in 1606 Reading exported 5,753 broadcloths, more than six per cent of the national total. However, by the 1630s it was now clear that the traditional manufacture could never again be able to boast the long-term boom it had enjoyed before 1614. It was in the middle of an extended history of decline, painful adaptation and widespread redundancy. (Goose)

The market for Reading cloth had become difficult. European wars and outbreaks of the plague made exports more difficult, and manufacturers elsewhere began producing lighter, more colourful cloths that became more fashionable. Large quantities of cloth lay unsold in the town and the Corporation held crisis meetings with the clothiers, insisting that they must have all their wool spun by people within the town, rather than put it out to the countryside. This goes some way to explaining the virulent opposition to outsiders, discussed later.

In addition to cloth, the town was also an important leather and shoemaking centre, with some of the leading manufacturers serving much more than a local trade. An inventory of one of them, Henry Bourne (1563), showed he carried a stock of 1,440 pairs of shoes, and others operated on a similar scale. Other craftsmen found it less easy to make a living. William Knight, a bell-founder, was paid £4 10s. 0d. in 1584 for casting the great bell of St Mary's, but by 1622 his son was having to supplement his business as bell-founder by manufacturing cooking pots.

For many struggling craftsmen, the small-scale (and illegal) trade of unlicensed brewing, or tippling, provided a financial lifeline. Brewers generally operated from near to the water supply of the Kennet (and with that as a water source, drinkers could be thankful for the antiseptic qualities of beer!). The earliest records of the malting of barley as a local industry date from 1630. Towards the end of the century, much more of the wealth of the town would start to be concentrated in the brewing industry, and in particular malting. Much of this went by barge to quench the thirsts of Londoners, who at that time made up about a tenth of the national population. By the 1660s, maltster would rank second among Reading's leading occupations and bargemaster seventh.

Some industries were being wiped out by industrial obsolescence; for example, fletchers went out of business as the longbow was replaced by the gun. But this worked both ways; by 1618, the town had Richard Reddat, its first gunsmith. Other new trades also begin to appear around this time – glaziers by 1570 tobacco and pipe-making (early 17th century) and upholstering and market gardening from the 1630s. Bricklayers are recorded in the guild records from about 1570, though the first mention of a local brick-making industry does not occur until the 1620s. However, the industry must have been reasonably well-established and on a significant scale by then for, in 1626, the mayor and Corporation were able to order 200,000 bricks and 20,000 tiles from William Brockman of Tilehurst, for the construction of the Oracle.

There is evidence of Reading's licensed victuallers enjoying increased trade during this period. Up to 1600, those innkeepers whose inventories survive all listed a secondary occupation, suggesting that innkeeping did not provide a viable living by itself. This was certainly not the case for the victuallers of the 17th century, some of whom did very well indeed. The volume of trade going on in the town meant good business for its inns and taverns, a dozen of which were recorded in a survey of 1552. Some were quite substantial establishments; the *Cardinal's Hat* on the north side of Minster Street had 14 bedrooms and no fewer than 45 beds, and stocked drinks like malmsey, sack and gascon wine, which suggests that they attracted a good class of clientele. The Earl of Essex stayed at the *Bear Inn* in 1588, and it was in the *Bear* that Oliver Cromwell received gifts from the Corporation, somewhere between 1651 and 1653. But other dignitaries, in particular some of the assize judges, did not consider the local inns suitable places to stay. They would stable their horses there, but would prevail upon the hospitality of leading local citizens for their own accommodation. The *George* (which still survives on King Street) was the favoured dining place of those king's justices who did not billet themselves on the local gentry.

The records show that most business was conducted on the basis of credit, and that there was a very high level of bad debt.

Reading sat at the centre of a large rural hinterland. Farm produce came to the town from miles around, both to feed the urban population and for onward distribution to other markets. These areas also provided the raw materials for Reading's manufacturing industries – things like leather and wool, as well as non-agricultural products. The rural population would descend on Reading on market days, to sell their wares and to buy whatever they needed in the way of manufactured goods.

While some goods went to and from Reading overland, the poor state of repair of the roads made the waterways a much more important means of transport. Scheduled services appear to have been in operation at this time, since it was advertised that 'the Reading boat is to be had at Queenhithe

26   *The Broad Face in Market Place, one of Reading's many coaching inns, pictured c.1926.*

weekly'. Given the high capital cost of a barge, it was not uncommon for several businessmen to club together to buy one. Abraham Edwards was a waterman who died in 1639. He owned a one-eighth share in a barge and its equipment, which was valued at his death at £40. A lot of the town's trade was with London. Almost one-fifth of all the debts among the town's merchants at this period related to goods purchased from the capital. Some of the town's merchants even had their own accommodation in London.

Home Life

Most people would still have lived in a traditional timber-framed house, one or two examples of which still survive in Castle Street, Market Place and elsewhere. But by this time the authorities were trying to get rid of thatched roofs, which represented a fire hazard. A 1589 council ruling decreed that:

> all such persons as have builded any hovel, or building which shall be thought by the Mayor and Burgesses to be inconvenient shall forthwith take away all the thatch from such buildings, and no persons shall henceforth build any hovels or buildings except the same shall be covered with tile.
>
> (Reading University Extra-mural Department).

As ever, the local residents did just whatever they liked, and the records show several prominent citizens being prosecuted for breaches of this regulation. The council ruling was reinforced in the town's 1638 Charter from Charles I: 'because it often happens that whole towns are in danger of being burnt by roofs thatched with straw, no house in the Borough be hereafter roofed with straw, stubble or any other combustible thing'.

The houses stood on long, narrow plots (perhaps as little as 16ft wide, the aim being to give as many properties as possible a frontage in a good trading location). Where the house belonged to an independent craftsman, the front ground-floor room would be given over to retail space, with the family and any apprentices (plus any lodgers, who were not an uncommon feature of Tudor life) living in the rooms behind and above it. Family life would have centred around the main hall, with its long dining table and its fireplace. Only the more well-to-do had a separate parlour, and these would often double as an extra bedroom. Bedspace was at a premium and children in particular would often sleep on a truckle bed, one that could be slid under the main beds during the day. Where space was particularly tight, even the retail space at the front might double up as a bedroom at night. Another luxury that was not universal was a staircase. In some houses, access to the upper floor was by a primitive ladder. Glazed windows became more common during this period. No reference was made to any pre-1570 properties having any but, by 1590–1609, 28 per cent of the properties for which records survive had some. The price of glass certainly fell during this period but, at between 3d. and 6½d. a foot in the 1590s, not everyone could yet afford it. It was also rare for houses to possess fireplaces in anywhere other than the hall (and the kitchen, if separate).

Most people rented, rather than owned, their properties and it became the custom for the wealthy to purchase these leases as an investment (probably, given inflation and population growth, rather a good investment). Thomas Aldworth, for example, owned five houses in 1552 but left 10 houses in Reading in his will in 1576.

We know something of the range of diet available to those who could afford it: all sorts of meat, purchased from local farms and slaughtered in the Shambles (with all the consequent offal polluting the streets), and a vast array of fish (Berwick and Scots salmon, Newland fish, herrings, cod and ling, salted and dried or fresh fish, with cider vinegar or salad oil as garnish). Bakers produced fine white bread, coarser wheaten bread and household bread, along with horse loaves.

A very mixed picture emerges of the role of women in Tudor Reading. On the one hand, married women were very much the chattels of their husbands, not being allowed to own property in their own right. Women generally could even find themselves being ordered about by their husbands and fathers from beyond the grave, through their wills. Thus, Andrew Bird made his £250 bequest to his daughter Anne in 1636 conditional upon her not marrying a certain John Dennison 'who hath wilfully attempted to marry her without my consent'. John

27   *Elizabethan housing still survives on Castle Street. This picture is taken from the* Victoria History of Berkshire.

Blagrave similarly threatened in 1597 to reduce his daughters' inheritances by 90 per cent if they dared to marry without the consent of the executors of his will. Thomas Stevens in 1625 called upon his widow to enter into a bond for £200 to bring his daughters up until they were eighteen, but if she refused to be executrix she was to have £40 and 'be gone'. But most wills showed a good deal more affection between the couple and a genuine concern to make adequate provision for the widow. Many wills made provision for the widow only until such time as she might remarry, bearing in mind that, in that event, all the wife's property passed to her new husband.

A woman who was widowed or single had a much more independent position in the eyes of the law. Many of them carried on business (often, possibly the business of their late husbands) in their own right. About ten per cent of traders brought before the Court Leet in 1582 for misdemeanours were women. Some, to judge from the content of their own wills, did very well indeed from their enterprise. As we saw, it was not uncommon for widows to use any capital left them by their husbands as the basis of a money-lending business, in the days before there were banks to carry out this role. Depending upon their skill in deciding who to lend to, part (or a very large part) of the capital left in their wills could take the form of debts (of either the good or the desperate varieties). One Reading widow, Mary Symonds, left a total estate of £294, of which £270 was in the form of unpaid debts. However, her case was exceptional. Few others held debts exceeding half the value of their inventories.

The 16th century was a period of constant change in religious orthodoxy, as was reflected in the churchwardens' records for that period. In 1549 and 1550 they were pulling down altars, lime-washing the walls of St Laurence's to rid them of popish images of idolatry and buying service books in English; by 1553 the English service books were being replaced by the old Latin ones, while 1559 saw them knocking down altars again, removing statues and yet again ordering new bibles and books of common prayer. To judge from research into the forms of words used in wills, which can indicate the deceased's religious leanings, the great majority of Reading people gradually conformed to the Elizabethan Protestant orthodoxy after 1560; outside the town, there is much more evidence of Catholicism surviving.

The importance of religion in the life of the community is difficult to understand in these more secular times. The church was the only source of education for the majority of the people and the Bible the only book to which many of them would have access. In uncertain times, Christian doctrine provided the only basis for understanding what was happening in the world around them. The church was a centre of social life and, for those at the bottom of the ladder, parish relief provided the main protection from poverty and starvation.

Prior to the Civil War, the town had existed for centuries under the dominance of, first, the abbey and then the King. We saw in the previous chapter how non-conformist ideas had started to penetrate the town. By the time of the dissolution, it had become 'a very microcosm of heresy'.

Holidays in Tudor Reading were still strongly associated with the festivals of the Church. The first festival of the year was Hocktide, two weeks after Easter. During this, men and women would playfully steal each others' hats and attempt to ransom them back; there would be minstrels and a supper, generating money for church funds. May Day was celebrated at St Mary's with minstrels and a hobby horse and in the Forbury the traditional stories like Robin Hood and St George and the Dragon were acted out. At Whitsun it was the turn of the morris dancers to provide the cabaret, while a meal of bread, meat and 'church ale' was consumed in the church or churchyard. By 1600, much of this frivolity, and in particular the church ale, had disappeared, possibly under the influence of Puritanism, and the gap that was left in church funds was filled by the altogether less festive and more socially divisive means of seat rents in the church.

Visiting companies of actors, including companies under the patronage of the Queen, the Earl of Leicester and the Earl of Essex, were engaged to perform in the town. On a less cerebral note, the tanners organised bull and bear baiting, though they stood to be fined 12 pence if their 'entertainment' clashed with Sunday church services. Gambling appears to have been widespread among all classes, and drinking even more so.

Since medieval times, one compulsory form of leisure had been the practising of archery at one of the town's butts, or archery ranges. This continued until the mid-16th century, at which time many of the town's citizens listed a bow and arrows among their possessions. However, the practice seemed to have died out during the second half of the century. By 1602, all three parishes had been prosecuted in the Court Leet for failing to maintain their butts. After 1618, no Reading person was on record as possessing a bow and arrows when they died, and the town paid £3 'to redeem the inhabitants from the penalties of the statute for not using bows and arrows'. At the same time, the ownership of books spread, reaching even members of the working classes. For the most part, these were bibles or other devotional works.

Finally, discussion of the recreational tastes of Tudor Reading in their widest sense cannot fail to record that the birth records show little evidence of pre-marital sexual activity. Only 16 per cent of births in three studies occurred within eight months of the marriage and a very small number of actual illegitimate births were registered.

Chapter Five

SIEGE

May it therefore please your most excellent Majesty to take into your most princely consideration the miserable estate of your petitioners, who, through the general distractions of the kingdom, the decay of trade, the daily charge of your Majesty's army billeted upon us, and the miserable cry of the numerous poor, are so impoverished that most of your petitioners are scarce able to support themselves.

(Petition from Reading Corporation to King Charles I: January 1643)

Prelude: The Path to War

As we have seen, Reading's staple cloth industry was already in decline when Charles I ascended to the throne in 1625. Rival manufacturers had started to threaten the town's supremacy at home and foreign wars had denied them access to overseas trading centres such as Delft and Emden. By the end of his reign, the industry – and the town – would be on its knees.

Charles himself did little to endear himself to the people of Reading. When the plague visited London in 1625, he fled to Reading as a safe haven. The plague soon followed him and many of the townspeople fell victim to it. He imposed what were seen – not just in Reading – as unjust taxes on his people. Perhaps the most notorious of these was ship money. This was a tax that funded the upkeep of the navy, and was normally only collected from coastal counties. But Charles sought to extend the tax base to inland counties, such as Berkshire, on the not-altogether unreasonable grounds that everyone benefited from the protection the navy afforded the nation. But he did so without the authority of Parliament. The tax was wildly unpopular – Reading was assessed to pay £260, which in 1635 was the cost of a fully-equipped naval ship. When some of the local people refused to pay it, a reluctant Corporation (who were none too keen on the tax themselves) were forced to using the power of distraint, seizing the non-payers' goods and selling them to raise the required sum (often back to their original owner, as a means of them paying the tax without conceding the principle and losing face).

One of the leading opponents of the tax was closely associated with Reading. John Hampden was a Buckinghamshire Puritan landowner, and married into some of Reading's leading families. His second wife, Letitia, was the daughter of

Sir Francis Knollys, who owned the Battle estate, and the widow of Sir Thomas Vachell, whose family was related to Oliver Cromwell. After his marriage, Hampden acquired Coley House in Reading from the Vachell family. Hampden tried to oppose the tax through the courts and, although he narrowly lost the case, it won him enormous respect among those who shared his views. The Long Parliament finally declared ship money illegal in 1641 and the Reading Corporation proposed 'that those persones within the towne, which were distreyned for Shipmonyes, shall be agreed with and have their monyes repaid unto them by the hall'. Hampden was an influential Member of Parliament, and was one of the five MPs Charles sought

28   *Finches Buildings in Hosier Street, shortly before their demolition in about 1960. It was from here that Lady Vachell, the wife of John Hampden, watched the progress of the Civil War siege of Reading.*

to have arrested in 1642. He went on to be a leading light in the Parliamentary army, until his death at the battle of Chalgrove Field in 1643.

William Laud

Charles I had chosen a local man as his Archbishop of Canterbury. William Laud was the son of a Reading clothier, born in 1573 in a house that stood roughly where Broad Street and Queen Victoria Street meet today. He was sent to Reading School and, at the age of 16, won a scholarship to St John's College, Oxford. St John's had been founded in 1555 by Sir Thomas White – like Laud, the son of a Reading clothier – and it was a scholarship he had endowed upon Reading School from which Laud now benefited. To say that Laud had a successful student career is something of an understatement. He became a Fellow of St John's, then its President, then Chancellor of the university itself. During this time, he secured a new set of statutes for the university, secured the future of the Oxford University Press and made major donations of manuscripts to the Bodleian Library.

The King's favourite, Lord Buckingham, obtained a bishopric for him, and his ultra high-church views endeared him to both James I and Charles I. In 1633, Charles made him Archbishop of Canterbury, and he immediately set about imposing his views about uniformity of worship upon the nation, much to the fury of the Puritans. They claimed he was a Papist and referred to him as 'The Little Vermin, Little Hocus Pocus' and the man who made the Sabbath 'the

29   *William Laud, Reading's controversial Archbishop of Canterbury.*

Devil's Day instead of the Lord's Day' by allowing such activities as archery to be practised on a Sunday.

But wise Puritans made such comments quietly, for Laud was not a man to cross. Ludovic Bowyer, a nobleman's servant, made the assertion that Laud was in negotiation with the Pope to the wrong people. The Mayor of Reading had him hauled before the Court of Star Chamber, where he was fined what was then the unimaginable sum of £3,000 (nobody expected him to be able to pay), was sentenced to hard labour for life, to have the letters L and R (for Liar and Rogue) branded on his forehead and to stand in the pillory, twice in London and once in Reading. The pillory had its own terrors – for Bowyer it meant having his ears nailed to a post and a paper outlining his crimes fixed to his forehead.

On the credit side, Laud was a generous benefactor to Reading. He got Charles to grant the town a new charter in 1638, one that formed the basis for its government until 1835, and he restored the fortunes of the mismanaged Oracle charity and endowed local charities with his own land and money. But he was ambitious, tactless, harsh and domineering, making many enemies. His downfall began with the attempt to impose a high church prayer book on a largely Puritan Scotland, who rebelled against it. Laud has traditionally got the blame for this, though some suggest it was more the work of the Scottish bishops, supported by King Charles. But whoever was to blame, the King needed money to quell the rebellion and, to obtain it, had no choice but to recall Parliament. They in turn sent Laud to the Tower of London, where he remained until his trial in 1643.

The trial was rigged against him; the prosecution was led by a man on a mission – one William Prynne, a Puritan author who had had his ears cut off by the Star Chamber. Laud was given just two hours to prepare his defence against each of the charges laid against him, and a heavily edited (not to say falsified) edition of his diary was published during the trial. Despite these disadvantages, Laud made what even Prynne had to concede was 'as full, as gallant, and as pretty a defence of so bad a cause as was possible for the wit of man to invent'. The House of Lords and the judges found Laud not guilty of treason, but this was the wrong answer for the Commons. They signed an ordinance condemning him to death, regardless of the verdict.

After a long spell of imprisonment, the 72-year-old Laud was finally executed on 10 January 1645. He met his end with dignity and unbroken faith, preaching a last sermon and asking for the crowd beneath the scaffold to be moved 'lest my innocent blood should fall upon the heads of the people'. History has judged Laud harshly, describing him variously as 'the greatest calamity ever visited upon the Church of England' and 'an ayatollah of rigid theological views and liturgical preferences'. Others, however, suggest that he was less dogmatic about doctrine, and was trying to use common forms of worship to heal controversy, not to provoke it. Wherever the truth lies, Reading's only Archbishop of Canterbury was almost certainly the most controversial person ever to hold that post.

Civil War

During the Civil War, Reading was to learn again that there were disadvantages to being a centre of communications. The town was strategically placed, midway between Oxford, the King's capital, and the seat of Parliament in London. Its location on the river enabled it to control the important barge traffic between those two cities. One of the main roads between them crossed Caversham Bridge and the highway between London and the west country also ran through the town. The town also commanded the Goring Gap, the easiest way through the Chilterns, so the parliamentary forces could not attack Oxford without control of Reading, since it would have left their backs exposed to any royalist garrison stationed there. No less important than its strategic position, it was seen as a relatively large (and therefore, it was assumed wealthy) borough, and both sides in the war were desperate for funds. Reading, therefore, became an important prize to both sides. The town changed hands several times in the course of the war and was bled dry by the demands of its successive occupiers.

Like so many other communities, Reading's loyalties were divided by the Civil War. Some of the town's most prominent families, like the Knollys, were supporters of Parliament; the Blagraves and Vachell families had members in both camps. But the mayor and some of the other leading citizens, as well as some of the landowners in the surrounding area – Sir Charles Blunt at Maple Durham, Sir Francis Englefield at White Knights, Lord Craven at Caversham Court – had royalist sympathies. A silent majority just prayed for the nightmare to end.

The tensions between the two sides soon made themselves felt. Tanfield Vachell, the County Sheriff and a cousin of both John Hampden and Oliver Cromwell, consistently ignored instructions to circulate the King's proclamations in Berkshire and, when it became known in the spring of 1642 that the Earl of Berkshire was abroad in the county, trying to canvass support for the King, parliamentary forces had him arrested and imprisoned in London.

From June 1642 the town was occupied by a small parliamentary garrison. It had been organised by Henry Marten, the Member of Parliament for West Berkshire and a man of decidedly republican views. They left in a hurry on 1 November 1642, on hearing reports that a much larger royalist army under the personal command of the King was advancing on the town. Some of the town's pro-parliamentary families, including John Milton's brother Christopher, also took the opportunity to flee. Charles' army stayed for just a few days, extracting what they could from the town in the time available and terrorising the local people:

> Here wee have been in grate fear this two or three days of Prince Robert (sic – presumably Rupert) and his cavalieras, who like roaring lions go about seeking whom they can devour, plundering and pillaging the countrye round about us. No man's estate being his own, or secure from the fingers of these Harpies …
>
> (Griffin)

The Royalist Occupation and the Siege

> … a testy, forward, imperious and tyrannical person hated … by God and man.
>
> (Sir Arthur Aston, in the estimation of Oxford antiquarian Anthony Wood)

The King's army then left for London, leaving behind a garrison consisting of some 3,000 fairly raw infantry and 300 cavalry, with a few cannon and precious little gunpowder. They were under the command of Sir Arthur Aston, an experienced soldier, but 'a great and notorious Papist' and a man who, it was said, 'had the fortune to be very much esteemed where he was not known and very much detested where he was'. He soon began to make his presence felt, as parliamentary spies reported: 'There is masse constantly in the towne in severall places … The minister of the towne was put out of his house on Saturday last and a papist one mr Plowden was put into ytt'. (Griffin)

Aston immediately set about turning the town into a fortress. The entrance to the town from the west, along the Bath Road, was guarded by a fortification whose occupiers must have derived much comfort from its name – the Forlorn Hope. Behind it, earthworks ran from Castle Hill down to Greyfriars Church (now pressed into use as a guardhouse). From there, the fortifications ran eastwards, parallel to Friar Street, beyond the abbey as far as the Orts Bridge. They relied on the natural defensive barrier of the River Kennet, as far as the line of what is now Sidmouth Street, where a new earthwork began, following the line of Sidmouth Street, across Sunninge Avenue (what we know as London Road). It then turned west up to the top of Whitley Hill (where a barn large enough to house 50 men was fortified) and thence back down to the Kennet. The area between the Kennet and the Holy Brook again had the natural defence of being drowned meadows and west of Holy Brook a further earthwork ran up to Castle Hill to complete the circle.

These were no modest defences. The earth walls had wide ditches in front of them and some of the fortifications were said to be as tall and as wide as houses, incorporating forts and other features that enabled any attackers to be caught in a crossfire. Stones, extracted from the walls of the ruined abbey with

30 *Forbury Hill from the east, thought to be part of the Civil War fortifications and illustrated c.1800.*

gunpowder, and all the town's available bales of wool, were taken to reinforce them. Remains of the fortifications were visible when Daniel Defoe visited the town in the 1720s, but the only trace of them that remains today is the mound in the corner of the Forbury Gardens (subject to the reservations about its possible medieval origin, mentioned earlier). In addition to these structures, there was defence by dereliction. Bridges, barges and ferries that might provide a means of access into the town were destroyed; roads were dug up or deliberately potholed. Essex, once he had secured the north-western outskirts of the town, added to the dereliction by further dismantling Caversham Bridge to secure his northern flank. On market days, traders wishing to cross Caversham Bridge would have to manoeuvre their carts across rickety improvised arrangements of planks, which were removed at night.

The town's economy rapidly plunged towards disaster. The war had brought Reading's staple – but already declining – cloth industry to a virtual standstill. Both sides imposed strict prohibitions over communications with enemy-held areas, making trade impossible. The parliamentary side even blockaded the Thames to prevent munitions, food or intelligence passing along it. Laurence Halstead, a man from Sonning who had betrayed the parliamentary cause to join the King, tried to compound the problem by getting Reading's cloth industry relocated to Dartmouth and Exeter. None of this stopped the occupying forces making heavy financial demands on the town. Despite its parlous state, the clothing industry was asked to provide 1,000 suits of clothes for the soldiers; the Corporation was asked on 2 January 1643 to 'lend' the King £2,000 and another £2,000 just four days later. The Corporation accounts for the period show such items as '£102 and 4 shillings towards the provision of horsemeat for His Majesty's army', fuel for the guardhouses and fodder for the cavalry horses. Not only was the town of Reading (population 5,000) being asked to support a garrison of 3,000, but food and goods were also being shipped out of the town to help support royalist strongholds at Oxford and elsewhere. Wealthy individual citizens were also targeted: brewer and former mayor Thomas Harrison was required to supply the army with free beer and lent £600 to the cash-strapped Corporation to pay its dues. He also had his barn (which stood near the junction of the present day Whitley Street and Christchurch Road) appropriated to form part of the town's defences, as described earlier.

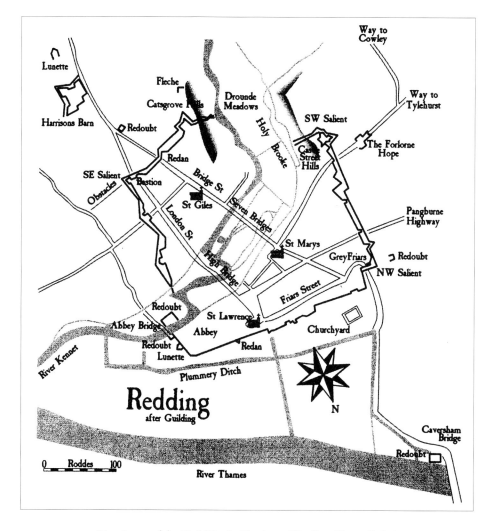

31 *A map of the Civil War fortifications of Reading. (Barres-Baker)*

The troops garrisoned on the town caused massive overcrowding in the town's insanitary tenements, something that would later help spread disease. Local people provided bed and board in return for tickets, which could – in theory – eventually be redeemed for payment. For their part, the cavalry complained of 'want of accommodation … and of all things necessary for the subsistence of men'. Many of the ordinary soldiers, who often went unpaid during the war, sold their equipment to local people, and many more deserted. By contrast, Aston paid himself a salary of £7 a week as head of the occupying forces, enabling him to maintain a more than comfortable standard of living, even to the point where he lent the cash-strapped Corporation £100 (on interest), which he duly extorted back from them.

The Corporation was very soon deeply in debt, its assets mortgaged to meet these demands. Things got so bad that the Corporation petitioned the King to be relieved of some of these demands, on grounds of poverty. The King unsurprisingly refused, and suggested instead that parliamentary sympathisers in the town be made to pay double. Some of those sympathisers had precious little more to give. In one such attack Battle Farm, the estate of Sir Francis Knollys, was plundered by some of the royalist troops, who generally behaved so badly that Aston was forced to hang three of his own men for some notorious crimes. Knollys at least survived the attack, dying in 1648 at the age of 98, still an active Member of Parliament: 'Honest old Sir Francis Knowles, the ancientest Parliament man in England, had much prejudice done to his house and tenants'. (Quoted in Coates)

Discipline would have been difficult for Aston to maintain; many of the troops were pressed men, in some cases captured enemy soldiers who had been given the option of changing sides or death. Aston had to deploy many of his more reliable troops to guard these men, and told the King that he 'needed not have sent him more enymies, for hee had enowe already'.

Those aldermen and others who did lend the Corporation money to help it pay the King's demands were later assumed to be royalist sympathisers when the town fell into parliamentary hands. They would find their entire estates confiscated and themselves, very possibly, imprisoned. Similarly harsh treatment was meted out by the royalists to those who tried to evade payment. Where the head of the household was absent on war service for the parliamentary cause, their wives or relatives could find themselves going to prison in their place.

Despite the harsh penalties for doing so, a steady stream of intelligence about the state of the royalist forces continued to reach the parliamentary side. In part, at least, this was driven by a desire to persuade the parliamentarians that the town was theirs for the taking, in the hope of getting the royalist forces out. A plot was even hatched to kidnap Aston, who – it was learned – was in the habit of dining at the homes of Sir Charles Blunt at Maple Durham and Sir Francis Englefield at White Knights, both outside his defensive wall. Only a last-minute change of plans by Aston frustrated the plot, and the would-be kidnappers ended by blowing some of their number up, as they tried to blast their way into Maple Durham House.

In April 1643, Reading became the scene of the first major siege of the Civil War. The Earl of Essex advanced on the town with forces numbering 16,000 infantry and 3,000 cavalry. They also bought with them some heavy artillery, including two of the biggest cannon from the Tower of London – huge 12ft cannons called Roaring Megs that required 24 horses to pull them.

There are differing accounts of Essex's line of attack. The traditional version has it that they attacked from the north, driving off a royalist advance guard stationed in Caversham, and shooting the spire off St Peter's church (where royalist artillery was installed). But more recent research (Barres-Baker) suggests that the destroyed spire of St Peter's may have been confused with that of St Giles, to the south of the town. The suggestion is that the earliest accounts of the siege were written by London journalists or serving soldiers, neither of whom had much knowledge of, or interest in, Reading's geography, and that these errors were perpetuated in later accounts. Essex in fact went around the south of the town and assembled his troops on its western flank. This came as a surprise to Aston, who had not expected an attack from this quarter and had failed to clear some of the hedges and other obstructions to his firing line. Essex made his headquarters in Southcote House, the former home of Sir John Blagrave, about a mile from the Forlorn Hope.

Once his troops were in place, Essex invited Aston to surrender the town, or 'he would beat it about his ears'. There appear to be two differing accounts of the royalist response, one or both of which may be the product of the wartime propaganda that was endemic throughout this siege. In one version, Aston said he would 'keep the town or starve in it', adding, ominously for the people of Reading, that 'he would not deliver the town until wheat was forty shillings a bushel, and as for the women and children they should dye with him'. The other has Aston offering to surrender if he could be allowed to march away 'with bag and baggage'. In this version Essex dismisses the offer, saying 'we came for the men, not the town'. Whatever the truth, Essex and his army settled in for a long siege. Neither side was at this stage in a dominant position. Parliament could not yet surround the town entirely, until the remainder of their forces arrived, and the royalists for their part did not have sufficient forces to relieve the town. Only by 19 April did the parliamentary forces complete the encirclement of the town.

The previous day, the townspeople's woes had been compounded by the start of an artillery bombardment. Within two days, the royalists were able to bring in reinforcements from Sonning, but the opposition responded with more forces of their own. Aston was standing outside a shelter on Castle Hill when a cannon ball dislodged a roof tile, which struck him on the head. At first they thought he was dead, but on further examination it was 'proved to bee that he had his pate broke with a tile'. A modern diagnosis would be 'a fractured skull and subdural haematoma'. The primitive surgeons of the day had to bore a hole in Aston's skull to relieve the pressure and, although the operation was successful, Aston was seriously injured enough to hand over to his second-in-command, Colonel

Richard Feilding. There was a further reverse for the royalists when one of their limited array of cannon was buried as the parliamentarians brought down the steeple of St Giles's Church, in which it had been deployed. Its activities had apparently 'very much annoyed some part of the Lord General's army'.

Throughout the siege, the royalist forces suffered from a shortage of gunpowder and munitions. This led to claims of them firing curious material, such as stones, from their cannon, and of them manufacturing low-grade, soft lead musket balls within the town. These latter acted as a primitive form of dum-dum bullet, causing horrific wounds that: 'chanked and furled, which poisons where it placeth, unlesse the flesh be immediately cut out'. (Barres-Baker)

On the night of 22 April, a brave royalist soldier named

32 *An artist's impression of the Civil War battery installed in the tower of St Giles's Church.*

Rupert Flower climbed through the trees in Caversham Park to avoid troops stationed there, swam the river and crept past the ranks of besieging forces into the town. He bought the news that reinforcements were on their way. But when he attempted the return journey he was captured and, under torture, made to reveal the royalists' plans. An alternative version has it that Flowers did not betray the plans, and that the relieving party simply blundered into a body of parliamentary troops by accident. Either way, Feilding did not get his supplies. That same night, an attempt by a deserter from Essex's troops, who had joined the royalist troops but had been paid £5 to blow up their store of gunpowder, was foiled. The guilty party was executed on the spot.

With the parliamentary forces forewarned, attempts to bring reinforcements and provisions into the town by barge were foiled. Further reinforcements, led by the King himself, were ambushed at Dorchester and some of them forced to retreat. But the remainder of the force, including Charles himself, were able to make their way to Wallingford, where they were joined by the King's nephew, and his cavalry commander, Prince Rupert.

Barres-Baker explains Charles' apparently irrational decision to attack Reading from the north. His army was far inferior to Essex's and he had the Thames between him and his objective. He could not really hope to get his troops across the bottleneck of a partly demolished Caversham Bridge in any numbers. One theory is that he planned to capture the bridge and, with Feilding's help, force a corridor through to the town centre, which he could hold for long enough to enable the garrison to escape. This seems optimistic in the extreme, given the time it would have taken to get all the garrison across the obstacle of the dismantled bridge. But the alternatives were even less palatable. He could not attack from south of the river and risk a pitched battle with Essex's superior forces – that could have lost him the war in an afternoon. But neither could he simply abandon this major garrison to its fate. Barres-Baker seems to think that Charles's decision involved a good deal of hoping that something would turn up.

Nonetheless, on 25 April, Prince Rupert led an attack on Caversham Bridge. During the attack, nature intervened decisively, as a Puritan historian reported:

> It pleased the Lord, in the midst of the fight, to send among them a very violent and vehement shower of hail and rain, which the wind blew into the faces of the King's Cavaliers, and greatly offended and molested them, while it was equally favourable to the Parliament's forces, being in their backs.
>
> (Hinton)

As one part of the royalist forces crossed a field in Caversham, roughly where Balmore House stands today, they were cut down by gunfire like ripe fruit in a strong wind by parliamentary troops, who were protected from both bullets and the elements by the mud walls of a barn. Local people for years after talked of the day Balmayer's field ran blood. Despite this reverse, the royalist forces made it in numbers as far as Caversham Bridge. Sir Simon Luke, one of Essex's commanders, takes up the account of the battle in his diary:

> They (the royalists) fell upon a loose regiment that lay there to keep the bridge and gave them a furious assault both with their ordinance and men, one bullet being taken up by our men which weighed twenty-four pounds at least. This was answered with our muskets; and we made the hill (St Peter's Hill) so hott for them that they were forced to retreat, leaving behind seven bodyes of as personable men as were ever seene and moste of their armes, besides others which fell in three or four miles compasse as they retreated. And it is sayed that within five miles there were five hundred hurt men drest in a barne, besides many prisoners which we tooke, and many hurt men within our precincts to which we sent the next morning our surgeons to dresse, and gave orders to have the dead bodyes buryed by the parish where they were slain.
>
> (Humphreys)

Luke's estimate of royalist casualties probably contains a large element of propaganda, but parliamentary casualties were said to be far fewer – possibly less than twenty overall. In the chaos of battle, the royalists finally managed to get further supplies of gunpowder into the town, but it was too late. Just before the battle had started, Feilding, apparently thinking the King had been comprehensively defeated at Dorchester, had surrendered. When, to his surprise, the battle to relieve him began, Feilding did not renege on the surrender terms he had negotiated with Essex. This was either a matter of honour or he had no faith in the prospects of Charles relieving him. He told the King that he would not withdraw his surrender. Long-term, this was a very bad career move on his part, but more immediately it allowed him and his troops to obtain free passage to rejoin the King at Oxford.

After the firefight around Caversham Bridge the royalists retreated northwards along a track that is now the old Peppard Road. Critics in the parliamentary infantry later complained that Essex's cavalry failed to harass the opposition sufficiently as they returned to Oxford.

Feilding and his men were allowed, under the terms of the surrender, to march out of Reading: 'with flying colours, arms and four pieces of ordnance, ammunition, bag and baggage, light match (the fuses used to fire muskets) bullet in mouth (where fighting soldiers held their next round), drum beating and trumpet sounding'. (Hinton)

The surrender terms may have made their departure sound more glamorous than the reality. According to one account (which again may well be propaganda) Feilding's army looked: more like a congregation of hedge-rogues than like soldiers and they were accompanied by a huge company of whores and Bastards, little lesse in number … than the soldiers themselves. (Barres-Baker)

The terms of surrender agreed by Essex do seem surprisingly generous. This may have reflected his desire to avoid the 5,000 parliamentary casualties he estimated would be involved in taking the town by storm. Feilding's decision to keep to the surrender terms, with would-be rescuers on the hills above the town, was equally unexpected. The incoming parliamentary forces were surprised at how relatively well provisioned the town was. As one of them said: 'If any man on the Parliament's side should have delivered up a place on those terms, he would have deserved no better than a halter (noose)'. (Hinton)

The same thought crossed the royalists' minds. Rumours circulated that Feilding had sold out the town for £16,000, using a woman spy to communicate with Essex. More to the point, one of the terms of surrender that Feilding had negotiated proved to be a major propaganda own goal. Feilding had agreed to hand back to Essex any man who had deserted to them from the parliamentary side for summary execution. Charles, meanwhile, had been doing everything he could to promote desertion from parliament's ranks, offering a free pardon and a 5s. gratuity to any parliamentary soldier who came across. Feilding was court-martialled and sentenced to death for betraying the town into enemy hands. Twice he was actually taken to the scaffold and twice reprieved, before being pardoned. But, despite the fact that his military career never prospered thereafter, he went on demonstrating unswerving loyalty in the service of the King.

Aston recovered from his wounds and returned to active service, initially as Governor of Oxford (where his popularity was such that even his own men found an opportunity to beat him up one dark night). He continued to serve even after losing a leg and, in 1649, was Governor of Drogheda at the time Cromwell's soldiers captured the town and committed their infamous massacre. Aston himself 'was hewn in pieces, and his brains beat out of his head with his wooden leg'.

Even though Feilding put a clause in the terms of the surrender that no harm should be done to the townspeople, Reading people continued to suffer. The consequences of unleashing 15,000 unwashed and battle-brutalised parliamentary troops on a town of 5,000 people could not be contemplated, and Essex forbade them to enter the town immediately. He even promised his men 12s. each, in lieu of the proceeds of looting. Despite this, the troops began drifting into town, without their 12s. gratuity, getting drunk and going out looting and 'enquiring for grand malignants' (that is, royalists).

The Corporation tried to placate their new occupiers. They ordered the church bells to be rung as Essex entered the town, and presented him with diamond rings and fancy clothes (thought to have been looted from dead Royalists, which did not endear them to Essex). He immediately demanded more money, for his troops were seriously in arrears with their pay. He demanded 1/60th (originally 1/20th) of the estates of the people of Reading. Pleas of poverty by the Corporation had as little effect on Essex as they had had on King Charles.

Pestilence

But Essex's army paid a high price for the living conditions under which they were forced to conduct the siege. Their resistance had been lowered and: 'It pleased Almighty God to visit the army with sickness, by which many of our young men perished, and the rest, on account of their weakness, were disabled from doing much service in the field'. (Hinton)

If the conditions for the royalist troops in Reading had been bad, with overcrowding and shortages, they were nothing compared to those endured by the parliamentary forces besieging the town. The ordinary soldier would normally have had no tent and, if he could find no shelter where he was stationed, would sleep under a hedge in the open, in a sea of mud. The weather was cold and wet (Britain was at the end of a mini Ice Age) and the ordinary troops possessed only the clothes they stood up in. They were almost continuously cold, damp and often under-provisioned – some had to live on whatever water they could find for two days at a stretch.

But there was a greater danger than cold and hunger. About a hundred and fifty years before the Civil War, a new disease had appeared in Europe. It was known as *morbus campestris* – the camp disease – and it flourished in verminous and closely confined conditions, such as prisons and battlefields. It produced violent headaches, complications for the nervous system and a high fever. The crisis came within two weeks, by when up to three-quarters of its victims would die. Typhus (as we now know it) was carried by lice and rat fleas, and came to its peak in warmer weather, so the main effects of it would only be felt in Reading after the worst of the siege. Some 250 Reading citizens would die of typhus between May and August 1643 and both armies were decimated by typhus, during and after the siege. By some estimates, Essex's army lost 3,000 men to it before the epidemic burned itself out in the autumn of 1643.

Their losses were added to by desertions. The parliamentary troops remained in and around the town until 26 May, but when they were moved to the healthier higher ground of Caversham Park the disease followed them, taking the lives of some 30 members of what was then the tiny community living north of the river. The town itself continued to have a parliamentary garrison until September 1643 (though this did not stop Colonel Blagge, the royalist Governor of Wallingford, sending the Corporation a further demand for money, which they for some reason paid). Shortly after the first battle of Newbury, a new royalist occupation began, under Sir Jacob Astley. He immediately demanded more money from the town and 'invited' the local people to work on restoring the defences (terms: 7d. a day for working, or a 12d. fine for non-attendance).

All their enforced hard work was cancelled out in May 1644, when Charles withdrew his forces and began destroying the fortifications. The parliamentary forces returned within days. It was at this stage that the royalist garrison at Wallingford kidnapped the Mayor of Reading, one William Brackston, and held him to ransom. They argued that, since Reading now had no royalist garrison of its own, it should pay £50 a week towards the cost of the one at Wallingford. They demanded £200 (which included an estimated three weeks' arrears) for the mayor's return. The Corporation pleaded poverty but managed to secure his release by some means.

The parliamentary forces strengthened their garrison to prevent a repetition of the kidnap and set to work restoring the defences. They remained in occupation for the rest of the war, and from July 1644 the town paid taxes to the parliamentary side only. But the town continued to be ill-used by the occupying forces. The townspeople petitioned Parliament in December 1644, saying that the soldiers:

> break down our houses and burn them, take away our goods and sell them, rob our markets and spoil them, threaten our magistrates and beat them, so that without a speedy redress we shall be constrained … for the preservation of our lives, to forsake our goods and habitations, and leave the town to the will of the soldiers.
>
> (Hinton)

Plague returned to haunt the town in the three years from 1646, and in 1647 Cromwell billeted a large force on the town, at the local people's expense. They also faced the added burden of supporting wounded soldiers returning to the town with no means of support but begging to sustain them now that the woollen industry had all but been destroyed. Gradually, the town returned to some sort of normality under the new regime. In 1652, most of the fortifications in the Forbury were levelled: 'whereby the faires may be kept and the Inhabitants of the towne maye enjoy their privilege as formerly'. (Barres-Baker)

Of the two main protagonists of the siege, the reputation of the victor, Essex, suffered more than that of the defeated Aston. Essex emerged with his reputation for ineffectual leadership enhanced. Aston was relieved of any responsibility for the defeat on account of his injury.

33 *Some of the houses in Market Place, from which Reading people fired on the hated Irish troops during the so-called 'bloodless revolution' of 1688.*

Postscript: Bloodshed in the Bloodless Revolution

Seventeenth-century Reading had not seen the last of strife with the ending of the Civil War. James II succeeded to the throne in 1685 and was deeply unpopular on account of his Catholic sympathies. The birth of a male heir, seeming to promise a Catholic succession, prompted both Whig and Tory interests in England to persuade William of Orange, James's son-in-law, to invade and remove James. William landed in Torbay in November 1688 and began marching towards London.

James had stationed several hundred Irish Catholic troops in Reading. They were hated by the local people, who feared they were going to murder them in their beds. As soon as William's forces reached Hungerford, the Corporation sent a message to him seeking his help. William despatched 250 troops to relieve the town. The Irish expected William's men to advance on the town along the Bath Road. Accordingly, they posted lookouts in the tower of St Mary's Church, which then dominated that part of the town, placed cavalry in Castle Street, other troops in the churchyard and Broad Street, and the main body of their forces in Market Place. The townspeople got wind of this and sent messengers to warn the Dutch forces. They moved over to what is now the Oxford Road, and were thus able to fall upon the Irish troops with total surprise.

They drove the Irish back down Minster Street and Broad Street, into Market Place. There local people joined in, firing down on the Irish from upper storey windows. In the confusion, the Irish failed to realise their superior numbers and fled in the direction of Twyford, pursued by the Dutch. In all, about fifty-three of the Irish were killed and wounded, for the loss of about six of the Dutch. Some of the dead are buried in St Giles's churchyard. For a century afterwards, the date of the battle – 9 December – was celebrated in Reading by the ringing of bells. Soon afterwards, James fled to France, bringing to an end the so-called Bloodless Revolution – which in Reading's case was anything but bloodless.

Chapter Six

ACROSS THE BRIDGE

Behold, all that remains of the best knight who ever lived.
Cardinal Langton, Archbishop of Canterbury, giving the funeral oration for
William, Earl Marshal of Caversham, in 1218.

The Town across the River

Until 1911, Caversham remained administratively separate from Reading, within a different county (Oxfordshire). But the fortunes of the two towns have been linked since the beginning of recorded history. There are varying interpretations of its name; the 'Cavers' part could have related to calves and the 'ham' could be a version of 'haim' or homestead, making it a homestead for calves. But the 'ham' could also have been 'hom', or meadow, reflecting the fact that the area near the river may have been low-lying water meadows with streams running through, where cattle grazed. Street names like Gosbrook Road and Westbrook Road hint at other streams that may have run through the area. Another theory is that the 'Caver' part was an individual's name, so it could be 'Caver's home'. Other speculative efforts have it translated as a wooded hollow. None of this is helped by the fact that Kift identifies 22 spellings of the name, other than the present one. What we can say is that the earliest appearance of the name is in Domesday Book, where it appears as Cavesha.

Equally uncertain is the location of the earliest settlement on this bank of the river. Possibly it was centred around the original medieval manor house, which is thought to have been to the east of the present Caversham centre, near Caversham Park but closer to the river – possibly near Dean's Farm. It is thought that a separate settlement would have grown up around St Peter's Church, built in about 1100 on land donated by the Lord of the Manor, the Earl of Buckingham. They are still shown as two separate settlements on Thomas Pride's map of 1790. There was a mill at Caversham before Domesday Book was drawn up (which could well be the one that survived into the 20th century, at Mill Road, beyond Gosbrook Road). By 1493 there were two mills listed and 50 years later they had been joined by two fulling mills, to support the local cloth industry.

The bridge linking Caversham and Reading has been central to their relationship from the earliest days. It was built some time between 1163 (when

34 *Caversham had its own mill from medieval times, which survived to have its*
photograph taken in 1911.

the famous duel was fought on nearby de Montfort Island) and 1231, when
it was referred to in a letter from Henry III. In it, he commanded the Sheriff
of Oxfordshire:

> to go in person, taking with him good and lawful men of his county, to
> the Chapel of St Anne on the bridge at Reading over the Thames one side
> of which is built on the fee of William Earl Marshal and by the view and
> testimony of these men see that the abbot has the same seisin of the said
> chapel as he had on the day on which the said earl died.

The background to this is that William Marshal, the Earl of Pembroke, had
died at his home at Caversham Park in 1218. He had been a towering figure
in the affairs of the nation, and had been the Regent during the first years of
Henry III's minority, effectively running the country. The bridge was evidently
built partly at the expense of the Earl Marshal and the King was taking steps to
ensure that the rights of his family (whatever these were) were being properly
asserted over the bridge.

At this time a ferry existed alongside the bridge and, that same year, Henry gave an
order to the keeper of Windsor Forest to deliver to Andrew, sergeant of Caversham,
one good oak to make a boat for ferrying the poor people over the water of Caversham.
This reflected two probabilities; the first that the poor could not afford the bridge
tolls and the second that the early bridges often got swept away by floods, making the
alternative of a ferry indispensable. Prior even to this, it was said that the Thames could
at this time be forded at Reading and that people would have done so from somewhere
near where one or other (or both) of the current bridges cross. This was not to be
unreservedly recommended; there are records from 1329 of one John Waley drowning
while attempting to ford the river near Caversham Priory on horseback.

It is not hard to understand why a bridge would have been built in this location at about this time. On one side of the river stood one of the richest and most influential abbeys in the land, one with which the King had regular contact. On the other stood the family home of the most powerful minister in the land. Added to this was the arrival in Reading in 1224 of a community of Franciscan monks, who made their home on the south bank of the Thames, near the site of the bridge. They were greatly devoted to committing acts of piety, of which the building of bridges counted as one, and was one that had the added attraction of making contact with their brothers in Oxford easier. There would also be the not inconsiderable incentive of the toll-paying traffic between the shrines at the abbey and Our Lady at Caversham.

Over this period, the Abbot of Reading and landed interests to the north of the river shared responsibility for the upkeep of the bridge, admittedly with mixed results. But, after the dissolution, Henry VIII failed to reassign clear responsibility for its maintenance and the bridge soon fell into disrepair. Local business interests were concerned at the effects of this on the town's trade, but hesitated to take on what could be a bottomless commitment themselves. Queen Elizabeth settled the responsibility for their end on the Corporation, sweetening the pill by giving them materials to help with the works.

35 *Caversham Bridge – the picturesque ruin of the 'half and half' bridge that served the needs of Reading and Caversham, however inadequately – for centuries until 1869.*

John Leland visited Reading in 1536 and singled out the bridge for mention:

> There is a main bridge of timber over the Thames where I marked that it
> rested most upon foundations of timber and in some places of stone. Towards
> the north end of the bridge standeth a fair old chapel of stone, on the right
> hand piled in the foundation for the rage of the stream of Thames.

Navigational improvements to the river in the years that followed meant that larger barges could use it, and they had difficulty navigating through the narrow medieval piers. Their frequent collisions with the bridge did nothing for its state of repair and, although the boatmen were supposed to stop, report and pay for the damage, in practice this never happened. In 1638, the new charter that Charles I granted the town included the right to charge a toll of 4d. for every boat going beneath it, as well as payments for road traffic crossing it. This was supposed at last to resolve the problem of its upkeep and, in August 1642, the town council resolved 'that Caversham Bridge shall be viewed and soe much thereof shal be amended and repaired as is needful'.

However, as we saw, Civil War soon engulfed the nation and the bridge became a strategic target for both sides. In 1642, Henry Marten, the head of the parliamentary force then occupying the town, had several spans removed and replaced by an improvised drawbridge. Charles issued orders that the bridge should be restored to enable his troops to enter the town:

> Whereas I have received information that the bridge over the River of Thames
> at Causham was lately broken down Our will and express Command is that
> you imediately on sight hereof cause the said bridge imediately to bee rebuilt
> and made stronge and fitt for the passage of our Army and Artillery by to
> morrow eight of the clock in the morninge as thee Bearer shall direct of this
> you may not fayle at your utmost peril.
> (Letter from King Charles I to the Mayor of Reading – 3 November 1642)

This the Corporation ignored. When Parliament retook the town, the Earl of Essex issued orders that a substantial drawbridge should be erected (at the expense of the townspeople, naturally) but this work was not completed until February 1646, when a master carpenter, one John Hancocke, was engaged to maintain the Caversham end of the bridge for a period of five years.

But it was not just the state of the bridge that acted as a barrier to communications between the two settlements; the low-lying land between the Reading end of the bridge and the town suffered from severe and frequent flooding. In 1631 calls were made for a causeway to be built to link the two, but this was not taken up until the 18th century.

Disputes about the responsibility for maintenance flared up again in the early 19th century. The Corporation had repaired and widened their end of the bridge but, notwithstanding the ruling from Elizabeth I, they tried to pass responsibility for the north end back to Caversham. The Oxfordshire authorities showed no great interest in taking the job on, and ongoing disputes over maintenance meant that the bridge spent many of its intervening years in a ruinous state. J.M.W. Turner and the local artist William Havell both painted the picturesque results of this mismanagement. Less happily, in 1812, a carter named Barefoot is recorded as having fallen to his death from it, as a result of most of the parapet being missing. That same year, Reading Corporation won an action against the Oxfordshire authorities for failure to maintain the bridge and, in 1815, Earl Cadogan, the owner of the Caversham Park estate, was forced to repair it. But this work did not provide a long-term solution to the problem.

The River Thames has been central to the life of the town since its earliest days, and boat-building has been one of its staple industries. The Reading section of the Thames had a thriving barge building-industry until after the First World War. On the Reading bank at Caversham Bridge were Talbots; Lewis's had their yards on de Montfort Island, while the ancient firm of Freebody were said to have traded from the Caversham side as ferrymen, bargemen and boat builders from 1257 to 1964, when the last of the family retired. Maynards built steam launches, and Freebody and others doubled building boats with operating them for pleasure trips. At least one of them – the *Britannia* – went to Dunkirk during the epic evacuation in the Second World War. In addition, the marine engine company Thorneycroft operated from here until the early 1960s.

Lords of the Manor

The history of the Caversham Park estate and its Lords of the Manor is remarkable for the number of them who have been at the centre of the nation's government. After the Conquest, Caversham was granted to Walter Giffard, a relative of the Conqueror, who in 1070 became the Earl of Buckingham. His name is apparently a disrespectful nickname meaning 'fat cheeks'. He lived in Crendon in Buckinghamshire, near Notley Abbey (which would feature later in the history of Caversham). Through his family, it passed to the Earls of Pembroke.

The first of these, Richard de Clare, was known as Strongbow and was an important figure in the conquest of Ireland. He died in 1176, leaving his estate to an unmarried daughter, Isabel, who became the ward of King Henry II. Henry married Isabel off to the younger son of his Earl Marshal and the tutor to his own son, William Marshal. William inherited both the Earl of Pembroke's estate at Caversham and, eventually, the title of Earl Marshal. He was a man of world-wide renown, tall and with handsome features and of such fine bearing that it was said 'he resembled an Emperor'. Trusted by both sides in the dispute between King John and the barons, he was instrumental in getting the King to sign the Magna Carta in 1215. The following year, John died and his nine-year-old son succeeded him as Henry III. William Marshal, by now in his eighties, served as regent during the next two years of Henry's minority and effectively ran the country. In 1218, he was brought back from

36   *Caversham Park – one of several grand buildings to stand on this site. The present one was built by Victorian ironmaster William Crawshay.*

London to Caversham to end his days, the entire royal household travelling with him. His body was later conveyed in state back down the river to London, to be interred in the Temple Church.

By 1313 the estate was held by Gilbert, the Earl of Hertford and Gloucester, who was married to Edward I's eldest daughter, Joan of Acre, and who was held to be the most powerful subject in the land until his death at the Battle of Bannockburn. It then passed to the wife of Hugh Despencer. He was chief adviser to Edward II and his son the King's companion. It was said that the two of them virtually ran the country until 1326, when Queen Isabella took against them. Before the year ended the father was hanged and quartered at Bristol and his son was hanged at Hereford. One Thomas Despencer also held the manor under Richard II but, as a supporter of that king, when Henry IV succeeded to the throne he lost his title, his lands and, in 1400, his head. By 1449 it had passed to the wife of Richard Neville, better known as 'Warwick the Kingmaker'. After he was killed at the Battle of Barnet in 1471, it was confiscated by Parliament.

It then came to the daughter of the Countess of Warwick, Isabel, who was married to the brother of Edward IV – George, Duke of Clarence. He was found guilty of high treason in 1477 and was taken to the Tower of London, where he was famously drowned in a butt of malmsey. He and his wife's possessions were forfeited to the Crown and, in 1493, Henry VII leased large parts of the manor to the monks of Notley Abbey. He retained the moated area around the great house and the properties within it (the great house in which the Beauchamps and the Despencers had lived was by this time apparently in a ruinous state). The dissolution of the monasteries led to the manor once again reverting to the Crown.

In 1543 Henry VIII granted to Anthony Brigham the office of Bailiff of the Manor of Caversham. The previous year, he had leased the site of the manor and some of the lands attached to it to Francis Knollys (also spelt Knolles and pronounced Knowles); by 1552, Knollys had acquired the Lordship of the Manor itself. He was married to Catherine Carey, the daughter of Anne Boleyn's sister Mary and thus first cousin to Queen Elizabeth I. Catherine became the Chief Lady of the Queen's Bedchamber, the most intimate of her servants, and Francis a Privy Councillor, Captain of the Guard (responsible for the Queen's personal safety) and Treasurer of the Chamber (responsible for her personal finances). Knollys's son, William, in time became the Earl of Banbury and Queen Elizabeth's Comptroller. He entertained the Queen at Caversham in 1601, during one of her stays at Reading Abbey. Knollys apparently made great cheer and entertained her 'with many devices of singing, dancing and playing wenches and such like.' Anne of Denmark, the consort of James I, also visited the house. After William Knollys died, the house was bought by the Earl of Craven. Charles I visited there during the siege of Reading and, in 1647, the doomed King had a final meeting with some of his children at Caversham Park, en route to his execution. It was described by one who was present as the tenderest sight his eyes ever beheld.

Craven's property was seized by the Commonwealth and Caversham Park fell into the hands of a speculator, George Vaux, who vandalised the house for its saleable building materials and its woodlands for their ship-building timber. Craven got back what was left of his estate after the Restoration in 1660 and sold it on for £8,700 to the Earl of Kildare in 1681. From their family, it passed in 1718 to William Cadogan. He was a soldier who had served with distinction in Ireland (Battle of the Boyne, 1690), Scotland (suppression of the 1715 Jacobite rebellion) and in Flanders under the Duke of Marlborough, eventually succeeding him as the overall commander of the British army. By the time of its acquisition, he had also acquired titles to go with it – Earl Cadogan and Viscount Caversham. He was also a Member of Parliament (Woodstock 1705–16) and sought to become Reading's M.P. in the notorious general election of 1715, which was ruled null and void due to the amount of corruption involved.

Marlborough left the magnificent Blenheim Palace as his monument, and Cadogan evidently sought to rival him. He pulled the old house down and built a new one on higher ground, farther from the river, on the site of the present house. This was a truly stately home with a 320ft frontage, a great terrace of 1,850ft and cost the huge sum for the day of £130,000. One needs to imagine the stately home at Cliveden, but a quarter bigger again, to get an impression of its scale. Some were greatly impressed by the new development; it was described 'as one of the noblest seats in the kingdom'. Others, such as Sir John Clerk, thought rather less of it, describing it as 'a vast expense but laid out without either taste or judgement. The house consists of various parts irregularly put together as his Lordship's fancy or occasion required it'. His marble statues of Goddesses, imported from Holland, came in for particular criticism: 'There are

37   *There were many fires in the various houses on the Caversham Park estate. This one in 1926, while the Oracle School was in occupation, did not cause irreparable damage.*

several Goddesses but of such a clumsy make as one may see they were made in a country where women are valued by the pound of arse'.

William died in 1726 and his brother Charles bought the estate for the knockdown price of £15,000. He bought in Lancelot 'Capability' Brown to redesign the landscaped grounds. It was said that his designs rivalled his finest, at Blenheim. The property remained in the family until 1784 when, for reasons that are shrouded in mystery, they were forced to sell it, to Major Charles Marsack. Marsack was a nabob – the name given to those who had made their fortunes in India – and was himself a mysterious figure. His mother, Marguerite, Comtesse de Marsac, was a Huguenot, whose father had been forced to leave France by Louis XIV in 1685. It was claimed that Charles was the illegitimate son of George II, though proof of this seems elusive, and Marguerite ended up married to a commoner, one John Holcroft. Marsack was not popular with his neighbours, being overbearing, ostentatious and felling many of the fine trees in his estate. Thomas Jefferson, the future American President, visited the estate in 1786. At some time during the 18th century, the house was destroyed by fire and replaced by a smaller property. In due course the property passed to Marsack's son, but he was forced by gambling debts to sell it in 1823.

Chapter Seven

A VERY GREAT TOWN: EIGHTEENTH-CENTURY READING

… a very great one, I think bigger than Salisbury.
> Samuel Pepys's view of Reading at the threshold of the 18th century

Communications: The Canals

Pepys was perhaps over-generous in his estimation of Reading (even if correct in its pre-eminence over Salisbury). Reading was still suffering from the aftermath of the Civil War as the 18th century began. Its pre-war cloth industry never really recovered, and new businesses were slow to fill the gap it left in the local economy. Reading's importance as a centre of communications had always played a vital part in the town's fortunes, and the 19th and 20th centuries saw two revolutions in travel that helped to change the town beyond all recognition. But the transport revolution really started in the 18th century, with improvements in the construction and maintenance of the roads, the growth of the stagecoach industry, and the development of its waterways. But each of these improvements in Reading's communications attracted opposition, often from vested interests or landowners who felt threatened by change.

From the earliest days, the waterways were vital to the town's prospects. We have seen how the abbey sought to benefit from the trade along the waterways to London in medieval times. But by the end of the 18th century, the town was at the centre of a network of communications that gave it water-borne links with many parts of the country.

There had been talk of linking London and Bristol via the Thames and the Avon since the time of Elizabeth I. As early as 1626, Henry Briggs, the Professor of Geometry at Merton College, Oxford, surveyed the two rivers and found them, at one point, to be only three miles apart and with relatively flat terrain in between them. Only Briggs's untimely death prevented a link being made at that time. Others, including the Earl of Bridgewater in 1668, also tried without success to promote an east-west route. The alternative to the Thames-Avon route was to provide that link via the River Kennet, and a first step towards creating it was taken in 1715 when the Kennet Navigation Act was passed, permitting the river between Reading and Newbury to be made navigable. All the other towns

38 *For centuries, commerce rather than leisure was the raison d'etre of the Kennet and Avon Canal. This must have been one of the last commercial barges to pass along it, in the early 1950s.*

along the route were fully in support of the scheme, but Reading people were none too pleased about it. Up until then, Reading had been the navigable limit of the Kennet, and this drew much trade into the town as a consequence. In 1720, the town's opposition turned to violence. A mob of about three hundred people, including the mayor, Robert Blake, attempted to destroy part of the canal works. The rioters' efforts were in vain, and a threat of legal action against them deterred any further attempts at sabotage. Ironically, the name Blake is commemorated in the first lock on the canal, though this may refer to an earlier Blake, John, who owned a wharf on the Kennet within the abbey precincts in about 1650.

Local opposition was not the only problem the canal company had to face. They had employed an incompetent engineer, who spent the small fortune of £10,000 on locks but did nothing to reduce the meandering length of the route. His replacement, John Hore, put in 11½ miles of cuttings, to reduce the distance between Reading and Newbury to 18½ miles, just a mile longer than the road journey. But this in turn plunged the company deep into debt by the time the navigation opened in 1723. They owed money to everybody, including their staff and local landowners, and to add to their problems the company was badly run.

But it did not take bad debts to fuel the continued opposition of Reading people to the canal; the early bargees were stoned as they passed through the town and, in 1725, a death threat was issued against a Maidenhead bargee called Peter Darvall. Whatever it lacked in literary merit, it certainly left the recipient in no doubt as to its menacing intent:

> Mr Darvall, wee bargemen of Redding thought to Aquaint you before 'tis too Late, Dam You, if y. work a bote any more to Newbery wee will Kill You if you ever come any more this way. We was very near shooting you last time, wee went with to pistolls and was not too Minnets too Late. The first time your Boat Lays at Redding Loaded, Dam You, wee will bore hols in her and sink her so Don't come to starve our fammeleys and our Masters, for Dam You if you do we will sent you short home…

> (Phillips)

There were other problems for the new canal to contend with, not least of them being a lack of water supply – particularly with mill owners along the banks competing with the canal for water. Simon Finch, the miller at Sheffield Mill, diverted almost all the water supply through his mill-wheel, denying barges passage through the nearby lock. One barge-load of coal was delayed there for eight days, before giving up and returning to Reading. Other bargees were less tolerant and attempted their own impromptu engineering works to secure a navigable water supply, leading to confrontations with the local people. The company made almost no profit for the first 25 years, and even then was forced in 1756 to drop its prices in response to a new flying coach service between Reading and Newbury. But improvements to the canal were begun two years later, which enabled it to take larger barges and that led to a marked improvement in its profitability.

However, it soon became clear that, far from bankrupting Reading, the canal was ushering in a new period of prosperity for the town. In 1794, plans for the Kennet and Avon Canal received parliamentary approval and the long-awaited link between London and Bristol could be completed. This million-pound project was carried out by the young (but soon to be eminent) engineer John Rennie and was opened to traffic in 1810. There were other additions to the network: the Oxfordshire Canal, which opened in 1790, gave Reading links with the Midlands and Birmingham, and the Thames and Severn Canal (1789) gave a route to Shropshire and Wales. In 1802 the earliest navigable length of the Kennet, between High Bridge and the Thames, was itself canalised. Improvements to the navigation of the Thames were made from 1772, but it remained a bottleneck for many years. There were even plans put forward in 1793 to construct a canal from Reading to Isleworth, by-passing the worst parts of the Thames entirely, but this never got past the planning stage.

Reading benefited enormously from the canals. Before they were built, the only coal available in Reading had to be brought by sea, via London. Now, cheaper supplies could be had from Staffordshire, Shropshire, Wales and Somerset. Manufactured goods from all over the country – ironware from Birmingham, stone from Bath, pottery from Staffordshire – could all be delivered to Reading as cheaply as – or in some cases, cheaper than – they were available in London. At the same time, the produce of Reading and its hinterland could now be sold to a far wider market, and could be moved on a far larger scale, than before. The Newbury barges that now traded along the Kennet and Avon were up to 109ft long, 17ft wide and weighed up to 128 tons. They could carry 1,200 quarters of malt or other merchandise worth as much as £2,000 yet, going downstream, a fully laden barge required just a single horse (plus its human crew, of six men and a boy). But the days of horse-drawn transport on the canals were already numbered. 1813 saw the first steam barge pass through Reading, en route from Bath to London.

The importance of the canals to the town may be gauged from the fact that, in 1835, of the goods coming into and out of Reading, 50,000 tons were carried by canal and just 100 tons by road. The economics explain why. In 1814, the carriage of goods from London to Reading cost 2s. 6d. per hundredweight by road, but just 11d. by water The importance of the canal network was felt in a negative way when they became frozen and un-navigable for weeks on end during the dreadful winter of 1813–14, creating dire shortages and paralysing the local economy.

It is sometimes forgotten that the canals also carried passengers. The records for 1832 include a party of 43 emigrants boarding a barge at Caversham Bridge, at the start of their long journey to Liverpool and their even longer one to a new life in America. But from 1840 the coming of the railways meant the canals were doomed, whether carrying goods or people. The receipts of the Kennet and Avon fell in a single year from £51,000 in 1840–1 to £39,000 in 1841–2. It was the start of a long period of decline.

Coaching

Travel by road had been in an even longer period of decline nationwide, some say dating back to the seventh century. Such goods as needed carrying by road were mostly borne on the backs of horses and men, and wheeled traffic became a rarity, due to the sheer difficulty of moving it around. From 1555, an Act of Parliament made parishes responsible for the upkeep of their roads and gave powers to fine those who failed in their duty. But while some parishes took the responsibility seriously, many ignored it. The roads out of 17th-century Reading were impassable for as much as six months of the year. The Bath Road to the west of the town was described by Celia Fiennes in 1690 as 'sad clay deep way'. These roads were not only difficult to travel along, but also dangerous. The *Reading Mercury* for 24 September 1785 reports a wagon breaking a wheel on the rough road while going down a hill at Shiplake, rolling over and killing the two women and the boy who were riding on it.

But during the 18th century, the practice of turnpiking – carrying out road improvements that were funded by tolls charged on the users – started to become common. Combined with improved techniques for constructing roads, this

Hone's General Coach Office
KING-STREET READING.
(Adjoining the George Inn,)

Reduced Fares to LONDON
BY THE
OMNIBUS.
Inside 8s. Outside 5s.
Mornings at 10 o'Clock.

TO LONDON
THE TELEGRAPH FAST COACH,

Through MAIDENHEAD and SLOUGH, every day at Twelve (except Sunday,) to *Nelson's* Black Bear, Piccadilly, and Blossom's Inn, Lawrence Lane, Cheapside; from whence it returns every Morning at 11; and Black Bear, Piccadilly at a quarter before 12.

——ooo——

"STAR" Coach to BATH and BRISTOL,
Through MARLBOROUGH, DEVIZES, and MELKSHAM, every Morning (except Sunday) at a quarter before Nine o'Clock to the York House Bath, and White Lion, BRISTOL.

TO LONDON.--The ZEPHYR, through WINDSOR,
Every day at half past One.

——ooo——

COACHES DAILY TO

Oxford	Brighton	Marlow	Portsmouth	Windsor
Wallingford	Guildford	Bath	Basingstoke	Wantage
Maidenhead	Petersfield	Bristol	Newbury	Faringdon
Winchester	Odiham	Horsham	Marlborough	Cirencester
Alton	Horndean	Southampton	Monmouth	Gloucester &
Farnham	Wycombe	Gosport	Hereford	Worthing.

Wm. HONE & Co. Proprietors·

	£	s.	d.
PAID OUT......			
CARRIAGE......			
BOOKING			
PORTERAGE...			

SOCIABLES to Streatley, Newbury, Basingstoke, Windsor, Wallingford, Henley and Maidenhead, daily

White, Printer & Binder, Reading.

39   *A poster dating from around 1800 advertises some of the coach services from Reading.*

40   *Castle Hill from the turnpike road, looking east, c.1823.*

brought about a revolution in road transport, with both costs and journey times falling dramatically. However, turnpikes were not generally popular with local people, and it was not at all uncommon for troops to have to be called out to suppress riotous attempts to destroy the toll barriers. Many of Reading's main roads, being on some regionally important routes, were among the earlier ones to obtain the private Act of Parliament required for a turnpike. The section between Reading and Theale, complained of earlier, was turnpiked in 1714 and that from Reading to Twyford in 1736. This latter section was the last part of the London to Bristol road in Berkshire to be turnpiked. It was only delayed because of fears that it might interfere with the town's profitable barge traffic to London, or deter local farmers from bringing their livestock to Reading for the market. To this end, traffic related to the woollen trade was made exempt from tolls. However, by no means every road was improved by this means. Even at its height, never more than a fifth of the national road network was turnpiked. Nor was turnpiking an automatic guarantee of a good road. One traveller in 1754 complained about the lack of widening of the Bath Road turnpike, its deep puddles, the lack of a proper surface and unkempt hedges. He concluded 'tis the worst public road in Europe, considering what vast sums have been collected from it'.

But eventually a sufficient network of trunk roads had been turnpiked and improved to make possible a reasonably reliable national set of stagecoach services. These again were not universally loved, one early opponent describing them as one of the greatest mischiefs to have happened of late years to the kingdom – mischievous to the public, destructive to trade and prejudicial to lands. The first record of a stagecoach service between Reading and London was an advertisement dating from 1657. This was part of the service between London and Bath, a journey that took three bone-shaking days (God willing, as the advertisement encouragingly put it) in an unsprung coach, seating just four people. In the early part of the 18th century, Queen Anne made it fashionable for London society to take the waters at Bath Spa, and Reading found itself on a rapidly growing route between the two. By the 1830s, improvements to both the roads and the coaches had reduced the journey time for the fastest services to Bath to 11 hours. Thirty-three stagecoach services a day now passed through Reading. For Reading people, the five-hour trip to London was the most popular, costing 12s.–16s. (inside) and 6s.–10s. (outside). In addition to London and Bath, other services from Reading ran to Oxford, Cheltenham and Bristol, and the town's streets were constantly busy with the clatter of their hooves and wheels.

A good number of coaching inns also prospered on the back of this industry. In addition to the *George* on King Street and the *Sun* on Castle Street, which still survive, they included the *Crown* at the junction of London Street and Crown Street, the *Angel* on Broad Street, the *Bear* on Bridge Street and the *King's Arms*, which stood at the western limits of the town. Many other people in the town also made their living from travel – in addition to the 11 coaching inns in Reading by 1826, the town could also boast four coachbuilders, seven farriers, four horse dealers, six saddle-makers, four wagon proprietors and four wheelwrights.

The close association between the coaching industry and inns, and the need for the drivers to fortify themselves against the effects of bad weather, meant that the coaching industry was not always noted for the sobriety of its staff, at a time when drunkenness was generally more tolerated. This newspaper report was by no means unique:

> The London mail did not arrive so soon today by several hours as usual on Monday, owing to the coachman getting a little intoxicated on his way … and falling from his horse into a hedge, where he was found asleep by means of his dog.
>
> (Dils)

Another hazard to the coach traveller was highwaymen – and the road between Maidenhead Thicket and Reading was notorious for them. The coaches responded by carrying guards, often armed with a fearsome blunderbuss. These guards became almost as much of a nuisance as the highwaymen themselves, for their habit of discharging their pieces gratuitously in built-up areas and disturbing sleeping neighbours. One guard fired in the middle of a village and had his weapon blow up, sending shrapnel through all the nearby windows. As the newspaper reported, 'it so terrified a woman … that she was instantly seized with fits which, it is much feared, she will never get the better of'. Worse still was the fate of one would-be passenger, who tried to flag the coach down, only to be shot as a suspected highwayman.

Some of these coaches also carried mail. During the reign of Elizabeth I a network of routes was set up, principally for the delivery of the government's mail, but also carrying a limited number of private letters. One such, between London and Ireland, came through Reading from 1579. One Richard Spignall was made the postmaster for the Reading section, which principally involved supplying horses and any other help needed for that stage of the journey. Charles I threw the service open to all private mail in 1635, as a means of offsetting the cost of the government part of the operation.

From the 1780s, private letters received in Reading would be delivered free to a small area around the post office. Beyond that, people were supposed to collect them from the post office themselves. But postmasters soon saw a way of making more by charging extra for delivering to a wider area (in those days it was quite usual for the postal cost to be borne by the recipient of the letter). Local carriers were hired to deliver mail to convenient places (such as the local inn) in outlying villages. They would style themselves as postmen. It was strictly illegal, but a blind eye was turned to the practice.

By 1839, mail for London left Reading in the evening and arrived in the capital at about 7a.m. Any post for onward delivery to the provinces then had to wait until the coaches left London the following evening. The introduction of the penny post in 1840 saw a massive increase in the volume of mail traffic. The mail from Reading increased from 3,800 letters a month to ten thousand. A main post office in Broad Street and two sub-post offices in the south and east of the town were opened, and a public subscription was raised to provide the town's six postmen with uniforms.

But it would be too late for the coaches to benefit from this increase in trade; the railways had robbed them of the London mail traffic as early as May 1840. The local turnpikes also suffered from the competition of the railways, with their revenues falling disastrously from 1840 onwards. Twyford Tollgate, which in 1832 had an income of £1,215, was down to £234 20 years later.

The Gentlemen of the Press

Before 1723, Reading people who wanted to read a newspaper had to have one mailed to them from London. This was a slow and costly process, given that postage costs had to be added to the crippling newspaper stamp duty and a separate tax on newsprint. By 1815, stamp duty alone represented over half the cost of 7d. for a newspaper. Their cost, and the limited spread of literacy, made newspaper reading a minority activity. The other factor that limited their availability was the technology of printing them, which had barely changed since the invention of the printing press. Their hand-operated presses could barely turn out 250 sheets an hour, printed on one side only.

In July 1723, Reading saw the birth of its first newspaper, the *Reading Mercury or Weekly Entertainer*. Initially, it got round the newspaper stamp duty by having itself classified as a pamphlet (a widely used loophole, and one that the government closed within two years). It was produced by William Parks and David Kinnier, two printers who had set up in business next door to the *Saracen's Head* in the High Street. They appear to have been the first printers to have established their business in Reading but, to judge from some of their earliest editions, they seem to have been printers first and journalists a rather distant second. Most of its content consisted of an assortment of titbits of national and international news gleaned from the London papers. At this time, this was the standard method for producing most provincial papers. If the *London Gazette* and the *Times* were late arriving in town, then the publication of the local paper was correspondingly delayed. In addition, they provided lists of the merchandise passing between Reading and London, a great deal of detail about the price of corn in every market town for 20 or 30 miles around and just a few local items of (to our eyes) doubtful news value.

For example, much space was devoted in the second week's edition to a minutely detailed description of the town's boundaries. In subsequent weeks, the readers were treated to a list of the town's mayors over the past 300 years. This item was serialised, possibly on the basis that too much excitement might be bad for their readers. If neither of these seemed to cry out 'Hold the front page!' one apparently local item that did cause a stir turned out to be misleading. From the first issue, they ran a weekly bill of mortality, which claimed to list the causes of death among an undefined local population. Looking at the list, the weekly death toll seemed disturbingly high for a town the size of Reading (whose population was at this time probably no more than 8-9,000). For example, the very first week's list included 42 deaths from smallpox alone, and prompted a complaint from the Reading authorities that local people and visitors alike were alarmed by these figures. They turned out to be the figures for London. As an aside, modern readers will no doubt be interested in some of the other causes of death that were being diagnosed at the time. They included: 'dropsie, fever, griping in the guts, 'teeth', 'evil', looseness, mortification, purples, rising of the lights, stoppage i'th' stomach, water in the head, twisting of the guts, horseshoehead, 'suddenly' and 'lunatick and worms'. If these did not leave the readers of the *Mercury* with a renewed sense of their own mortality, I do not know what would.

The initial circulation was small – around four hundred copies, rising to about a thousand by the end of the 18th century. Even by the time in 1855, when the removal of stamp duty made newspapers much more affordable, the *Mercury* was still only selling about 4,000 copies and its rival, the *Chronicle*, a mere 800 or so. The newspaper was cross-subsidised by selling a host of other products from its offices, notably, in the case of the *Mercury*, quack patent medicines. So visitors to their offices might be offered Daffrey's Famous Cordial Purging Elixir, Stoughton's Grand Stomach Drops and Lisby's Never Failing Eye Water, as well as a newspaper.

No actual news gatherers were employed until well into the 19th century; the 1841 census records only one person in Reading (or anywhere else in Berkshire) listing their occupation as journalist. Such local news as was published was the result of people volunteering it. It seems there may have been little attempt to check its accuracy for, in March 1799, the *Mercury* carried a letter from a Mr J. Phipson, complaining that reports of his death had been greatly exaggerated. It was perhaps not surprising that the two printers did not remain proprietors for long. Within

41 *A map of the town as it was in 1813. (Childs)*

a year, Parks had emigrated to the United States. A man named John Newbery
was hired as an apprentice to the newspaper in 1730. Seven years later the new
owner of the paper, William Carnan, died, and Newbery not only inherited half
the business but also married the other half, in the form of William Carnan's
young widow, Anna Maria. On her death in 1809, it passed to her son-in-law
Thomas Cowslade, in whose family it remained until 1913. The *Mercury* ceased
publication in 1987, when it was absorbed by the *Chronicle*.

The *Reading Chronicle* is a relative newcomer. Its earliest claimed origins go
back to a paper first produced in Wokingham in 1770. However, this early
Berkshire Chronicle was circulated as far afield as Sussex, Surrey, Hampshire,
Wiltshire, parts of Gloucestershire, Hertfordshire, Northants and Middlesex,
and was thus hardly local. This only survived until 1775 and there appears to be
no evidence to link it directly with the modern newspaper of that name. The most
obvious ancestor to the newspaper that finally became the *Reading Chronicle* in
1962 was first produced in January 1825, as the *Berkshire Chronicle, Forest, Vale
and General Advertiser*. Among its promoters was a pillar of the Establishment,
Mr J.J. Blandy, local solicitor and Town Clerk to the Corporation. From the
start, the paper went for the throat of its older rival:

'It has long been a matter of surprise, among those who know how to estimate the vast importance of the Press, that the town of Reading should not possess an impartial newspaper, conducted with that talent and ability which the enlightened state of Public Opinion demands and maintaining those sound constitutional principles, which are most deeply rooted in the hearts of all loyal and patriotic Englishmen … the only newspaper here put forth is of a character so manifestly different from that which we have described … That the journal alluded to may be adapted to the readers of a certain class we do not dispute.'

(Berkshire Chronicle – 29 January 1825)

The article goes on to accuse its rival (justifiably) of selecting its news by 'the old jog-trot method' of snipping extracts from the London press. By contrast, the *Chronicle* promised a mixture of local, national and international news (a single newspaper in those days having to perform all the functions now undertaken by our various local and national newspapers and other media). If relations between the two papers started off badly, they rapidly got worse. In April 1826, the *Chronicle* threatened to sue the *Mercury* over an alleged libel, committed under the guise of reporting a speech by a Parliamentary candidate, Mr Fyshe Palmer. In this, he allegedly described the *Chronicle* as: 'a weekly paper abounding with more personal abuse and more frequent attacks on private character than any other town in England, but which from its very confined circulation was an evil of little consequence to either town or neighbourhood'.(*Reading Mercury* – 2 April 1826)

This action came to nothing. But shortly afterwards the *Chronicle* was successfully sued by a third party – a member of the gentry, whose honour in a small matter had been wrongfully impugned by the paper – with the active support of the *Mercury*. As we will see later from the great railway debate, the two papers developed their own positions and their own readership. Both of them edged the pages in black when reporting the death of a member of the Royal Family. But only the more radical *Mercury* did the same when covering the failure of the first Reform Bill.

Another weekly paper, the *Reading Standard*, was published in the town from 1891. This was taken over in 1965 by the Thompson Organisation and replaced by the first daily evening newspaper in the country to be published since the Second World War – the *Reading Evening Post*.

Religious Divisions

This was a time of great religious diversification in the town. John Wesley noticed a change in the people of Reading, when he visited in 1777. He commented: 'For many years we were beating the air at this town, stretching out our hands to a people as stupid as oxen. But it is not so at present'.

Reading became a breeding ground for all sorts of non-conformity. Wesleyan chapels were founded in London Street (1814) and Church Street (1817). All sorts

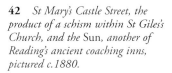

42 *St Mary's Castle Street, the product of a schism within St Giles's Church, and the* Sun, *another of Reading's ancient coaching inns, pictured c.1880.*

of other sects flourished in the town; Primitive Methodists were worshipping in Silver Street, Unitarians in Mill Lane and then London Street and Presbyterians in Minster Street. There were also less familiar non-conformists, such as Cudworthians (who practised the equally obscure corpuscular philosophy), Sandemonians and Universalists.

Religious disputes continued to divide the town, from the 18th into the 20th centuries. One of its most visible manifestations today is the Independent Congregational Chapel of St Mary's in Castle Street, built on the former site of the town's prison. This was the result of a schism within the congregation of St Giles's Church. Between 1767 and 1774, St Giles's had a popular and strongly evangelical vicar, William Talbot. He was succeeded by William Cadogan, the son of Lord Cadogan of Caversham Park. After a hostile start, he was even more firmly won over to the cause of evangelism until his early death in 1797 at the age of forty-six. His successor, Joseph Ayre, was described as a tepid rationalist, whose charisma may be judged by the title of one of his sermons, 'The probable causes and consequences of Enthusiasm'. He plunged St Giles's into a rapid decline and, as early as December 1798, those who had deserted his ministry flocked to the thousand-seat chapel in Castle Street, which they were able to fill each week.

Non-conformists in Reading at this time were disadvantaged at every turn. Universities and posts in national and local government were closed to them; for marriage (except for Quakers and Jews) and burial they had to look to an Anglican church; they even had to pay rates to a church they did not attend. Despite this, all sorts of non-conformism flourished. There had been an Anabaptist congregation in the town since the 17th century – John Bunyan had preached to them in 1688. Their numbers grew in the late 18th century, particularly among the poor of Silver Street. The Baptist minister in Reading between 1820 and 1837, John Howard Hinton, used to preach to the crowds on Forbury Hill during the cheese fairs, and was the driving force behind the building of their chapel in King's Road in 1834. Many others flourished, some creating impressive places of worship. One of these, the independent chapel on Broad Street, dating from 1800, is now well known as a bookshop.

Reading's Catholic congregation had its origins in a group of émigré French priests who lodged at the *King's Arms* on Castle Hill. They worshipped at a building on Vastern Lane until 1838, when James Wheble of Woodley Lodge commissioned the eminent architect Augustus Welby Pugin to design the church of St James, which stands in the shadow of the gaol and the abbey ruins.

The emancipation of Catholics came with the repeal of the Corporation Act in 1828, which allowed non-conformists to hold public office for the first time since 1661. But that was not the end of discrimination for Reading's Catholic congregation. As late as 1909, the priest and congregation of St James Church went on a Palm Sunday procession through the streets of Reading. Harmless though it may sound, this was objected to by a body called the Evangelical Lay Churchmen's Union, who cited legislation dating back to the Reformation banning the wearing of Roman Catholic robes or the conducting of Roman Catholic worship in the street. They called upon the Police to ban any further such activities. This led to complicated legal arguments involving the Catholic Bishop of Portsmouth and, at one stage, the Home Secretary, before it was decided that such processions could now be allowed.

Jews had to wait until 1858 before they could become Members of Parliament, but Reading was one of the first constituencies to take advantage of it. Sir Francis Goldsmid served as Reading's MP from 1860 until his death in a rail accident in 1878 and, in the 20th century, Rufus Isaacs would be the town's MP, and much more besides.

Sauce, Sailcloth and Silk – Some More Reading Industries

No single industry developed in 18th-century Reading to take up the dominant position formerly held by cloth-making, but a number of important industries emerged. From the middle of the century the town became a centre for the malting of barley, supplying the London brewing industry. By 1760, Berkshire was the nation's most important area for malting, producing some 15,000 tons a year. It would be money from malting that made possible the establishment of the Huntley and Palmer empire. It was around that time, too, that the local brewers set up a cartel that fixed beer prices and, working in cahoots with the local magistrates, restricted the entry of competition by refusing licenses to new public houses.

Silk weaving, an industry started in the time of Queen Elizabeth, still employed numbers of people in the Oracle and elsewhere. As late as 1841, Messrs Baylis were erecting an extensive silk manufactory in Kings Road. Sailcloth was also made in the Oracle, as well as in Katesgrove. Large quantities were supplied to both the East India Company and the Royal Navy. Musgrave Lamb produced so much sailcloth for the Royal Navy from his 140 looms that locals used to claim that the Battle of Trafalgar was won in Katesgrove Lane. There were also important brickworks in Tilehurst and Katesgrove by the end of the century, and Katesgrove Lane was also the location for Benjamin Williams's iron foundry,

43   *A horse tram passes the famous Cocks Reading Sauce factory on King's Road, c.1890.*

which was started in 1790. This grew into the Reading Ironworks under Messrs Barrett, Exall and Andrewes, and was one of the largest suppliers of agricultural machinery in the country until it failed in the slump of 1887. Their Berkshire plough was famed in farming circles, and they also produced horse-driven and steam-powered farm equipment.

Charles Cocks was a fishmonger who went into the manufacture of his sauce recipe from premises in Duke Street in 1789. So successful was he that, in 1814, he took legal action against a Mr Shout, a London oil dealer, for trying to counterfeit his product. It was the first of several lawsuits against imitators and the manufacturing process was thereafter carried out in great secrecy, lest spies obtained his recipe. For over a century, Cocks' Reading Sauce was almost as famous throughout the nation as the Worcestershire variety, and even enjoyed the fictitious endorsement of Phineas Fogg in Jules Verne's *Around the World in Eighty Days*. The business later moved to Kings Road and survived until 1962.

Civic Improvements

The town was relatively run-down and shabby at the start of the century, but a number of civic improvements were undertaken, particularly in the latter part of the century. As we have seen, as long ago as the 13th century, the flooding of the area between the town and Caversham Bridge had blighted the efforts of the Grey Friars to establish a community there. It remained a problem until the start of the 18th century, with Caversham Road also being known as Watery Lane. In the 1720s an energetic mayor, John Watts, used a public subscription to raise the money to import over a thousand wagon-loads of gravel to raise the road above flooding level.

King Street was created in 1760. Up until that time, it had been split down the middle by a row of run-down houses, creating two narrow lanes – Sun Lane and Back Lane. The name of the new street commemorates the accession of George III to the throne in that year. Its extension, Kings Road, was not built until around 1830. The land on either side of it, owned by the Crown Estate, was sold for development over the following few years, and many of the grand houses built along it were of Bath stone, imported by the town's new railway or the canals.

A bridge across the Kennet at Duke Street had been part of the town since the construction of London Street in the middle of the 13th century. A new wooden bridge was erected in 1707 but, by 1787, it was in a ruinous condition and heavy vehicles were not allowed across it. The council brought in the London architect Robert Brettingham to design a new stone bridge at a cost of £3,500. The result, High Bridge, was an elegant structure that survives to this day as one of the town's three scheduled ancient monuments. However, it did not make life any easier for the bargees who had to navigate this particularly difficult stretch of the Kennet. There was an island in the middle of the river, just upstream of the bridge, and the 109ft barges had to go through the narrow archway of the bridge at a slant. To this day, this stretch of the canal is unusual in being controlled by traffic lights.

Other civic improvements of this period, such as the refurbishment of the Oracle, the construction of a new town hall and the work of the paving

44   *For centuries, Caversham Road – also known as Watery Lane – was prone to flooding, until its level was raised in the 1720s. In this 1905 scene, it was still apparently safe for sheep to wander about in the road.*

commissioners, are described elsewhere in the book. But one part of the town was by no means being improved:

The Abbey – More Rack and Ruin

The years immediately after the dissolution were the period of greatest destruction of the abbey, but the catalogue of neglect and vandalism continued down through the centuries. The use of abbey materials for the Civil War fortifications is documented elsewhere in the book. In May of 1644, when Charles I ordered the slighting of the defences, it seems he may have discharged a mine under the abbey, part of whose foundations appear at some time to have been shattered and tipped by a great explosion. In 1754 stone from the abbey was used to build a bridge between Wargrave and Henley and in 1786 a new council hall, the first phase of the current town hall complex, was built on the site of the former abbey refectory. Another part of the site was sold to house the new house of correction on the Forbury in 1791. One contemporary described the prison as being placed so conspicuously among the ruins. During its construction an unusual lead coffin was unearthed. With the town's usual respect for both antiquity and the deceased occupant, the coffin was sold to a plumber for its scrap value.

The Compter Gate, adjoining St Laurence's Church at the west end of the abbey site, was demolished in about 1800 and in 1811 a school for national education, large enough to take between two hundred and four hundred pupils, was erected in the midst of the ruins, prompting laments about this disfigurement of the finest and most perfect remains of this once beautiful abbey. This at least was relatively short-lived, itself being demolished by 1837. Meanwhile, the abbey gateway was slipping from disrepair into dereliction. Safety dictated that it had its battlements removed and parsimony meant that they were replaced by several courses of unsightly brickwork. The 1791 illustrator of the abbey, Thomas Tomkins, said the effect was 'so unpleasant to the eye and take(s) off from the grandeur of the gate'. But worse was yet to come.

Chapter Eight

CRIME AND PUNISHMENT:
READING'S PRISONS, POLICE AND VILLAINS

…'tis a pity we have no guardians who might prevent property being stolen by fear of their presence, but lacking them, you must pay for the lack with eight years in Botany Bay.

(Judge at the 1827 Berkshire Assize, sentencing a thief to eight years' transportation – quoted in Wykes)

Before 1403, anyone could run a prison and they were virtually unregulated. The earliest recorded prison in Reading was run by the abbot and consisted of three small rooms over the main gateway to the abbey, next to St Laurence's Church. It was called the Compter, and was used to incarcerate misbehaving monks and wrongdoers from the town. During the reign of Richard II, a prisoner starved to death in it, and the coroner's jury were unable to establish who should have been responsible for feeding him. After the dissolution of the abbey, the Compter was used for debtors and civil prisoners. The structure, if not the function, survived into the early 19th century and the Compter House itself, where the head constable lived, was not demolished until 1973.

The town had other early lock-ups for short-term detention. Minor offenders could find themselves in The Hole, a single cell built on the end of the Blagrave Piazza. A further lock-up was provided to the rear of the *Shades* public house in Gun Street, for the use of the nightwatchmen in the unlikely event that they ever caught any miscreants. The use of this was discontinued in about 1850, around the time of the demolition of the original Oracle.

In 1403 Henry IV ruled that Justices of the Peace should incarcerate prisoners only in the common gaol, which was under the control of the county sheriff. Reading's county gaol stood on Castle Street, on the site occupied today by the town's other St Mary's Church. The main priorities of the gaoler in these days were security and income generation. There was no thought of prison conditions themselves being used as a form of punishment, or of trying to rehabilitate the prisoners. The gaoler rented the premises and recouped his (or her – when prison reformer John Howard visited, the gaoler was a widow) outlay by selling privileges to those prisoners who could afford them. These ranged from extra food and strong liquor (the gaoler had a licence to sell the prisoners alcohol),

45   *The Blagrave Piazza, on the south side of St Laurence's Church, was long used for the storage of the town's instruments of justice – the pillory, stocks and tumbrel.*

through additional bedding, to lighter manacles. Each debtor and felon also had to pay 13s. 4d. to the keeper and 2s. 6d. to the turnkey on their release. Those prisoners without private means had to rely upon the none-too-generous provisions of the Poor Law, or beg to passers-by from their subterranean cells through a grating in the street.

The first records of the county gaol date from the last quarter of the 16th century. The register of burials at St Mary's for 7 July 1585 record John Greenwoode, who had been pressed to death. At that time, if someone was charged with a felony they could refuse to enter a plea since, if they were found guilty, all their property would be forfeit to the Crown and their family would be left destitute. In order to extract a confession from the accused, the authorities used to press them, piling weights 'as heavy as they can bear and more' onto them, until they either confessed, or expired. The formal name of the punishment was *peine forte et dure.* During this drawn-out process, the prisoner was only fed every other day with 'but three morsels of barley bread and water from the gutter nearest the gaol'.

Conditions in the prison, while not intended as a punishment in themselves, were awful. There was severe overcrowding, no segregation of the sexes (except for sleeping), the food was poor (unless you could afford to supplement it), debtors, felons and those of unsound mind were mixed in together and sanitation was minimal, leading to outbreaks of gaol fever (typhus). So it was small wonder that the gaolers found a ready market for their over-priced alcohol. In March 1661 there were complaints to the Corporation that 'there is great disorders in the gaol by reason of the gaoler's keeping a common alehouse there'. Sales of spirits to the prisoners were only banned after the opening of the new prison in 1792, but beer continued to be sold to them well into the 19th century.

The county gaol contained mostly debtors and remand prisoners, although there were also religious dissenters – John Bunyan served time there – and people who had been press-ganged for service in the Royal Navy and were awaiting transport to their new 'careers'. When the prison reformer John Howard visited the prison in 1779, he found that the prison, with a nominal capacity of 20, contained 18 felons and debtors and 19 victims of the press gang.

By the 1780s, the old county gaol was in serious disrepair. Plans were put in motion to provide a new house of correction for the county and these were extended to include a replacement county gaol, all on the site of the modern-day Reading Prison. They were designed by an eminent architect of the day, Robert Bressingham (who also designed Longleat House and Reading's High Bridge) but the buildings were soon found to have been jerry-built. They also became overcrowded. By 1830, a prison that had a nominal capacity of 100 was housing 142 prisoners.

As part of keeping the prisoners occupied, a treadmill was installed in the new prison in 1822. It was linked to a mill to grind corn for the prison bread. By 1834, this contract was found to be operating at a loss (remarkably, given the unlimited supplies of free labour available, and probably due to fraudulent accounting). The milling of grain was therefore discontinued and a friction brake was fixed to the treadmill. Thereafter, the prisoners climbed the equivalent of 13,300ft each day, to no useful purpose. It survived in this form until the demolition of the old prison in 1841.

Food for the prisoners in the new prison was at first just bread and water, with occasional portions of vegetables or meat. This was relaxed somewhat in 1825 to include 'sufficient quantity of bread and water and other coarse but wholesome food as the Justices may direct'. By 1865, more detailed central control of the prisoners' diet was in place. Short-stay prisoners got a pint of gruel and four ounces of bread for breakfast and six ounces of bread for dinner and supper. Long-stay inmates had the relative luxury of a pint of gruel and six ounces of bread for breakfast and supper, with a dinner that might include some potatoes, cheese or bacon. They also suffered the indignity, until 1828, of having to wear a uniform that was half-blue, half-yellow to ensure that they would stand out from the crowd should they try to escape.

Despite the deterrent of the uniform, there were a number of attempts to escape from the prison. Perhaps the most original of these, in 1799, involved trying to burn the building down as a diversion. Not surprisingly, the other inmates saw certain problems with this arrangement, locked as they were in their cells. For once, the idea of honour among thieves did not apply, and the would-be escapees were betrayed to the authorities.

Conditions for the staff in the prison were scarcely better than those of the inmates. They worked a 14-15-hour day, could not leave the prison without the permission of the keeper and had to be back by 10p.m. The *Reading Mercury* carried this tempting advertisement in January 1822:

> Wanted at the County Gaol and bridewell immediately, a steady, honest and sober middle-aged man who can bear confinement, as an ASSISTANT TURNKEY, at the said Gaol; if he is a married man, he cannot be accommodated with apartments for his family; he will himself be expected

> to sleep at the Gaol, and never to absent himself therefrom without leave. A
> single, middle-aged man without encumbrances would be preferred.

During the construction of the Great Western Railway the gaol was filled with
wild and lawless navvies. The Berkshire Justices complained at so much space in
their prison being taken up by these outsiders, and the local taxpayers having to
foot the bill for them. Not surprisingly, neither the Great Western Railway nor
their contractors rushed to help finance the prison.

Victorian prisons operated on two different systems. Reading started out with
the silent system, where prisoners were allowed to associate with each other, but
in strict silence. This was difficult to enforce in overcrowded and understaffed
prisons, especially when the prisoners had developed an effective system of sign
language, and in 1863 a solitary system of strict segregation of prisoners became
the national norm.

Under the solitary system, every effort was made to deprive the prisoners of
their individual identity. They were known by their cell number rather than
their name – the prison's most famous inhabitant, Oscar Wilde, became C3.3.
All their personal possessions were removed, and a minimum of prison-issue
items were provided for their daily needs. Even their daily supply of water was
rationed. They left their cells only for exercise or to attend chapel, both of which
they did out of visual contact with the other prisoners. Should they by chance
encounter another prisoner they wore caps, which they were supposed to pull
down over their faces to prevent recognition. The prison was supposed by law to
provide the inmates with work, but the only activity given to them in Reading
was the learning of whole books of the Bible by rote. This was criticised in an
inspection report in 1850, and the authorities eventually established a system of
hand-grinding of corn to provide the inmates with 'coarse but wholesome bread'
and the breaking of rocks to provide road stone. Once again, despite the supply
of free labour, this enterprise somehow managed to lose £10 in its first year.

A mere 50 years after John Howard began campaigning, Sir Robert Peel began
putting Howard's proposed reforms into effect, with the construction of the first
new model prison at Pentonville. In 1841 the Home Secretary received reports
about the lack of security and other shortcomings at the Reading County Gaol,
and was told by the Inspectors of Prisons that it was a stigma and detriment to
the county, which answers none of the purposes for which it was established
– the deterring, correcting and reclaiming of offenders. The Inspector of Prisons
also told the Justices that a new prison for 150 prisoners, along the lines of
Pentonville, could be built for £15,000. A competition was held, in which some
of the country's leading architects participated, and a contract was awarded in
1842 to George Gilbert Scott and William Moffatt, a practice whose other work
included the Home Office, *St Pancras Station Hotel* and the Albert Memorial.
Their tender price, at £24,000, far exceeded the Inspector of Prisons' estimate;
even so, this rapidly increased to £33,000 and, by the time of its opening in
1844, to £43,648. The new prison became Reading's largest public building

46 *Abbots Walk by the Kennet in about 1910, showing some of the original detailing of Reading Prison that was apparently inspired by Warwick Castle.*

and certainly its most striking one, its medieval-looking towers and battlements originally modelled on those of Warwick Castle.

In parallel with the history of Reading's county gaol, the town had another place of incarceration. The idea of prison as a form of punishment in itself grew up with the Elizabethan Poor Laws, when houses of correction, or bridewells, were set up. Their aim was to punish (and thereby, it was hoped, reform) vagrants, the idle, harlots and others by means of strict discipline and hard labour, generally by being locked up for short spells. It was to this end that the ruinous remains of the old Greyfriars Church were put from 1631, once they ceased to be used by the burgesses as their guildhall. We have a description of the bridewell as it was at the start of the 19th century. By then, the central roof had been removed, for fear of it falling in, and the centre of the church had become an open exercise yard. Its floor was green with moss and slime and its central feature was an earth privy. The side aisles had been partitioned off into individual cells, measuring about 14 feet by six, which had been known to take up to six prisoners. They had no light, air only through a small grille, no heating even in the depths of winter, no furniture, no fresh water and no facilities for the sick. Rats ran freely between the cells and one even had the added amenity of its own cess pool. The prisoners slept on a bed of straw and lived on bread and water. As one 19th-century observer put it: 'The ingenuity of man, one would have supposed, could not have contrived a place so well adapted to reduce their fellow men below the condition of beasts'. A prison inspector visited the bridewell in 1837 and declared only three of the cells fit for human habitation.

Another contemporary report confirms the horror:

> In the felons' ward was a cesspool … the place was infested by rats. The felon's cell had been previously occupied by the horse of the mace-bearer of the Corporation. There was no water within the walls of the prison; the whole interior of the prison was out of the gaoler's view; there was no infirmary or sick room; the magistrates of the borough seldom pay their prisoners a visit; no religious or moral instruction was ever conveyed to the prisoners.

The mayor in 1829 declared that this building was good enough for its purpose, but public opinion began to press for the improvements that led to its eventual closure.

In addition to incarceration, there was also the option of community sentences. Until the early 19th century these took the form of the stocks, pillory and whipping post. These were potentially more than just unpleasant; the materials used to pelt the prisoner included not just rotten vegetables and eggs, but also the waste products of nearby slaughterhouses and even stones. There was a real risk of suffocation, unless they had someone nearby to keep their mouth and nose clear of the debris, or of death by stoning.

Whipping could also be tantamount to a death sentence. In 1816, an unemployed workman living in one of the slums in Silver Street was sentenced to be whipped for stealing a loaf of bread from a baker in Castle Street. The man was stripped to the waist, tied to the tail of a cart and whipped as the cart made its way from the bridewell to his home. Despite it being a relatively short journey, the keeper of the bridewell at the time, a man named Paradise, carried out the sentence with extreme brutality. By the time they reached his home, according to one eyewitness, there was not a portion of this poor fellow's back that was not literally cut into shreds. The man died without ever leaving his home again.

Many criminals never even saw the inside of a prison cell for any great length of time. As at 1800 there were some 220 crimes carrying the death sentence, some as minor as stealing an object worth as little as 1s. (5p). Juries were often unwilling to convict on these lesser offences, and the courts would respond to this by lowering their valuation of the goods stolen to just below the capital punishment threshold. Even then, the death sentence was not automatic. The judge had powers to commute the sentence, as did the monarch until 1837 (when it was considered an unsuitable burden for the young Queen Victoria, and the Home Secretary took the role over). During the French Wars, convicted offenders could be let off if they joined the navy. This was no easy option, for conditions on board ship were generally reckoned to be worse than in prison. Transportation was also an option, at first to America, until the War of Independence put a stop to that from 1776, and then to Australia, until the practice ceased entirely in 1857.

Before the new prison was built at Forbury Road, public hangings used to be carried out at Gallows Tree Common, Earley. Tradition had it that the condemned man and his gaoler would stop at the *Oxford Arms* public house in Silver Street for a final drink en route. A similar story is told of the *Marquis of Granby* public house at Cemetery Junction, which used to be known as the

Gallows Tavern. Perhaps they stopped at both? One would need more than one stiff drink to get you through a hanging, especially if you were to be the victim. After the execution, the prisoners would be buried in the north-west corner of corner of St Mary's churchyard that was reserved for them. One body was later disinterred from there, still wearing its chains. Once the new prison opened, an area at the eastern end of St Laurence's churchyard was reserved for those who died in custody.

Hanging continued to be a public spectacle until 1862. The top of the front gate of the prison provided a suitable stage for a scaffold, and crowds of up to 10,000 would gather outside, filling the meadow opposite and, in some cases in later years, climbing up the railway embankment for a better view. The last man to be publicly hanged was John Gould, who went to the scaffold on 14 March 1862 after being found guilty of slitting his seven-year-old daughter's throat with a razor. It was claimed that he had come home drunk and became enraged on finding that she had failed to clean the house. But many of those executed in public were guilty of property offences – such as theft, robbery or issuing forged banknotes – rather than murder. After 1862, hangings continued in private at the prison until the last one took place in 1913. But the most famous death on Reading's gallows was that of a trooper in the Horse Guards, one Charles Thomas Wooldridge, who was hanged in 1896 for the murder of his wife. He went on to find posthumous fame as the CTW of Oscar Wilde's *Ballad of Reading Gaol*.

Reading has had its share of murders over the years. One of the most notorious of these was that of a Roman Catholic priest, the Revd Mr Longuet in February 1817. He was murdered on the Oxford Road, near where Brock Barracks currently stands, for his purse. His murderer was never found, though a member of a well-connected local family was widely suspected. The suspect died himself shortly afterwards, and the community's suspicions could never be tested.

But Reading's most notorious murderer was hanged at Newgate on 10 June 1896. An unlikely mass murderer – Wilson describes her as 'a stunted old woman only 5ft tall with scanty white hair scraped into a meagre bun' – Amelia Elizabeth (Annie) Dyer was 57 years old when she died. She was born of a respectable family in Bristol and continued to live in or around the area until the last year of her life, when she moved to Reading. She first came to the attention of the authorities in 1880, when she was sent to prison for six weeks for running a baby farm. In those days, single mothers or others who were unable to keep their children would pay people to look after them, in return for a monthly board payment (or in Mrs Dyer's case, sometimes the payment of a single capital sum, claimed to be anything up to £80).

In 1891, 1893 and 1894, Dyer was admitted to various asylums, following more or less unconvincing suicide attempts. It was later claimed that she had staged these artificial bouts of insanity to evade the enquiries of parents who had left their children with her. In June 1895 Dyer went to live with her son-in-law and daughter, Arthur and Mary Ann Palmer, in Cardiff. They only stayed there until September when, badly in debt, they left and moved to Caversham. They eventually settled in Piggotts Road and Dyer immediately resumed her baby farming activities, advertising for custom in the newspapers, where she portrayed herself as a wealthy farmer's wife. During her short stay in Caversham she took in at least 11 children and, by April 1896, four of them were dead.

The body of Helena Fry was fished out of the River Thames by bargemen on 30 March. It had been strangled with white tape and wrapped in brown paper, on which could still be detected the words Mrs Thomas, Piggotts Road, Lower Caversham. Thomas was one of several aliases Dyer used. This, and the

47   *Annie Dyer – Reading's, and one of the nation's, most notorious murderesses.*

fact that she had subsequently moved from Piggotts Road, meant that there was a fatal delay in the police tracking her down. Over the next two days, Dyer acquired two more babies. Doris Marmon was the daughter of an unmarried mother from Cheltenham, and Harry Simmons was the child of a lady's maid, who had literally left her employers holding the baby. On the night of 2 April, the pair of them were consigned to the Thames in a carpet bag, not far from where the first child had been found.

The police finally caught up with Dyer on 4 April. While in custody she made two more half-hearted suicide attempts. By the end of April a total of seven infant victims had been fished from the Thames, all of them strangled with white tape and wrapped in a parcel weighed down with a brick, similar to some found in Dyer's coal-house. Her son-in-law was also arrested as an accessory to the murders. Dyer wrote a letter to the Superintendent of Police, denying any complicity on the part of her daughter or son-in-law and (by implication) confessing her own guilt. Palmer was released and immediately rearrested for abandoning a four-year-old child while living in Plymouth in 1895, for which he later served three months in prison.

When Dyer was brought before the committal hearing, her daughter gave evidence that argued her own innocence and incriminated her mother. Dyer's trial took place on 21 and 22 March. She was only tried on the one count of murdering Doris Marmon (presumably giving the prosecution a further chance if the first charge did not stick). Her counsel tried to argue a defence of insanity, producing the doctor from Gloucester Asylum, where one of her suicide attempts had taken place. Lurid accounts were given of her delusions, of the birds talking to her, her bed seeming to sink through the floor, of her taking her mother's bones from her coffin and of the voices that told her to kill herself. The prosecution produced contrary medical evidence, claiming her to be sane. The jury took just five minutes to find her both sane and guilty.

Dyer was taken back to Newgate to await her fate, but some other executions were scheduled to take place at the prison before hers. Rather than risk her witnessing the preparations for these executions she was moved temporarily to Holloway Prison until they were carried out. She spent her last days filling five exercise books with her 'last true and only confession'. The papers carried a detailed account (much of it probably invented) of her last moments, right down to her weight and the appropriate drop for the hangman to allow for a woman of her size.

A sale of Dyer's household effects was held at Kensington Road, her last residence in Reading. It drew a large crowd and, although the total sale of her meagre belongings fetched only £7 15s. 3d. one item attracted particular interest. It was a crude armchair, home-made from a wooden sugar box. It was claimed (or implied) that the compartment built into it was where Dyer used to conceal her murder victims. Although the intrinsic value of the item was no more than a shilling, lively bidding, much of it from showmen in the audience, drove the final price up to £1 9s. The proceedings were interrupted by a thunderstorm so violent that some saw it as a judgement on Reading's most prolific murderess.

48   *The Clappers – the rickety footbridge across the Thames from where Annie Dyer would throw her infant victims, seen c.1900. It was replaced by Reading Bridge.*

Dyer's case received national coverage and she became notorious. Victorian parents would warn their misbehaving children that they would be sent to stay with Annie Dyer, and her image appeared in Madame Tussaud's Chamber of Horrors. The baby-farming industry suffered a severe downturn. Nobody knows how many babies she murdered in a career as a baby farmer spanning more than fifteen years. Four years after her execution, the bodies of four more babies were found buried in the garden of a house in Bristol where she had once lived.

Perhaps Dyer's one faintly redeeming feature was her determination to protect the rest of her family from any complicity in the crimes, particularly given that her daughter's evidence, saving her own skin, was some of the most damning given against Dyer. But it is hard to believe that none of the household had any suspicions about the string of infants that suddenly appeared in the house and just as quickly vanished. Some time afterwards the Palmers were found guilty of abandoning an infant (chillingly, wrapped in brown paper) in a railway carriage in Newton Abbot. The child would have died there had its crying not attracted somebody's attention. They were both sentenced to three years' hard labour.

Law and Order: Reading's Police Force

Before 1836, the security of the town at night was in the care of a force of about thirteen nightwatchmen, appointed by the commissioners for paving. Their job – in theory – was to patrol the streets, shout out the time and the state of the weather and arrest felons. In practice they were, according to Wykes, 'a blackguardly lot whose watchfulness had been concerned mainly with the preservation of their own interests'. In the event of trouble, their first priority would be to put the maximum distance between themselves and it, assuming they were not too drunk to do so. The ill-lit streets were a dangerous place to be after curfew had been rung from St Laurence's Church. Darter recalls in around 1810 that the borough was reduced to just a single nightwatchman for the whole parish. The individual concerned, a man called Norcroft, 'seemed never to get into trouble but when necessary would call on a bystander to aid and assist in the king's name, and if his appeal was not responded to the delinquent was heavily fined'.

In the circumstances it was not surprising that some citizens took matters into their own hands. A Mr Patey, the landlord of the *Row Barge Inn*, suffered a series of break-ins during 1811. He installed a man-trap in his garden to catch the perpetrator, but instead caught his son in it, who was shot and lamed for life.

London got its police force in 1829, but it was the 1835 Municipal Corporations Act that gave Reading an elected local authority with the power to set up its own police. Reading's watch committee decided in 1836 that a force of 21 (almost immediately increased to 34) would be needed for a town of 18,000 people, and the successful candidates were kitted out with blue uniforms, top hats, a rattle (for summoning help), a short staff (for dispensing on the spot penalties), oil lamps and a 24-page rule book, and were sent out to keep the king's peace in all

49 *Reading's police station and magistrates' courts were established in Valpy Street from 1912.*

matters and especially in ridding the town of 'Beggars, Unseemly Drunkards, and others who by noyse or action offend the Burgesses of the Town'. The total cost of the original force was £1,200 a year, with constables being paid 13s. a week, sergeants 16s. and inspectors 20s.

However, many of the new officers appear to have been nearly as bad as the nightwatchmen they replaced, for the early records were full of disciplinary measures for drunkenness, insubordination, neglect of duty, gossiping with women, failing to account for money handed to them, sleeping on duty and forming improper and indecent intimacy with females. But the bad lots were gradually weeded out and the force reformed.

The first police station was at 6 Friar Street, which was then a residential area, and it provoked complaints from the neighbours about the noise and nuisance from arrested drunks being brought there at night. The station soon moved – in 1840 – to 2 The Forbury, where living accommodation could also be provided for unmarried constables. In 1912 it migrated to Valpy Street, taking over the former premises of the Reading University Extension College. Until 1839 the watch committee ran the force themselves, at which time it was decided to appoint the first chief constable, a former Metropolitan Police sergeant called Henry Houlton. By the end of the century the force had grown to 62, but the town had also grown, to 60,510, giving a ratio of about one officer for every thousand people. By now, a newly appointed constable was earning £1 3s. 4d. a week, and could look forward to a pension and seven days' paid leave a year. In a later chapter we will see how a 20th-century Reading police force gradually embraced new technology in the fight against crime.

Chapter Nine

GASLIGHT AND ALL PERFECTION:
EARLY NINETEENTH-CENTURY READING

Unmarred by smokestacks and railway banks, neither a haunt of fashion nor a seat of manufacture, without straggling suburbs, masking its squalid courts behind the staid demeanour of streets in which the gabled fronts and overhanging storeys of an earlier style were intermixed with houses of Georgian dignity, Reading presented the characteristics of an English country town of those days.

(Childs)

The Reading of the early 19th century was little bigger than it had been in the earliest maps, drawn 200 years before. Most of it could still be contained within a triangle with the abbey, Greyfriars Church and Whitley Hill as its three corners, and its residents could enjoy a country stroll along New Street (or what we now call London Road) to a rustic public house called the *Marquis of Granby*. Caversham too was separated from Reading by countryside, as well as by a river. Some of the Civil War fortifications still survived on Castle Hill, on what was still the western edge of the town, and ploughing matches were held on the fields of Redlands. No railway embankment obscured the views from the Forbury across the meadows to the Thames and Caversham beyond.

But change was slowly beginning to happen. In 1816 the row of houses along the north side of Gun Street, backing onto St Mary's churchyard, would be demolished. Housing growth was just beginning to happen, particularly along the Oxford Road where there was no turnpike to constrain development. The opening of King's Road and Queens Road by 1832 signalled a new direction of growth to the east. But John a Larder's almshouses, a group of buildings that had blocked off the western frontage of St Mary's churchyard from the Butts since 1476 and the row of houses that stood along its centre, would survive until the late 19th century. The eastern end of Broad Street would also continue to be divided into two for much of the century.

One of Victorian Reading's staple industries was already in place; a state-of-the-art brewery stood along the banks of the Kennet. But the others were still no more than a gleam in their founders' eyes at the turn of the century.

The town's skyline had been dominated since medieval times by its churches, including the abbey ruins. Now they were joined by the water tower, St Giles' Mills

50   *Reading, as it looked from Whitley Hill in 1847.*

in Mill Lane and the new County Gaol. The original Oracle still stood on the north
bank of the Kennet, though it was entering the period of its final decline. The first
phase of the complex of buildings that we today refer to as the old town hall had
been erected in 1785–6, and stood next to the buildings of Reading School. One
literary visitor to the town complained that it had 'neither the society of the town
nor the freedom of the country' but it was not entirely without its amenities; 'a
neat little theatre' had been opened in Friar Street and 'cold, warm, vapour and
shower baths' were opened in Bath Court, near Mill Lane, in 1819. For better or
worse, the influences of the metropolis were carried into the town by the constant
stream of coaches passing between London and the fashionable spa at Bath.

The financial underpinning of the town was also in transition. We will see in a
later chapter how William Simonds of the brewing family set up a bank in 1790.
Another of the town's banks, Marsh, Deane and Company, went bankrupt in
January 1816. Virtually everybody in the town had some sort of dealing with
the company and there was widespread panic. So great was the fear of public
disorder arising from this that the Secretary of State ordered all local militia
weapons to be deactivated and placed in the county gaol for safe-keeping. When
a meeting of the bankruptcy commissioners was held at the *Bear Inn*, the crush
was so great that the only way of leaving the building was through the windows.
In July of that year, debtors were promised a payment of just 3s. 4d. in the
pound, but the mess took over twenty years to sort out. In 1838 the total debts
of the bank were announced to be in excess of £100,000. One of those badly
affected by the collapse was the fledgling corn and meal business of Suttons, and
this limped along in a much-reduced way for some years.

At the other end of the financial scale, a national shortage of small change was causing such a headache for local shopkeepers that they were either having to turn trade away or give credit on very small sums. So bad did the problem get in 1812 that J.B. Monck of Coley Park, one of the town's Members of Parliament, took to issuing local tokens in silver and gold, the circulation of which he said would be lawful until March 1813. Monck undertook to attend at the *Bear Inn* at specified times to exchange his tokens for banknotes.

Thus far, our account of early 19th-century Reading has drawn heavily on the work of W.M. Childs. But we are fortunate in having a good many other accounts of the town in those days. To some, the Reading of the early 19th century was a town of infinite charm. According to William Fordyce Mavor, Reading was

> delightfully situated, its houses well-built and commodious, and, as for its residents … An air of gentility is thrown over the place; and there is an elegant sociability in the manners of the inhabitants which is irresistibly attractive to strangers … There is not a county town in the Kingdom that unites so many charms and advantages to persons of independent fortune and cultivated minds … [it is] in every respect the first town in Berkshire.

Then there are the views of John Man. First, we need to set his views in context. The governance of early 19th-century Reading was shared between the paving commissioners and the ancient Corporation, which still operated under the 1638 charter granted by Charles I. The community had no say whatsoever in the activities of the Corporation, which was entirely self-appointed and held office for life. The income of this body in 1833 was £1,137, of which £362 was derived from tolls charged at markets and fairs. However, the Corporation was at this time in debt, due to their having had to lay out over £2,500 on repairs to the town's bridges in 1830. The Corporation were accused by their unappreciative constituents of a host of malpractices – of eating and drinking the rates away, fraud, partiality, failure to publish accounts, and so on. The municipal commissioners investigated them in 1833 and, while finding them not guilty of some of the worst excesses of which they were accused, neither were they lavish in their praise. A system where the Corporation had been made up of members of the same families for the past 50 years and where the same person could be both town clerk, mayor, presiding magistrate at the Court of Record, partner of the attorney engaged in the case before him and taxer of the bill of costs in that case did rather leave itself open to challenge. All of this would be swept away by the Reform Act of 1835. But among the things the Corporation were not responsible for were the paving, lighting and cleaning of the town's streets, which is where John Man comes in.

In 1810 a retired schoolteacher, John Man, published a book called *A Stranger in Reading*, which purported to be a stranger's view of the town (Man himself was a long-standing resident). It ruffled a good many local feathers because of the unfavourable light in which it cast Reading, but it is useful for our present purposes for Man's obsession with the paving and lighting of the town's streets. He shows us vividly that moving about the town was still a dirty, unpleasant and dangerous experience.

Up to 1785, every householder was responsible for the state of the highway outside his or her house. As we have seen, this produced a standard of maintenance that it would be charitable to describe as variable. But 1785 saw the passing of the Reading Improvement Act. This was: 'An Act for paving the footways in the Borough of Reading, in the county of Berkshire, for better repairing, cleansing, lighting and watching the Streets, Lanes, Passages and Places in the said Borough; and for removing Encroachments, Obstructions and Annoyances therefrom, and preventing the like for the future'.

According to the Act, the streets were in some places very incommodious and unsafe for travellers and passengers. Man could not have agreed more, but said so in rather more colourful language. Here are a few of his judgements on the town's streets in 1810:

> As to the pavement before the houses I cannot say much in its favour, for though there is on one side, for a small distance, a spacious piece of flat pavement almost four inches wide, the rest is so miserably pitched with vile flints with their sharp points upwards, that it is almost impossible for a foot passenger to make his way over them, without either cutting his feet or breaking his legs in the attempt.
>
> (Man)

In Castle Street, he comments on the custom of:

> Having a pretty little dunghill before each house, composed of road dirt, ashes, straw, dung, turnip parings, cabbage leaves, &c, &c but these last are not so plentiful as might be wished, owing to some all-devouring hogs who are continually plundering these precious compounds of the greater part of their beauty.
>
> (*Ibid*)

While in Friar Street: 'I … pursued my walk along main street, without meeting anything worth noticing, except filling my shoes at every step from the puddle water that lay concealed under the beaux-traps' (loose paving stones). (Ibid)

It was not just your feet you had to look out for; in Gun Street (and in other places in the town) the butchers used to hang their wares up outside their shops. Man describes how: 'Half a dozen fat hogs were hanging across the footpath, apparently just killed, with their reeking entrails hanging on each side'.

He emerged from the experience of walking past the shop covered in blood and lard. And if none of these got you there were always the gaping cellar doors, left open to swallow up the unwary. In short, there was little sign of improvement in the streets since medieval times, and no sign that the 1785 Act had achieved many positive effects. This was not for lack of activity – over 200 paving commissioners had been appointed. They had appealed for voluntary contributions to carry out works (since their tax-raising powers were limited) and spent all the money. In 1787, scavengers were appointed to keep the streets clean.

The 1785 Act had also required every householder to hang a lamp in front of their house between Michelmas and something called Lamp Day. When this did not work, the commissioners started providing their own. In 1797, they tendered for the maintenance of 156 street lamps; by 1808, the number had grown to two hundred and fourteen. These were only lit between 13 September and 14 April, and even then not when there was a full moon. By 1818, the Reading Gas Company had set up shop (by some strange coincidence in Gas Lane) and the following year some of the town's main streets had their first gas lights. At first these were praised as being 'not only ornamental but a great protection against nocturnal predators'. But even these fell out of favour, and by 1832 their inadequacy was being blamed for night-time coach accidents.

In short, none of it seemed to work, and the criticisms of the commissioners began to multiply. The street lamps were inadequate, the streets were dirty and the scavengers were not doing their job (though they must have been doing something, since people used also to complain of the scavengers' large dungheap disfiguring the Forbury). In 1823, the *Reading Mercury* asserted that 'There is no town in England where there was less attention paid to keeping the streets clean, in good order, and passable to traffic'. For, in addition to the lack of cleanliness and lighting, many of the streets were totally congested with carts, carriages, wheelbarrows and other vehicles, parked and driven without any consideration for any other road users. As if to add insult to injury, the 1785 Act also plunged the town into debt, and additional charges had fallen on the townspeople as a result.

Eventually the weight of criticism made itself felt and in 1825 the old legislation was swept away, to be replaced by a new so-called 'All Perfection Act'. This set up a new group of commissioners with similar responsibilities to the old ones, but greater powers. From 1841, the town's roads began to be surfaced with tarmacadam, making them more even and easier to clean. These new commissioners continued with their work until 1850, when their powers transferred to the local Board of Health.

Occasionally, Man manages to tear himself away from his preoccupation with the streets to give us an insight into other aspects of Reading life. Reading got its first purpose-built theatre in Friar Street in 1788, part of a chain of 20 built around the country by Henry Thornton. Man (who is not always the most impartial of observers), claims that the actors played to near-empty houses, due to the meanness and philistinism of the Reading public. He lists the preferred pastimes of Reading people as 'reviews, balls, assemblies, coteries, card parties and concerts for the ladies; fishing, hunting, coursing and shooting for the gentlemen'.

Markets and fairs were still big business in Reading. During 1800, the twice-weekly market sold £120,588 worth of wheat, barley, oats, beans and peas, with separate markets being held for livestock. The cheese fair in the Forbury in 1795 sold an estimated 1,200 tons of cheese, with an estimated value of £60,000. The cattle market by 1840 had to be moved from Friar Street and Broad Street into the Forbury, owing to the immense numbers of cattle being bought to market. There were also markets in human beings, with farm workers of both sexes coming to seek a new employer.

The year 1814 saw one of the cruellest winters in the town's history. A bitter 12-week frost saw the canals frozen and unusable, the roads impassable, with 12ft snowdrifts reported in Watlington's Lane and the London coach being forced to turn back after four miles. With virtually no goods coming into or going out of the town, the price of everything went through the roof and there was widespread unemployment. On the positive side, people could walk across the frozen Thames at Caversham Bridge. Had the ice lasted until May, this might actually have been useful, since it was then that the bridge collapsed, making it impassable for carriages. It had been in a ruinous state for some considerable time and, about twelve months previously, had also collapsed and been repaired (though obviously not very permanently) by W. Blandy esquire, who was in turn repaid by public subscription.

Reading's Prime Minister

> Pitt is to Addington
> As London is to Paddington
>
>   (A George Canning jibe from *c.*1803)

Reading has produced just one Archbishop of Canterbury and one Prime Minister. Just as William Laud was the most controversial holder of the archbishopric, so Henry Addington turned out to be one of our least distinguished premiers. His father, Anthony, was a leading doctor, who came originally from Twyford but settled in Reading in 1744, when he married the daughter of the headmaster of Reading School. Henry was born in 1757 but was not a native of the town, his father having moved to London in the meantime. Among Anthony's patients in London were the family of Lord Chatham, whose second son, William Pitt, became a friend of the family – and, in particular, of Henry – after his father had restored him to health following an illness. When Anthony retired, he returned to the family home at 73 London Street in Reading, which still stands. His reputation was such that he was called out of retirement to treat King George III during one of the King's periods of so-called 'madness'.

Henry studied at Winchester and Brasenose College, Oxford and planned, on his graduation in 1778, to pursue a career in the law. But William Pitt persuaded him to come into politics instead, and in 1783 Addington was elected Member of Parliament for Devizes. That same year Pitt formed his first administration, while still in his mid-twenties. Although Addington hardly ever spoke in Parliament, he was loyal to his leader and liked by his parliamentary colleagues and, in 1789, Pitt secured for him the post of Speaker. He occupied this post, with some success, for the next 11 years.

Pitt resigned as Prime Minister in 1801, in part because of the King's opposition to his plans for Catholic emancipation. George III asked Addington to succeed him (attracted by his anti-Catholic views). But many of the leading politicians of the day refused to serve under him for the same reason, and he formed what was regarded as a mere caretaker administration, pending Pitt's return. The *Dictionary of National Biography* characterised his performance as Prime Minister in the following terms: 'His industry and good intentions could not make up for his own dullness and the incapacity of his colleagues. The pompous manner and sententious gravity which became the Speaker's chair was ill-suited for debate'.

51   *Henry Addington, Lord Sidmouth – the only Prime Minister Reading has produced, and later a repressive Home Secretary.*

For a short time, it seemed that his term of office would at least be distinguished by one success. The Treaty of Amiens (1802) brought an end to the war with the French that had been going on since 1793, and that had reached a stalemate. In practice, it turned out to be no more than an armed truce, with each side dragging its feet in fulfilling its treaty obligations. Britain declared war again in May 1803, and Napoleon began planning an invasion of Britain in a war that was to drag on until 1814. Pitt returned to replace Addington in 1804.

Addington was made the First Viscount Sidmouth in 1805, and went on to serve as a minister in successive administrations. The most significant of these was as Home Secretary in Lord Liverpool's government, a post that he held from 1812 to 1821. In this post he made his reactionary views most clear, opposing Catholic emancipation and any reform of the parliamentary system. He had earlier caused a huge controversy with a Bill requiring all dissenting ministers to be registered, which proved too much even for the House of Lords, who threw it out.

Addington's period as Home Secretary coincided with a period of considerable unrest in the country. Poverty and unemployment were rife and the threat of revolution was in the air. Addington suppressed the Luddite riots against the mechanisation in the textile industries with great severity – 14 demonstrators were hanged in a single day at York. He sat at the centre of a huge spy-ring, concentrated particularly in the growing industrial areas of the north of England, which Addington regarded as powder kegs of revolution. These spies fed Addington and his brother Hiley (who was Under-Secretary of State at the Home Office) with often highly-coloured accounts of subversive activity in places like Manchester. In response, Addington introduced ever more repressive measures.

Mail was routinely intercepted and the freedom of the press, the rights to free assembly and to form trades unions were all restricted. For a period, even the law of habeas corpus, protecting the citizen from arrest without trial, was suspended.

When a group of protesters, known as the blanketeers, sought in 1817 to walk from Manchester to London to present a petition about the suffering of the urban poor, Addington (through the local forces of law and order) had the leaders arrested and chained up. The rest of the marchers were ridden down by the cavalry. One was killed and hundreds arrested. But worse was to come. A peaceful gathering, numbered at anything between 30,000 and 150,000 in St Peter's Fields in Manchester degenerated into chaos, when a poorly trained local volunteer militia went into the crowd on horseback to try and arrest the main speaker, Henry 'Orator' Hunt. The cavalry wielded their swords against the unarmed crowd, leaving an estimated 11 dead and 420 wounded. This rapidly became known as the Peterloo Massacre. Although this was due more to local incompetence than to malign direction from the centre, Addington's official response was inflammatory: 'I am gratified equally by the deliberated and spirited manner in which the magistrates discharged their arduous and important duty on that occasion'. (Hylton)

During his time as Speaker of the House of Commons, Addington lived at Woodley Lodge, which stood on the site of Bulmershe Manor. There he set up a volunteer force, the Woodley Cavalry (with himself in command) who were ready to throw back the French forces in the event of Napoleon invading. They consisted of three officers and 54 men, with their barracks in a row of cottages in Church Road, Earley and their supreme headquarters in the *Three Tuns Inn*. The nearest they got to action was parading before King George III on Bulmershe Heath in 1799 and entertaining the King at Woodley Lodge thereafter.

Addington remained in the Cabinet until 1824, married a rich woman 30 years his junior and died aged eighty-six. His last speech in Parliament was to oppose the 1832 Reform Bill. He is remembered in Reading for the streets that

52 The Three Tuns *on Wokingham Road – seen here in about 1890 – was where Henry Addington and his Woodley Cavalry would meet to plan the downfall of any invading French army.*

bear his name (Sidmouth Street and Addington Road), and for his gift to the town of the land on which the Royal Berkshire Hospital would be built.

Napoleonic Wars

In 1804, England found itself in real and immediate danger of invasion. Napoleon had an army of 100,000 camped around Boulogne and an armada of 2,300 vessels waiting to carry them across the Channel. The whole of the nation was mobilised against the threat. A Defence of the Realm Act required a national list to be drawn up of all able-bodied males aged between 17 and 55, from whom a home guard would be formed, should the invasion come. Over 800,000 of the men between those ages – one in five of the national total – were engaged in the defence of the nation by late 1804, of whom 386,000 were volunteers. In common with every other town, much of the manpower of Reading was mobilised in one way or another. Some were directly recruited into the armed forces. Five of the public houses on London Street were used as recruiting stations by the army, sometimes duping or using force to get farm labourers and others, who had come to town on market day, to sign up. Some of those press-ganged in this way went to extreme lengths to extricate themselves:

> Yesterday two young men, who had enlisted with a recruiting party of the 4th Regiment of Foot in this town, came to the shocking resolution of cutting off their fingers to render themselves unfit for the service. To effect it, they repaired to a tombstone in St Mary's Churchyard, on which with a knife they deliberately cut off the fore and next finger of each other's right hand.
> (*Reading Mercury* – 9 March 1801)

The press gang had a long history in Reading. In the years leading up to the Seven Years' War with France (1756–63) the navy had an urgent need for more men. Reading was one of six inland towns chosen by them as rendezvous or recruitment centres – most such 'recruitment' being done in the coastal towns. A regulating captain would be sent to the town with a squad, whose job it was to enlist men either voluntarily or by force. A number of the 'volunteers' may have offered their services when it was put to them that the alternative form of recruitment open to them was far more painful. Some would also volunteer to join the press gang, as an alternative to being pressed themselves. In addition to getting new recruits, the gang was also on the lookout for deserters. The civil authorities sometimes tried to assist the process by offloading undesirables onto them but, contrary to popular belief, the navy of those days was not crewed by the absolute scum of the earth – most criminals were not accepted, though, for some reason, debtors and smugglers were. All recruits were also subject to a medical examination.

Many other Reading men became members of locally based volunteer forces. Two companies were raised in the town when the war broke out in 1795. These two hundred or so men were paid by the Government, but had their uniforms provided by public subscription. In 1798, as the danger of invasion grew, three more companies were raised locally, this time unpaid and providing their own equipment. The troops were disbanded with the false dawn of the Treaty of Amiens in 1801, but hastily recalled when this unravelled in the following year. The unpaid part of the force took the title of the Loyal Reading Volunteers. These latter continued until all immediate threat of invasion had passed, in 1809. At this time, some were transferred into the local militia and the remainder disbanded.

The militia, who were commanded by the Marquess of Blandford, were drawn largely from the town's tradesmen. Each parish was expected to provide 50 men, and volunteers were not easy to come by. The overseers were forced to resort to a combination of stick and carrot to fill their ranks. A bounty of two guineas was offered to aspiring heroes who signed up. The stick took the form of a ballot to conscript those who would not volunteer. However, the difference was that people could pay £10 for two years' exemption from the ballot, and up to £80 would buy you a substitute, were you unfortunate enough to have your name selected.

The town saw other signs of the war that was being fought in continental Europe. Companies of Wellington's troops marched through Reading on their way to serve overseas or returning from there to their barracks. Prisoners of many different nations were also marched through the town in their hundreds, and many of them were billeted there. Reading, for example, had the largest group of Danish and Norwegian prisoners of any town in the country. Most of these would have been officers – many of the other ranks were held in squalid conditions on board prison ships. They were subject to a curfew, but were otherwise free to travel around the town and up to a mile from it. Not surprisingly, there were a considerable number of escapes, and others – in particular, young boys – were even allowed to go home.

For the most part the people of Reading received them amicably, arranging concerts and medical treatment, buying the objects they carved from mutton bones and even organising a relief fund for them. Some even moved easily into middle-class society within the town. When a general amnesty was declared for them in 1809, to commemorate George III's 50th year on the throne, the prisoners gave a vote of thanks for their treatment and presented the Corporation with a carved model of a ship.

Just as industrialisation threatened the urban population of early 19th century Britain, so the threshing machine and the mechanical harvester threatened the rural workforce. In the winter of 1830–1 Britain found itself at war with hordes of displaced agricultural workers. Rural districts around Reading were terrorised by gangs of armed and often drunken men, burning hayricks and threatening the farmers who were introducing these innovations. Reading people could see the rick fires from Forbury Hill and guards were brought in from Windsor to ensure the security of the town.

By December 1830, the gaol was packed with prisoners, and a Commission of Judges was sent to clear it. They heard testimony from the farming families who had suffered at the hands of the rioters, and many of them were imprisoned,

53 *London Street c.1845 - another of Fox-Talbot's extraordinary early photographs of Reading.*

some were transported and three were sentenced to death. A campaign was mounted in Reading, seeking clemency for the condemned men, culminating in a local Member of Parliament, J.B. Monck, taking a petition to the King. Two of the men were saved by this but the third, William Winterbourne, was hanged at Reading.

The growth of early 19th-century Reading, and its picturesque decay surviving from earlier centuries, is captured in some of the earliest photographs that exist of any town in the world. William Henry Fox-Talbot, the inventor of modern photography, was lord of the manor at Lacock in Wiltshire and a Member of Parliament for Chippenham. In 1843, after three years of experimenting with his calotype process, he decided to begin producing photographs on a commercial basis. Reading was midway on the railway between Lacock and London and he chose a former school at Russell Street for his photographic establishment, converting a greenhouse at the rear into a print workshop. A Dutchman, Nicholas Henneman, was appointed as his manager and in the first seven months alone they produced some 10,400 prints, as well as his pioneering illustrated book *The Pencil of Nature*. Some of these were sold locally, at Lovejoy's stationery shop in London Street, which was also a gathering place for the local literary and scientific community. Much suspicion attended his work in the town, at a time when the idea of photography was virtually unknown. The people of Reading saw that these outsiders worked in total darkness, bought large amounts of paper from Lovejoys and that their hands and clothes were stained with chemicals. Worse still, the man in charge was a foreigner! Word soon spread that they were banknote forgers. The establishment closed in 1847, but in the meantime they left behind a unique record of early Victorian Reading.

Chapter Ten

Reading Man at Play

… a sport or pastime so full of delight and pleasure that no game in that respect is to be preferred to it.

(An early 19th-century Reading man's view of cock-fighting)

How did the people of Reading of the early 19th century spend their leisure time? At least some of their interests would have been familiar to us. Cricket has been played in Berkshire since at least 1793, in which year Maidenhead Cricket Club took on a team at Lord's for a purse of 500 guineas. In about 1850 a Berkshire team of no fewer than 22 players competed against an all-England side in Reading. County cricket proper in Berkshire dates from 1858, when a Mr Spencer Austen-Leigh established a side called the Gentlemen of Berkshire. Some of their home matches were played on some fields behind the *Duke of Edinburgh* public house on Caversham Road, which later became home to Reading's cattle market. During the 20th century, Reading's main claims to cricketing fame have been two England captains – A.P.F. Howard in the 1920s and Peter May in the 1950s.

The earliest recorded horse races took place in 1747 at Bulmershe Heath and were, from the start, attended by a degree of glamour. As the *Reading Mercury* records in August 1801: 'The races afforded great sport, with every heat being strongly contested. The balls were honoured with a most brilliant display of all the fashion and beauty of the neighbourhood'. This came to an end when a Mr Wheble enclosed the heath in about 1815, depriving the locals of not only their sport but also a source of peat for fuel and somewhere to raise their geese and pigs. Wheble allowed cricket matches and the drilling of the South Berks Yeomanry to continue on the heath after enclosure, but the horse-racing moved to what we now know as Kings Meadow. There it gradually declined in importance, and was discontinued in about 1873.

River bathing was a favourite – and free – pastime for the town's youth. A popular venue for this was the lock pool down at Kings Meadow. Boys being boys, they began to make a nuisance of themselves by running about among the neighbouring cornfields, and this degenerated into a war between them and the farmer, a Mr Tanner. Tanner retaliated by dumping several cartloads of broken bottles into the lock pool. This did not stop the boys swimming there, but many of them went home with cut feet.

The town boasts the oldest professional football team south of the River Trent, and we follow the story of Reading Football Club in a later chapter. But the history of the game locally goes back much further than their founding in 1871. As early as 1349 Edward III was complaining that the 'skill in shooting with arrows was almost totally laid aside for the purpose of useless and unlawful games', prominent among which was football. The first recorded game in the area was mainly notable for the murder of two players by one of the opposition. This was in 1598, and involved a rather robust game with unlimited numbers on each side, using the church doors as goals. Two brothers, Richard and John Gregorie, fell out with one of the opposition and his father, known as Ould Gunter. According to the contemporary records, 'These two men were killed by Ould Gunter: Gunter's sonne and the Gregories fell together by ye yeares at Football, Ould Gunter drew his dagger, and broke both their heades, and they died booth together within a fortnight'. Perhaps the oddest part of the story is that Ould Gunter was apparently the local parson, and there is no record of him being hanged for the offence, or even deprived of his living. Surely it must at least have been a sending-off offence?

Football was again a cause of disorder in this entry from the Reading Corporation records in 1628: 'John Barker junior, and William Booth, seeing the playing of the souldyers at Football in the Forberye, did endeavour to fetch the ball from them, which cause much trouble to the constables and officers and danger of hurt to many others'.

But some of the leisure activities indulged in by the Reading people of the 19th century would seem to us today bestial or even nonsensical. Berkshire was one of the last areas to practice bull-baiting. It was promoted, among others, by one George Staverton, who lived in the time of Charles II, and who had been gored by a bull. His unusual means of revenge was to make a bequest of £6 a year that was to be used to purchase a bull for baiting. Local people would send their bulldogs in to fight it. The outcome was never in doubt; the meat was to be distributed to the poor and the leather to provide them with shoes. Wokingham was a favourite venue for this spectacle and worthies of the Corporation used to be among the vast crowd. Darter recalled one such meeting in around 1815. The bull was tethered on a five-yard chain and then attacked by bulldogs. One of them bit the bull on a tender part and the maddened creature broke its chain and ran amok in the streets, before being recaptured and taken to the slaughterhouse. A fight then broke out among the spectators. A more brutalising scene could not well be imagined, Darter concluded. It was banned by law in 1835, but continued in the area into the 1840s.

Cock fighting was also popular throughout Berkshire. The *Reading Mercury* announced in 1798 that during Ascot races will be fought the 'great main of cocks … for five guineas a battle and fifty the odd'. The main is from the old French *à la main*, and is a reference to the steel spurs the birds used to wear. A bizarre variation on this was an activity known as throwing at cocks. In this the unfortunate creatures were tethered by a short length of string and the so-called sportsmen threw broomsticks at them from about twenty paces. This proved to be too much even for the sensibilities of the day, and it was outlawed.

Equally illegal was the sport of pugilism. Berkshire, being close to London, was a favoured location for the fights. They often used to take place near the borders of a given magistrate's area of jurisdiction so that, in the event of a raid, they could slip across the border in the hope of escaping arrest and completing the bout before the neighbouring magistrates caught up with them. The first recorded fight locally took place in 1759, when an ambitious cowman from Reading named Moreton took on the champion, the renowned John Slack, and received a good beating for his trouble. And a good beating in those days was no exaggeration. The protagonists could leave the ring with their faces reduced to raw meat, and deaths were by no means uncommon. Darter witnessed another bout, between Jem Burns and someone called 'White-headed Bob'. They fought each other to a standstill, their backs cut from the ropes and their fronts from bare knuckle blows. Bob was the winner but, according to Darter:

> his face and head presented a fearful spectacle; every feature was literally knocked out of him, and the wonder to my mind was how he, after such a fearful loss of blood, was able to sustain this protracted fight, for I think it continued for more than an hour and a half.

The condition of Burns, the loser, was left to the imagination. Neither fighter was able to raise his arms at the end of the contest, which was for a 200-guinea purse.

With the coming of the railways, Berkshire became an even more important venue for bare-knuckle fighting. In July 1842 a whole trainload of swells, nobs and fancy men, accompanied by 'the sweepings of St Giles and Whitechapel', travelled to Twyford station, where a bare-knuckle fight was being held in the station yard. After two hours' fighting the winner claimed his £50 purse and the loser – one Tom the Greek – was left dying of his injuries.

Moving from the bestial to the utterly bizarre, local people practised a number of other types of trial of combat between humans. Cut-legs and kick shins appear to be relatively unique to Berkshire, and understandably so. Cut-legs was a game in which Berkshire carters and others would engage. They would stand a short distance apart and hit each other with their whips about the legs until one cried 'hold'. In 'kick shins' the protagonists seize each other by the shoulders and attempted to kick each others' shins with their hob-nailed boots, until one yielded and bought the drinks. We are told that the local champion's shins were knotted and bent and twisted in the most remarkable manner, as a result of his numerous encounters.

Darter describes a Whitsuntide sports day at Bulmershe Heath in about 1812, at which the curious spectacle of Cudgel playing took place:

> Gypsies and fortune tellers, gentlemen in carriages, farmers in traps, besides horsemen, surrounded a roped ring of about 12 yards diameter … Someone threw his hat onto the ring, and shortly afterwards another did the same

in answer to the challenge, and the men, having divested themselves of all superfluous clothing, and being supplied with the referee with cudgels with basket handles, they began fencing. One of them received a blow on the head which drew blood, and there was a general shout of 'A Head!' Once again, the bout degenerated into a general brawl between members of the audience. This event was a favourite at local fairs, and the Chequers at Woodley was noted as a venue for it.

Great events in the life of the nation provided an excuse for the town to come together in celebration. In 1809, a sports day was held in the Forbury to commemorate the 50th year of George III's reign. There was donkey racing, climbing greasy poles to retrieve prizes and a host of fairground-type games. Shortly afterwards, on 25 July 1814, there were the (slightly premature) celebrations for the downfall of Napoleon. Darter again: 'A diminutive journeyman tailor of the name of Hilton, was dressed in the costume of Napoleon and rode a donkey through the streets, accompanied by a miscellaneous throng, some carrying loaves on the top of short poles with 'cheap bread' written on cards attached'.

A cannon was fired in the Forbury; Madame Mistayer's shop in London Street had 'Thank God' spelt out in coloured lamps in its window and the entire town joined in a celebratory street banquet. Eighty principal tables, each 40ft long, were laid out, stretching from the *Crown Inn* in London Street to the upper part of Friar Street. Four hundred and eighty stewards and an army of carvers served a splendid old English hot dinner to 6,000 diners. This was followed by sports in the Forbury in the afternoon, and bands with dancing until the early hours.

All the Fun of the Fair (and Other Attractions)

Fairs of a rather unsavoury kind (if Darter is to be believed) were held in Peppard and many other villages around Reading: 'From time immemorial a most demoralising revel has been held in the village every Whit Monday; vast concourses assembled; drinking, fighting, brutalising sports, and the most awful immorality characterised the scene.' We have a number of accounts of Reading's fairs, from various points in the town's history.

From medieval times, the Forbury was one of the focal points of the town's leisure, and this continued well beyond the period of the abbey's dissolution. During the Napoleonic Wars, the voluntary (or not so voluntary) militias of the day used to parade, fire volleys and hold band practices in the Forbury, in eager anticipation of old Boney ever daring to march into town. There were the Reading Volunteers, the Loyal Reading Volunteers, the Reading Armed Association (consisting of 'upwards of two hundred of the most respectable tradesmen and housekeepers of this borough') and the Woodley Cavalry. In 1840, a recruiting party of the Rifles set up their stall in the market and managed to enlist almost fifty Reading men in two days.

But more commonly the focus of events was business, pleasure or both. The showmen were constantly on the search for new attractions to catch the customers' eye. In 1798, 'caravans of wild beasts and shows of other descriptions' filled the Forbury. Wild animals were clearly a great attraction since, in 1814, we had the first visit by Gillman and Atkins' Grand Menagerie 'consisting of the most Wonderful Productions of Nature (admission: 1s. ladies and gentlemen; 6d. children and servants)'. One of the particular attractions was a 'tremendous serpent' (a live 16ft boa constrictor). There was also a camera obscura on the largest scale. 1821 boasted wild beasts, giants and dwarfs, and in 1823 there were Adam's celebrated pedestrian troop, Wombwell's extensive menagerie and the Vauxhall Gardens in miniature. 1847 bought us the bizarre confection of a brass band conducted by the youthful Miss Chapman on an elephant, and Hughes' Royal Mammoth and Grand Oriental Establishment was led into town in that same year by: 'The Egyptian Dragon Chariot or perambulating Temple of Isis and Osiris, purchased at the enormous cost of 200,000 piastres, drawn by four gigantic camels'. (Slade)

The fair of 1829 included a waxworks, which was further developed in 1844:

> Among the chief attractions of the Forbury may be ranked Mr Purchase's Collection of Wax Figures, not only on account of the novelty of the subjects produced (which include the murder of Sir William McNaughton during the insurrection at Cabool, and the death of Nelson) but from the circumstances of it being worked by powerful machinery to represent nature, so that all classes of visitors will, no doubt, be both amused and instructed.
>
> (Slade)

There were 19in female dwarves, a 10-minute version of *Macbeth*, wizards, fortune tellers, peep shows, firework displays and the ascension of a magnificent Montgolfier balloon, which rose from the green 'to an immense altitude'.

In between times, there was always the opportunity for people to make their own entertainment. As we saw, to mark the rather premature peace celebrations of 1814, it was announced that:

> The evening will be devoted to the exhibition of rural and ludicrous sports which will take place in the Forbury at six o'clock consisting of donkey races, jumping and running in sacks, a pig hunt, gingling (possibly some form of alliterative word game?), grinning (presumably pulling faces through a horse collar – what we would today call gurning), and smoking matches, dancing, etc.
>
> (Slade)

The level of sophistication had not greatly increased half a century later, when the residents gathered in March 1863 to celebrate the marriage of Edward, Prince of Wales with an afternoon of rustic sports, including:

> jumping in sacks, bobbing for oranges, hurdle races and hurdles, treacle roll amusement, diving for eels, apple scrambles, climbing the greasy pole,

running after a pig, the bucket race, the French omnibus, ball in the ring, winding up the string, donkey race, grinning through a horse collar, race up two greasy poles, etc.

(Slade)

The traditions of criminality that were seen in the medieval fairs were carried on by their 19th-century successors. Before Reading had its own police force, the magistrates used to bring in troops to maintain order. Pickpockets could expect to get three months' hard labour and a horse thief could face the gallows. This did not deter horse theft, and many a test-drive by a would-be purchaser ended up as a one-way gallop. In 1814, it was reported that the Earl of Abingdon's steward, who came here to buy grey horses for his master, had his pocket picked of £270. Prigs (petty thieves) were a constant nuisance, which the presence of the troops or police did not entirely discourage.

After 1840, Reading's fairs used to attract a whole new rail-borne clientele (including less desirable elements) from a wider area. But the railways also proved to be the kiss of death for the town's cheese fairs. It now became much easier for the dealer to buy direct, and Reading's cheese fair – which had once been just about the biggest in the country, selling up to a thousand tons in four days – went into a decline and ceased in 1860.

Culture

But some Reading people, at least, tried to bring a more serious side to the town's leisure. Theatrical performances were held for the more literary-minded inhabitants. Charles Dickens came to Reading, performing at the town hall and other venues. Darter recalls that on one occasion Dickens required a guarantee of £200 for appearing in Reading. As the great man explained:

> It is not only because the expenses of moving the theatre and company are very large (the machinery being exceedingly ingenious and the scenes rare works of art needing great care) but because we have already agreed upon a certain list of excursions always combining two or three towns in one trip, which greatly lessens the charges.

(Darter)

A book club was founded (albeit briefly) in 1802, followed by a rather longer-lived permanent library and literary institution five years later. A philosophical institution introduced science to the town in 1831, becoming the forerunner to the Athenaeum a decade later. While the Athenaeum was more like a gentlemen's club, the Mechanics' Institution pursued a much more missionary goal to popularise education for the working classes from its premises in London Street. First set up in 1826, it only really took off in the 1840s. The Reading Pathological Society, based in the Royal Berkshire Hospital, discussed medical matters, one of the first medical societies in the Country. The theatre apparently survived in the town despite the best efforts of the Methodists, who denounced it from the pulpit as dangerous to religion and (for some reason) the immoderate thirst for gain that pervades every class of shopkeepers. Music seems to have been rather better received, with triennial Berkshire Music Festivals being held in the town, attracting performers of national renown and filling the town with visiting concert-goers.

A Hot Time at the Hustings

Perhaps the wildest celebrations, and the most riotous behaviour, were reserved for the election of the town's Members of Parliament. Reading has returned Members to Parliament since 1295. For a long time after the dissolution of the abbey the Corporation had reserved to itself the exclusive right to select the town's Members of Parliament. Their appointment could prove controversial, even to the point in 1658 when attempts were made to establish a rival Corporation in order to appoint a different candidate.

But from 1659 the House of Commons Committee of Privileges ruled that it was not for the Corporation but 'the mayor, aldermen, and the whole commonality of the said borough, though not free to appoint the MPs'. This franchise (one of the widest in the country) applied until 1708, when new legislation limited the vote to those ratepayers and freemen of the borough who were not receiving alms. This prompted a rush among the town's citizens to take up the freedom of the borough. There followed: 'a period of flagrant corruption and sharp practice unmatched at any period of the town's history save perhaps in the early 19th century'.(Aspinall)

The mayor, as returning officer, did not hesitate to use harassment and violence to influence the outcome of the polls, and allegations of menaces, bribery, treats and other undue practices were made against the successful candidates in many of the early 18th century elections.

Huge sums were expended by candidates in feasts, designed to win over would-be voters. When the wealthy brewer Felix Calvert stood for a seat in Reading in 1713, his menu included '1 ox, 19 fatt sheep, 5 buck, 7 calves, 3 lambs, 100 fatt ducks, 100 rabbits, 100 poulates, 10 pigs, 7 flitches of bacon, 20 barrels of bear, 50 dozen bottles of wine, 1000 half peack loaves and a gift of 3 guinies to the biggars'. It seems his guests were inclined to abuse his hospitality for, among the incidental losses for which he had to refund the caterer, were '24 dozen knives and forks and a great deal of linin and a great many bottles'. It appears he held a similar feast for the women of the town the following week, none of whom even had the vote.

In 1715, the agent of another candidate, William Cadogan, was seen in the *Black Boy Inn*, with a bag of 50 or 60 guineas, offering to pay voters two guineas for each of their two votes (electors at this time had two votes, which they could divide between the candidates or cast both for one). He offered to double any bribe offered by another candidate and, for those who were implacably opposed to his man, offered three guineas for them not to vote, but to 'go out of their way fishing'. One elector gleefully accepted this last offer, secure in the knowledge that he had already voted. When this piece of disgraceful dishonesty came to light, the agent indignantly demanded his money back.

But Reading was not alone in its corruption, and the entire 1715 national election was declared null and void due to vote-rigging. The House of Commons ruled in 1716 that the vote should henceforth be vested in all inhabitants paying scot and lot (the tax that funded the poor rate). This reduced Reading's electorate from about 1,500 to 500 overnight. It would not get back to its 1715 level until the mid-19th century.

Reading's reputation as one of the nation's most corrupt boroughs continued during the period (1755–82) in which John Dodd was the town's MP. He was in receipt of a secret pension from the Government, which was dependent upon his support for them in Parliament, and hence upon him remaining a Member. It was alleged that he would pay up to 30 or 40 guineas for a vote. In 1768 it was reported at Abingdon assizes that four verdicts were obtained for bribery in the late election for the borough of Reading and 'divers other prosecutions, upon the same statute, are depending in that borough'. Apparently, several voters who had taken bribes and were then confronted with taking the anti-bribery oath were seized with either an attack of conscience or a loss of nerve, and had flung the bribes down on the hustings table in the face of the candidate.

The early 19th century was Reading's other golden age of political corruption. John Weyland, a candidate in 1818, wrote: 'A quantity of ale was actually broached in the town, certainly not by me or my friends, and the populace reduced in open day to a disgraceful state of intoxication. A poor man actually lies dead on his bed from the consequences of another convivial meeting …' (Ibid)

Violence was never far from the surface, and special constables were sworn in at election time in an often vain attempt to keep the peace. However, they could do nothing about the brawling when it reached the scale described by Darter, at the time of the 1826 election:

> After some delay a procession was formed with a military band at its head, followed by garlanded women, flags, &c … on reaching the town hall, the opposing parties met, and a fierce fight ensued; a Mr Webb, a farmer, who was very tall and powerful, struck away left and right, leaving three or four on the ground at a time, but whether they were friends or foes I could nor tell, neither do I think Mr Webb could; all were so excited.

On some occasions, the exuberance even escalated to the use of military ordnance. There was often a subscription raised to have a celebratory cannon fired in the Forbury on election night. But, at the time of the passing of the 1832 Reform Act, two slight mistakes were made amid the celebrations. First, Jerry Tibble, the firer of the cannon – who was no doubt as drunk as many of his fellow residents on that joyful night – moved the weapon into London Street, so that his fellow Whigs, dining at their headquarters in the nearby *Crown Inn*,

54   *Coley House in 1823, home of the Monck family, leading lights in the civic life of Reading and active participants in the riotous elections for the town's Members of Parliament during this period.*

could enjoy the celebration more intimately (The Tory headquarters was at the *Bear*). Second, he placed a charge into the cannon, forgetting that he had already filled it with gunpowder. This blew the cannon to pieces and destroyed most of the windows within a wide radius. There were no fatalities, but the promoters received a £26 glazier's bill.

It remained an expensive business becoming an MP in those days. Man estimates the cost of getting elected at this time at around £4,000, even before you started bribing anybody. This would include the cost of providing a public dinner for all the town's electors (which he apparently did not even count as bribery). The bribes themselves took the form of money or coveted positions as the landlord of an inn, or (later) a job on the railway. John Simeon (MP in 1792–1802 and 1806–18) bribed the electors with cheap loans, but his brother Edward upset local traders by distributing cheap produce that undercut their own sales.

Hostile voters might be threatened with being barred from a brewer's chain of pubs, or could alternatively be plied with drink until insensible, then removed to a place of detention until the voting had closed (which could take as long as eight days). Plying those voters who supported you with drink could, however, be counter-productive, as in the case of those who became so intoxicated they were physically incapable of placing their votes. Once again, even by the standards of the day, Reading had a bad name for electoral corruption. As the *Daily News* reported in 1849: 'Reading has got a dishonest reputation. With the single exception of Mr Talfourd, not a member has sat for this town for years except by the well-understood purchase of the voters'.

The rival candidates were also shamelessly abused and slandered by their opponents. In 1812, J.B. Monck was falsely accused of being a Roman Catholic; in 1826, Mr Spence was mocked for the fact that his father was a dentist, a profession then regarded with contempt; Dr Lushington was accused in 1830 of advocating the sale of dead bodies as a result of his support for the Anatomy Bill. Then there were the stunts; the prize for vulgarity beyond even the wildest dreams of a reality television show producer must go to a Mr John F. Stanford who promised in 1849, if elected, to select a bride from among the women of his constituency.

Once elected, the expense continued. It was the custom for the successful candidate to throw handfuls of money into the crowds who came to celebrate with him. When Charles Fyshe Palmer secured election in 1826, the celebrations were worthy of a Roman emperor. In fact, he entered the town in a Roman triumphal carriage, preceded by a herald, a long line of horsemen and a military band, and followed by a procession that, it was said, exceeded a mile in length and was populated by John Bull, knights and other figures depicting our glorious heritage. Public dinners were announced in 20 of the town's principal inns and the entire town was decked out in Whig flags and streamers. Bells were rung bands played. If only Mr Palmer's subsequent parliamentary career had equalled his manner of coming to it, Reading might have boasted an MP who eclipsed Gladstone, Disraeli and Wellington combined. Total expenses at the 1827 election were said by Childs to have exceeded £10,000. It would have taken a long time for the elected members to recoup those expenses by legitimate means. Reading's MPs received just two shillings a day attendance expenses; a sum that, given the shortness of the parliamentary sessions in those days, rarely came to more than £5 a year.

Notwithstanding all this largesse, which was no doubt enjoyed by some Reading people (not necessarily those entitled to vote), the town also harboured a strong movement in support of parliamentary reform. From 1809, large meetings were held in Reading opposing corrupt electoral practices and calling for reform. Indeed, many of the town's own elected members supported the movement (some of them, perhaps, mindful of the expense of getting themselves re-elected?). When the Reform Bill finally became law in 1832: 'the most exuberant joy was manifested everywhere … the bells of the parish churches rang merrily, cannon were fired at intervals, the farmers assembled in the market, and every man congratulated his neighbour on the triumph of reform'. (*Reading Mercury* – 21 May 1832)

The town resorted to its customary form of celebration – a street party – with 7,000 people sitting down at 116 tables lining the streets, each 50ft long, decorated with laurel and groaning under the weight of food. Beside those seated at the tables, nearly four thousand people joined in the feast.

In between elections, there was no shortage of opportunities for the more radical thinkers of the day to protest at a series of repressive measures brought in by the governments of the early 19th century. These included the Corn Bill of 1815, which kept bread as a luxury food as far as the working classes were concerned; the suspension of habeas corpus in 1817; the Peterloo Massacre two years later and what was seen in 1820 as the royal oppression of Queen Caroline, not to mention a wide variety of taxes, including window tax, which led one protester to complain that the very light of heaven is taxed! But none of the protests proved to be as lively as the elections.

Chapter Eleven

Beer, Biscuits and Bulbs

Though I cannot say much in praise of their beer, I think it is as good as the most skilful modern chymist could brew without malt or hops.

(An 1810 view of the Reading rivals to Simonds brewery)

No history of the town would be complete without an account of the three industries with which Reading was intimately associated for much of the past 200 years.

Beer – Simonds' Brewery

William Blackall Simonds was born into an affluent family from the Wokingham area. His father had established a malting business in Reading, which he left to his only son when he died in 1782. To this, Simonds was able to add a £1,000 legacy from his grandfather and a dowry of £2,000 when he married Elizabeth May, the daughter of a Basingstoke brewer. This enabled him to fund a state-of-the-art brewery on a large site in Seven Bridges Street (now Bridge Street) in 1785. No expense was spared; the eminent (Reading-born) architect Sir John Soane designed the buildings and, in 1797, Simonds installed one of the new-fangled Boulton & Watt steam engines. Most brewers would not have considered such an investment economic unless they were producing at least 20,000 barrels a year – three times his output at the time – but Simonds was from the start a man with ambition. He had already diversified into banking, as a co-founder of Messrs Micklem, Stephens, Simonds and Harris's Bank in 1791 (which later became a part of Lloyd's Bank).

But his brewing business faced competition from vested interests in the town. Reading's population at that time – 10,000 – had a choice of 68 pubs, all but two of them tied houses. But only 10 of these were Simonds houses (he had another seven outside Reading) and he was prevented from expanding by a cartel of the established brewers, who also fixed the prices so that his beer could cost no more than their inferior products (this at a time when beer was the staple drink of the entire population, including children, on account of the quality of the drinking water). Things got so bad that, by 1814, Simonds was considering getting out of brewing altogether and concentrating on banking. He left the

55   *Seven Bridges House on Bridge Street – said to have been the original family home of the Simonds family – or at least to have been on the site of their home.*

earlier bank he had founded in Market Place, and set up J. & C. Simonds Bank in King Street (this became part of Barclays in 1913, but Simonds's name is still to be found on the brass plate on Barclays' door. The J and C are John and Charles, his cousins and two of his partners in the venture).

But he did not sell his brewery. Instead it passed to his son, Blackall Simonds, while William enjoyed a long retirement in London and Pangbourne. Blackall was as entrepreneurial as his father, but rather more robust in his business methods. He threatened to fight a duel with another prominent townsman over a business dispute and, as an active Tory politician, was accused by his opponents of making 'practical appeals' to voters (ie bribing them) in the days before the secret ballot. His other passion was hunting, where he used his knowledge of the local countryside to spot potential pub sites.

Not until 1830 was the Beer Act passed, allowing beer shops to open without a magistrate's licence. The Reading cartel was broken and the quality of Simonds' products could start to make its mark. By 1839 they were the largest Reading brewer, with 37 tied houses and an output of 15,000 barrels a year. He had also produced a new type of beer – pale ale – that could survive even the rigours of export to Australia by sailing ship.

The company developed a scientific approach to the production of beer, producing new products to suit changing markets, and new techniques that improved the overall quality of the beer. They also developed new markets. One important market had been started as long ago as 1813, when Simonds had won the contract to supply the newly established Royal Military College in Sandhurst. In 1872 the brewery began to supply the canteen at Aldershot, which had become the home of the British army. This grew to supplying army canteens throughout Britain and the Empire, and a contract involving soldiers and beer was never likely to be a loss-maker. They also developed other markets in the railway refreshment rooms of the South-Eastern and South-Western Railways, and on a variety of seaside piers. By 1885, the company was producing 115,000 barrels a year and they became a limited company.

By the time of the First World War, the chairman of the company was George Blackall Simonds, better known as the sculptor responsible for the Forbury Lion and the statues of Queen Victoria and Edward VII in Reading, as well as commissions as far away as New York. Happily, given his artistic interests, he had the sense to give the able junior directors their head in running the business. One of these, Eric Simonds, became the driving force of the company from then until his death in 1953. Under his management, Simonds' became a leading brewer in the South and the West, taking over many local breweries and others further afield. In 1946, Simonds' took over the May Brewery of Basingstoke, into whose family William Blackall Simonds had married and received the dowry that had helped him on his way, back in 1782.

Simonds itself was absorbed into the larger Courage Brewery empire in 1960, and they moved to their current site at Worton Grange in south Reading, near junction 11 of the M4. By then, their production was 1.5 million barrels a year – over 200 times the 7,000 barrels they produced in the 1790s.

Biscuits – Huntley and Palmer

> Biscuit: a kind of hard dry bread, made to be carried to sea.
> (Dr Johnson's dictionary 1755)

Thomas Huntley and George Palmer, the founders of the Huntley and Palmer biscuit empire, were both Quakers, and this was an important part of understanding their business. The contribution that Quakers made to the growth of business in the 19th century was out of all proportion to their numbers, for a number of reasons. First, they had a highly individual method of self-discipline, based partly upon scrutiny by the fellow members of their church. Second, they had a strict and detailed moral code for conducting business at a time when business ethics were not always of the finest. They would not give short measure, compromise standards or profiteer from shortages, and it turned out that morally good business made good business sense. Third, there were complex family and business relationships between the Quakers – for example, all the original partners in the Associated Biscuits empire were Quakers – Huntley, Palmer, the Carrs (of Peek Frean biscuits) and the original founders of Jacobs.

56   *An aerial view of the old Simonds' Brewery, taken from Smith's* Reading Directory *of 1876.*

57   *Caversham Court, for many years the home of the Simonds brewing family, seen here in 1890.*

58   *The new Courage brewery at Worton Grange.*

They were nonetheless un-compromising non-conformists. They refused to swear oaths or pledge allegiance to the Sovereign, to pay tithes or fines or to serve in a militia. One ancestor of George Palmer was said to have harboured the fugitive Duke of Monmouth after the Battle of Sedgemoor in 1685, and to have been sentenced to death for it by Judge Jeffrey at the subsequent Bloody Assizes.

The Huntley family came originally from Gloucestershire. Thomas Huntley (1733–1813) was a schoolteacher and his wife Hannah started baking biscuits as a sideline. She sold some of them to passing stagecoach

59   *Thomas Huntley.*

passengers whose coaches stopped outside the school gate. Her son Joseph married a Quaker heiress, Mary Willis, part of whose dowry was a shop in London Street, Reading. Their eldest son (another Thomas) was born in 1803 and the family moved to Reading in about 1811. Joseph opened his biscuit and confectioner's shop on London Street in 1822, catering to the town's large middle-class clientele. Again, another group of customers available to them were the coach passengers, waiting at the nearby *Crown Hotel* while their horses were changed. In the meantime, Joseph's second son (confusingly, also called Joseph) had gone into the business of making tins and tin-lined boxes just a few doors away from Huntley's shop and, from about 1832, Huntley started supplying biscuits in these, as a means of keeping them fresh.

The business gradually grew, achieving a total turnover of about £1,600 by 1837. Joseph senior, 60 years old and in poor health, retired the following year and his son Thomas, who succeeded him, was also in poor health. He decided to find an additional partner to share the load. It took three years to find him, but the man they came up with was George Palmer. According to company legend, this was due to a chance meeting outside the *Crown Hotel*, when the coach Palmer was travelling in stopped there.

The Palmers were a west country Quaker family, tenant farmers from Somerset. They were another family with biscuits in their blood, so to speak; one of their ancestors had sold them on Yeovil market and George himself had been apprenticed to a biscuit maker at the age of fourteen. When the partnership with Huntley was formed in 1841, the business was valued at just over £1,000, £750 of which consisted of debts owed to them. It did not even have a bank

60 *George Palmer.*

account. The firm itself had debts of £400. Huntley was nominally the senior partner, but it soon became clear who the driving force behind the company was going to be. Palmer came forward with all sorts of ideas for mechanising the biscuit-making process and he got the local firm of Barratt, Exall and Andrewes (better known for making agricultural machinery) to convert his ideas into reality. They were not universally successful; breakdowns were frequent and one oven exploded, nearly killing the staff nearby. On the distribution side, Palmer created a network of commission agents all across the country.

At first, the business struggled to survive and was only kept afloat by a series of loans. Their turning point was when they acquired the rights to manufacture a form of patent unfermented bread, said to be particularly good for infants and invalids (despite one of its ingredients being hydrochloric acid!). By 1846 they were in a position to set up their own factory, which they did in a former silk mill in a largely undeveloped area to the north-east of the town. The site had a number of advantages; both the canal and the railway were near at hand, to aid their distribution (for many years, the canal was preferred, in that its gentler motion led to fewer broken biscuits). It also had as its next door neighbour the Reading Gas Works, making the heating of their ovens a simple task. Once again, Palmer was stretching them to the limit; they were only able to raise the £1,800 for the purchase of the silk mill as a result of the vendor himself giving them a mortgage.

But the business was growing; from £1,600 a year in 1837, turnover rose to £41,100 in 1850–1 and £105,000 in 1855–6. By 1857 both Joseph Huntley Senior and Thomas Huntley had died and, thereafter, Huntley and Palmer was in reality Palmers', as three new members of the Palmer family were brought into the management. New methods of promoting the company were found. One idea was to give every first-class passenger leaving Paddington a small packet of biscuits (restaurant cars were not provided on the Great Western Railway until the 1890s). By 1860, Huntley and Palmer were the biggest manufacturers of biscuits in the land.

But Britain was not the limit of their ambitions. The company began exporting as early as 1844. They were one of 17 Reading firms to display their wares at the Great Exhibition of 1851 and, by the mid-1850s, exports were 15 per cent

61   *The Huntley and Palmer factory in 1846.*

of their turnover, with markets as diverse as the United States, China, Brazil and West Africa. They sent a gift of biscuits to the King of Madagascar for his coronation in 1862, and the explorer Henry Stanley was equipped with tins of them as placatory gifts for the hostile tribes he met along the way of his search for Dr Livingstone.

   The tins in which they travelled became as coveted as the biscuits themselves (or possibly more so in some quarters). In 1904 they were found in the city of Lhasa, in Tibet, which was forbidden to westerners. Mongolian chiefs regarded the boxes as status symbols. They were used as ballot boxes in Switzerland and in Uganda to protect the Bibles of converts from the predations of white ants (special Bibles had to be provided to fit inside them). During the Battle of Omdurman the fanatical Sudanese followers of the Mahdi (not noted as fans of things western) were found to have decorated their sword scabbards with pieces of tinplate cut from biscuit tins, and when a landing party arrived at the uninhabited island of Juan Fernadez in the Pacific – used as the model for Robinson Crusoe's island – the only sign of human habitation they could find was a Huntley and Palmer biscuit tin. (Unfortunately Daniel Defoe wrote Robinson Crusoe in 1719, so it could not be claimed that his fictional hero had been sustained by a secret supply of Digestives.) Even the guarantee labels inside the tins became negotiable – these turned out to be the same size as colonial pound notes, and it is alleged that these were used by one fraudster to 'purchase' goods from illiterate Boer farmers (though this could have been anti-Boer propaganda during the war years).

The business became the town's biggest employer. From 41 staff in 1846, they grew to 535 by 1861 and 5,057 by 1898. The terms of employment were severe by modern standards. The working day in 1850 ran from 6.30 in the morning to 6.30 at night, with 40 minutes for breakfast and an hour for dinner. They also worked until 2.00p.m. on Saturdays, making a 58½-hour working week. Overtime was also available for the really enthusiastic. Staff had between 5½ and 7½ days of (unpaid) leave a year, including Good Friday, Whit Monday and three or four days at Christmas. Staff were also allowed the occasional half day off for major local events. Fines were payable for profane language, smoking, coming to work with unwashed face or hands, and other misbehaviour. The proceeds from this went into the staff Sick Fund Box, a benefit for employees that made no demands on the company's profits. From 1849, this was complemented by a contributory sick pay scheme, which operated until nationwide health insurance was introduced in 1912–13. Wage levels were initially set individually for staff, until the size of the company made this impracticable. They were low, given that the company had relatively little local competition for manual labour, as was illustrated by their low turnover of staff.

In other ways, though, the company went out of its way to care for the staff. There was a non-contributory pension scheme (albeit only available after 50 years' service). They organised excursions for the staff and their families – one of the first was see the Crystal Palace in 1857. By the early 20th century, these had grown to unimaginable proportions – 7,000 staff, requiring 10 special

62   *Huntley and Palmer even had their own railway, with smokeless steam locomotives without fires, for use within the factory buildings.*

trains and two different venues, to avoid one seaside town getting swamped by fun-seeking biscuit workers. There were musical soirees in the town hall and a Mutual Improvement Society, with a reading room, library and weekly lectures. A factory cricket club flourished from 1855, a recreation club came later and the Reading Temperance Band was almost entirely composed of their employees, and supported by the company. If you died in service, you could look forward to the company paying to bury you.

More generally, the Palmer family became one of the town's most important benefactors. They gave 12 acres of land at Kings Meadow for a cricket ground, and promoted the purchase of more land for public use there. In 1889, George announced that he was giving 21 acres to the west of Reading Cemetery to the town as a recreation ground, later extending the gift to 49 acres. This was what we now know as Palmer Park. He was outraged by the suggestion (from a local estate agent) that this land could have made him £100,000, if sold off as building plots. The public raised a subscription to erect a statue to him (this stood for many years in Broad Street, before relocating to its present home in the park). They also made him the town's first Freeman. William Isaac Palmer gave what was then the almost unimaginable sum of £25,000 towards the town's new free library. More generally, W.I. Palmer was one of the nation's greatest philanthropists. When he died, a very wealthy man, in 1893, it was found that his charitable bequests exceeded even his assets and his family, as a matter of honour, felt it necessary to make up the shortfall from their own pockets.

The Palmers also became active in public life. George served on Reading Council from 1850, was on the Board of Health and the School Board. He became mayor in 1857 (supporters celebrated with something of a Reading tradition, by firing the ceremonial cannon on the Forbury mound – loaded with stones and nails, this blew out many of the windows in the surrounding area and set fire to the fields across the river, in rural Caversham). George Palmer became one of the town's Members of Parliament (standing as a Liberal) in 1878. His maiden speech was in support of an early private members' bill to give votes to women and he served until 1885, when Reading lost one of its parliamentary seats. George Palmer later refused a baronetcy, though another member of the family, Walter, accepted one. George William Palmer in his turn was Mayor of Reading in 1889–90 and the town's Member of Parliament between 1892 and 1904.

The company by now had become a national institution – it received the Royal Warrant in 1884 – but all was not well by the end of the century. Competition was growing, from a range of manufacturers including Jacobs, Peek Freans and the Co-operative Wholesale Society. In addition, a number of the new chains of grocers were setting up as biscuit manufacturers in their own right. Their premises and their equipment were obsolete, and the management were slow to change their product lines and poor at advertising them when they did. By 1912, Peek Frean had overtaken them in the domestic market. It was part of a long decline that would continue for much of the 20th century.

63 *Gosbrook Road in about 1914, and a party of Huntley and Palmer workers set out on one of the works outings sponsored by their employers.*

64 *Palmer Park – one of the Palmer family's many gifts to the town – is opened in 1891.*

65 *An aerial photograph of the Huntley and Palmer empire at its greatest extent, c.1920.*

66 *Martin Hope Sutton, c.1870.*

Suttons Seeds

John Sutton founded a company in Reading in 1806, dealing flour, corn and other agricultural seeds. But it was his second son, Martin Hope Sutton (1815–1901) who introduced flower and vegetable seeds to the business. He joined the business in 1828, aged 13, and by 1836 was made a partner with his father. To say that he was enthusiastic about plants is something of an understatement. He would walk from Reading to Bagshot, Slough, Brentford and other centres of horticulture of the day to see prize specimens, and he is on record as having walked back the 25 miles from one of his visits overnight, in order to be at his work desk by 7 a.m. the following morning.

   Two factors contributed to the success of the business. The first was the scrupulous way they did business. Adulteration of seeds was widespread in those days. Expensive seed (like broccoli) would be mixed with much cheaper but similar-looking seed (like rape) which had previously been sterilised. Suttons were strongly opposed to this kind of practice and were supporters of subsequent legislation which outlawed adulteration. This also led to their advice being sought by the government in the wake of the disastrous potato famine that swept through Ireland in the 1840s. They supplied vegetable seeds that took the place of the lost potatoes, and doubtless saved many lives in the process. The other factor behind their growth was the establishment of a national postal system, which enabled them to transform their business from a local to a national one.

67   *Sutton's premises in Market Place, decorated for the Coronation in 1953.*

By 1857, the business employed 40 people and it continued to grow until, at its height, the Royal Seed Establishment (as it became) employed almost seven hundred people and covered a five-acre site to the east of Market Place, stretching from the Forbury Gardens and Abbey Street to Kings Road. Originally, this site was chosen as being close to the town's weekly farmers' market. In addition they had extensive trial grounds just outside the town (on what is now Suttons Industrial Park). The Royal in their title stemmed from an early business relationship established between John Sutton and the bailiff of the Royal Home Farm at Windsor.

In 1974, the company decided to realise the capital value of their prime sites in Reading and moved to Torquay. Few signs of their business remain, but some of their family homes (Hillcroft on Allcroft Road and Rosehill House in Emmer Green) remained after the move. The family are also remembered for their contributions to the life of the town – Martin John Sutton became the mayor of the town, and Herbert Sutton helped in 1893 to establish the University Extension College, which was to become Reading University.

Chapter Twelve

Nineteenth-Century Improvements: Health and Safety

… a town whose dignity may appear to be irretrievably lost in squalor but which can be captured by the united efforts of its citizens.

(Edward Oliver, champion of the Royal Berkshire Hospital)

The Reading that we know is, to a large degree, a 19th-century creation. In the following chapters, we will look at how some of the institutions that help to shape the modern town emerged during that time.

The Fire Fighters

Fire had long been a hazard for the people of Reading. As we saw in chapter four, the corporation in the 16th century and Charles I in his charter of 1638 had tried to reduce the danger. But 200 years later, the town was not conspicuously well-organised for dealing with it.

Under an ancient statute, which was in force until well into the 19th century, each parish was expected to maintain a fire engine in its vestry. The fire alarm was sounded by crossing the church bells or beating a drum. In this event, the following lightning-fast procedure came into effect. First, the fire engine would have to be released from its lock-up – at night, this could involve 'calling up the sexton and perhaps half a dozen other persons'. They would then proceed with it to the vicinity of the fire, open a plug in the nearest water main and (assuming anything came out, which was by no means guaranteed – see the section on water supply) flood and dam a portion of the gutter. This water was then gathered up in buckets, which were passed from hand to hand to the hand-powered engine, and thence pumped to the men on ladders, fighting the fire – assuming there was anything left burning by then. At least, that was the theory.

When, in 1843, the Corporation persuaded the three parishes to transfer their engines to the Superintendent of Police, they were found to be in such disrepair as to be useless. Small wonder, then, that Reading had suffered a series of disastrous fires in and around the town in the first half of the century. In one, at a stables on the future site of the Royal Berkshire Hospital, 35 stagecoach horses died; Aldermaston House, dating from 1636, was destroyed by fire in 1843; and, as is discussed elsewhere in the book, Caversham Park mansion went the same way in 1850. Small wonder, too, that

68   *Caversham Fire Brigade, c.1910.*

large employers like Suttons and Huntley and Palmer had their own independent fire brigades, as did some of the leading insurance companies. As late as 1928, the private fire brigades of those two Reading firms were called out to help the municipal brigade fight a major fire in the centre of Reading. Some older houses in Reading still bear the metal plate of their insurance company on their walls, telling any private fire brigade that appeared at the scene of a fire whether or not the property was insured with them. For those without insurance the consequences could be harsh. Darter recounts the case of a cork merchant on Friar Street whose premises went up in flames in May 1812. The owner, a Mr Nicholson, was uninsured and ended his days in the workhouse.

The Corporation invested in two new fire engines and a fire escape after 1844, but fire fighting remained a sub-section of the police, who kept the appliances in the police yard. The fire brigade only became a separate department of the council in 1893. Perhaps their finest hour came in 1945, when their own fire station in St Mary's Butts caught fire. Despite them apparently being on the scene very quickly, the firemen could not prevent the building being gutted, and three appliances and all their equipment destroyed.

The Royal Berkshire Hospital

The idea of setting up a hospital in Reading was first floated as long ago as the early 18th century. But it was decided that the facilities in London, Winchester and the John Radcliffe Infirmary in Oxford were quite close enough to serve local needs. In one sense this was true, in that there were few if any medical procedures that required a hospital to carry them out – these being the days before anaesthetics, X-rays and all the other complicated paraphernalia of life support.

69 *A fire at the cottages next to the* Duke of Edinburgh *public house in Prospect Street, Caversham, in 1907. The Caversham Brigade, pictured earlier, would have been despatched to deal with it.*

70 *Reading's fire station in St Mary's Butts goes up in flames in 1945, and the local brigade are unable to save their equipment.*

By the dawn of the 19th century, Reading's population of just under 10,000 was served by three physicians and seven surgeons. But they were among the leading opponents of a hospital, fearing the effect it might have on their practices. Others opposed the principle of a hospital on the grounds that it would attract delicate and sick people to live in the town. But in 1802 the doctors modified their position sufficiently to lead a public subscription to set up the Reading Dispensary, a medical facility to serve the industrious poor. This group was the one who had most difficulty in obtaining medical services, since the more affluent could buy them, while the destitute poor had them provided through the not always tender ministrations of the Poor Law and the workhouse. For the most part, the dispensary's activities were limited to the dispensing of advice and medicines, though it did provide a few beds at the dispensary house.

The dispensary was soon treating 400 in-patients a year, and by the 1830s this had increased faster than the growth in the town's population, to eight hundred. In February 1836 the governors of the dispensary received a report on the proposed establishment of a county hospital in Reading or its vicinity. It proposed that the dispensary give the first £1,000 towards the cost from its own funds. The doctors who had previously opposed such an idea were now converted to it, though whether from philanthropic motives or because they saw business opportunities is difficult to say. The funding was agreed, and their contribution was immediately matched by a local worthy, Richard Benyon de Beauvoir of Englefield House (who later gave a further £2,000). The great and the good of the town were lobbied for the remainder, and a sufficient sum was soon raised to enable serious planning to begin.

Much of the credit for the promotion of the hospital rests with a retired managing clerk at a London bank. Edward Oliver had lost much of his life savings due to a fraud perpetrated by a trustee of the bank, and lived in Reading on a very modest pension. He walked the length and breadth of Berkshire in pursuit of his cause, twice securing an audience with King William IV at Windsor to promote the idea. The King supported it to the extent of a 50 guineas a year contribution from the privy purse, and the patronage that enabled the word Royal to be added to its name.

Three sites were originally considered for the hospital. The one finally chosen was owned by Lord and Lady Sidmouth. Sidmouth (formerly Henry Addington) had been the only Reading-born Prime Minister, but initially he and his wife were unwilling to sell. While supporting the principle of a hospital in Reading, the loss of their land would be 'very objectionable to Lord Sidmouth and myself', as Lady Sidmouth told them. Fortunately, they were later won over to the idea, even to the extent of giving the land to the hospital.

A specification for a 60-bed hospital, capable of being expanded to 100 beds, was drawn up and an architectural competition was held. The winner of the 55 entries was Reading architect Henry Briant. The terms of the competition had set a price limit of £6,000 on the building, but the tender came in at £9,377. This was further inflated when the Kennet and Avon Canal froze over, cutting off the supply of building materials (Bath stone figured prominently) and delaying work, and the completed building came in at roughly twice its original budget.

71 *The Royal Berkshire Hospital, as originally built in 1840.*

The hospital opened on 27 May 1839, with as much pomp and ceremony as was consistent with 'due care for the preservation of order throughout the day' (as the instructions to the organising committee rather quaintly put it). Two thousand Sunday School children paraded to the hospital (each one rewarded with a bun), bands played, crowds cheered, public dinners were held in various places of assembly, cannons were fired and members of the public paid a shilling a time just to gain admission to the hospital grounds. It was the proud boast of the organisers that not a single person was injured throughout the proceedings.

But the hospital had no need to worry about a lack of business, with the Great Western Railway currently under construction nearby. Its first patient was one George Earley, a 15-year-old labourer on the railway. He was run over by a wagon train and his arm so badly fractured that it had to be amputated at the shoulder. In the first year, 61 out of the 86 patients treated for accidents were railway employees. The railway also provided the fledgling hospital with its greatest test when, on Christmas Eve 1841, eight people were killed and 17 put into hospital by the Sonning train crash. Moreover, it was claimed that the opening of the railway enabled many more sick people to travel from the ends of the county to overload the hospital further. The directors of the railway were therefore persuaded to make a contribution of 100 guineas and pay an annual subscription of 10 guineas towards the running costs of the hospital.

The initial staffing consisted of a house surgeon, a matron, three physicians and six surgeons, to whom were added nurses, a cook, a porter, a laundry-maid and other domestic staff as the hospital got up and running. The terms of their employment included a daily allowance of 1½ pints of beer (though staff were searched, to stop them bringing additional supplies of alcohol onto the premises). The 1839 concept of nursing differed markedly from the modern one. The nurses were all totally unqualified and their only medical duty was to ensure that the patients took their prescribed medicines. The rest of their time was spent cleaning, serving meals and looking after the general welfare of the patients. The records suggest that they were not always able to attract the cream of the labour market to these jobs. One of the nurses was found to be nearly blind, another was an alcoholic and the experience of a third in dealing with the severely incapacitated was limited to her previous employment as a barmaid. It was conceded that the nursing staff performed their duties 'in a matter-of-fact manner that jarred painfully on the sensitive nerves of a patient, and not infrequently retarded the progress of recovery', when they were reviewed in 1867.

The hospital's admission criteria also differed from those of the modern National Health Service in a number of respects. Admissions had to be worthy objects of charity and had to be recommended and sponsored by one of the hospital's benefactors (except in the case of emergencies). The more a benefactor donated, the more patients he could sponsor in this way. The sponsor also had to guarantee to meet the costs of the patient's removal from the hospital (including their funeral expenses, should this become necessary). The patients, for their part, had to write a letter of thanks to their benefactor on discharge. Failure to do so could result in them being black-listed for future treatment. By 1853, as pressure on places grew more acute, it was decided that people earning more than 18s. a week would not be eligible for treatment. However, private patients began to be accepted from 1851, as the high reputation of the hospital began to attract demand from that quarter.

The more impoverished patients, dependent upon the Poor Law, presented particular problems for the hospital. Many victims of illness or accident, having no savings to fall back on, technically became casual paupers and thus the responsibility of the various Poor Law Unions. The hospital asked the unions to contribute 7s. a week to their upkeep but they, for the most part, wriggled furiously to avoid payment – either disputing the principle of paying, claiming that their bills from the general practitioners they employed left them unable to pay, or trying to shuffle off responsibility to another parish. These disputes did not end in the event of the death of the patient. Their bodies would remain in the hospital mortuary for weeks, while responsibility for paying for the funeral was disputed. In some cases, the hospital conceded and buried the patient, but there were cases where they actually threatened to take the corpse round to the house of the Poor Law Union official and just leave it there!

The dispute with the Reading Union persisted until after the new workhouse was built, in 1867. By then, they were the only union for miles around that did not subscribe to the hospital. They resolutely refused to do so, arguing that their own medical officers were contacted to treat their inmates under all circumstances (and presumably regardless of whether or not they had the facilities to do so). But by now the new workhouse had a purpose-built infirmary. However, medicine had advanced since the hospital opened. There were now anaesthetics and antiseptics to improve the chances of surviving surgery, and the workhouse infirmary had no operating theatre and absolutely basic standards of nursing (one untrained nurse to look after up to 75 patients in the main infirmary and six cases in the fever ward). The guardians stuck out against subscribing until one of their inmates urgently needed his leg amputating. The union then finally relented and paid the six guineas that entitled it to sponsor three in-patients per year and to send four out-patients at any time. In 1873, there were 32 deaths among the workhouse population (well over 10 per cent of the total workhouse population) compared with a death-rate (itself high) of 18.4 per 1,000 population for the borough at large, though how far this reflects the vulnerable nature of the inmate population, and how far the quality of their treatment, is impossible to say.

Certain classes of illness were not treated. The hospital would not admit 'those apprehended to be in a dying state', pregnant women or children under seven (unless they were the victims of severe accidents). Those who were 'disordered in their intellects' were barred, as were those suffering from a long list of illnesses, from club foot and itch through consumption and epilepsy to venereal disease. Last but not least, patients had to be as clean as possible and bring with them their own tea, butter and sugar, and 'a sufficient change of linen' or a payment in lieu.

Accounts of the early years of the hospital present a strange mixture of the ancient and modern. On the one hand, they were apparently using water beds from 1839 and acupuncture from 1842. On the other, there were complaints in 1844 that they were using four times as many leeches as the Radcliffe Infirmary, which was twice its size, and there were no anaesthetics used until 1847. This last point seriously curtailed the number of operations they were able to perform (at least, with any hope of success). Only 96 patients had operations in the first six years. Despite all this, the hospital doubled in size by 1866. It treated 304 in-patients and 274 out-patients in its first year, and by 1878 this had risen to 1,079 in-patients and 1,620 out-patients.

Edward Oliver, the original champion of the hospital, ended his days in Benyon ward, after he was run over by a horse-drawn Huntley and Palmers wagon in London Street in 1855. He left two daughters more or less totally unprovided for, one of whom ended up in the workhouse.

The Reading Dispensary was not allowed by the courts to merge with the hospital, and continued its complementary activities for many years. By the 1870s, about a third of Reading's population were members of the dispensary, with those who could afford it paying a small weekly sum towards its costs. From around 1848, they occupied a rather impressive stone-fronted building on Chain Street, that was eventually knocked down in around 1975, to build the extension to Heelas (what is now the John Lewis department store). John Man was clearly unimpressed by their early efforts. In his 1810 book *The Stranger in Reading* he reported the dispensary's latest annual statistics. People treated: 409; those cured: 305; those still on the list: forty-five. This still left what was, to Man, a disturbing 59 of their patients unaccounted for. What had happened to them, he wondered? Had they fled? Were they dead?

The Workhouse

> Our object ... is to establish a discipline so severe and repulsive as to make them a terror to the poor and prevent them from entering.
> An Assistant Poor Law Commissioner on the operation of the Workhouse after 1834.

By the 1830s, the old Poor Law system described earlier was creaking badly, not just in Reading but throughout the land. A Royal Commission was set up to advise on changes to it. They found that there were far too many people permanently dependent on the system that the level of payments required was crippling many people and that it was impoverishing some of those who managed to stay in work and out of the system, by depressing wages. The result was the Poor Law Amendment Act of 1834. This merged the parish overseers into larger (and, it was hoped, more efficient) unions – in Reading's case, the three parishes came together and, along with Southcote and Whitley, formed a Reading Union. A much harsher regime was introduced, aimed at deterring all but the most desperate from using it. Outdoor relief was abolished and only the genuinely destitute would be admitted to the workhouse. The focus was to be very much on those too old, too young, too sick or too mentally infirm to work (for the workhouse also cared for 'idiots and harmless and chronic lunatics' not considered dangerous enough for committal to an asylum).

The first act of the new union was to close the former St Giles' Parish workhouse at Horn Street and to make modifications to the other two, which, they hoped, would be adequate to deal with the reduced demand arising from the new regime. This coped after a fashion until the 1860s, by when there was gross overcrowding, with some men having to sleep two to a bed. The Poor Law Inspectors said the overseers should do something about it; the overseers ignored them, so in April 1864 the inspector, a Mr R.B. Cane, wrote in much stronger terms: 'The only remedy for the most defective state of the accommodation ... is the erection of a workhouse which will remove the discredit which the existing buildings bring upon so important a Union as that of Reading'.

This had the desired effect and an eight-acre site on the Oxford Road, straddling the then borough boundary, was purchased. The process of getting the workhouse built appears to have been a nightmare of public procurement. First, the overseers tried (illegally) to incorporate a lunatic asylum into the plans, to save on the 10s. 6d. a week they were then paying to send each of the town's 40 more serious mental illness cases to the asylum at Littlemore, near Oxford. The authorities quickly rejected that. Then they decided to scale down the plans from 400 to 250 beds, again to save money. They pre-judged the cost of the scheme and set the competing architects the task of designing down to a budget, rather then to meeting a specification. A shortlist of two schemes was chosen but, when the alternative designs were displayed, the one preferred by the public (and the Poor Law Inspector, who was allowed an opinion, but not a vote) was not the one chosen by the overseers, and a furious public row took place. The Poor Law Board, who had to approve the plans, were scathing about them, forcing many redesigns (which increased the costs).

By 1867, the new workhouse was finally under construction, but it had already become clear that the new workhouse would be far too small for the needs arising from Reading's growing population. The architect proposed adding an additional floor to the workhouse infirmary, which was then under construction (more cost), but the growing numbers and changes in national standards for such premises meant that 75 per cent additional infirmary space was likely to be needed. Within three years of opening, the infirmary had to be extended again. As soon as the building was finished and occupied, further design faults emerged. The heating and hot water were found to be 'absolutely useless', the chimney in one room smoked so much that it was uninhabitable and some of the ungrateful inmates complained that they had been more warm and comfortable in their run-down former premises.

Every aspect of life in the new workhouse had to be planned. The food was to be: 'Plain and wholesome, the quantity sufficient without being excessive and the composition and cooking such as to render it palatable so that waste can be avoided, either from the food being more than the inmates require or from the food being distasteful to them'. (Railton and Barr)

One saving was achieved by not giving them milk, as well as sugar, in their tea, and beer was only to be issued to patients in the infirmary with the consent of the Medical Officer. The Poor Law Board laid down guidelines for the quantities of beer and spirits to be given to healthy inmates, and it emerged in 1870 that, in this area if in no other, the union was not stinting their charges. The Reading Union had the highest liquor bill in the county, spending £1 4s. 3d. per head per year, more than three times as much as the lowest spender. The Tilehurst Workhouse had also had a relatively lavish regime in the years leading up to the Poor Law reforms of the 1830s. The accounts for 1834 show high levels of spending on food and drink, including considerable amounts on wine, beer and gin.

One problem that was not anticipated was the residents being unused to such amenities as running water and proper toilets. They would leave the taps running and put all sorts of objects (such as builder's bricks) down the toilets, causing them to block or causing the cesspits to overflow. Neighbours complained of the smell and the health hazard.

Children were not kept in the workhouse but were sent to the district school in Wargrave, which dealt with the pauper children of both Reading and Wokingham Unions. This cost the union between £800 and £1,000 a year and, in 1870, a scheme was devised to export pauper children between the ages of seven and 12 to Canada, where they would be placed in work, or in service, or be adopted by a Canadian family. But only two shipments were sent before the scheme was abandoned without any explanation, at least in the workhouse records.

At this time, the workhouse also had a statutory duty to deal with tramps, and separate provision was made for them in part of the old St Laurence's workhouse. Essentially, this consisted of bed and breakfast (to wit, straw, bread and water) and a free police escort to the borough boundary in return for them picking a quarter-pound of oakum. Reading, being on strategic transport routes, was visited by a large number of tramps. In the first year of the new workhouse's operation the records show they dealt with 4,366 casuals (as tramps were called) passing through the town. They presented their own management problems; some would arrive late, to avoid the requirement for them to take a bath. This would result in complaints about verminous bedding from subsequent, more fastidious, customers (as the straw was not frequently changed). Another of the practices of the workhouse was to confiscate any cash found on the tramps, as a deterrent to them staying with the union.

Towards the very end of the life of the workhouse system, this group were to cause a further controversy. As part of a review of the service in 1928, a new site for the casuals' ward was found, just off the Bath Road in Woodley. The nearby residents of Wokingham and the Wokingham Rural District Council were outraged. According to them, the new facility would be in a 'particularly attractive' part of the parish and in a residential area. Tramps, 'a most undesirable class of individual', would cause 'serious depreciation in the value of property and would be a menace to the health of the community' and 'a disturbance of the peace'. The Ministry of Health nonetheless approved the scheme. Wokingham then refused to grant it planning permission and the Ministry overrode them yet again.

The boundary extension of 1887 also meant parts of the Wokingham and Bradfield Unions being absorbed into Reading – much against the wishes of those unions, since many of their costs were fixed and the unit cost of looking after their inmates was driven up by the loss of part of their areas.

After being commandeered during the First World War, the workhouse was returned into civilian hands in 1921. Many of the old inmates started moving back, but things had changed. It was now known as Battle Infirmary, and its inmates were referred to as patients, rather than paupers. Efforts were being made to get those with mental health problems (no longer called imbeciles or lunatics) treated somewhere else more suitable and epileptics were no longer classed as mentally defective. There was still strict discipline, but the routine was less dreary and there was no longer a distinctive uniform to mark them out.

However, the workhouse was not immune from the post-war recession. The increasing demands on the union from the growing band of the unemployed, plus the absence of the £48,559 payment still outstanding from the government for their wartime use of the facility, meant the union was plunged into financial crisis. Proposals in 1922 to reduce the scale of relief led to a noisy and potentially violent demonstration outside a meeting of the Board of Guardians, from which some of them had to be rescued by police. The guardians in turn lobbied the government for help, but were told that many of those in employment in Reading were receiving less than the 3,000 people in the town receiving relief. The guardians were sympathetic to the complaints of the working people, and provided food and shelter to a number of groups of those passing through the town on hunger marches, but the rates were still cut. They were reduced again in 1923 but, by the following year, 88 per cent of the Poor Rate was going on unemployment relief and the rate had risen from its pre-war level of 1s. 3d. in the pound to 3s. 2d.

The end of the Poor Law Union came with the Local Government Act of 1929, which transferred their responsibilities to the local authority. The guardians' last meeting took place on 31 March 1930. The end for Battle Hospital itself (as the infirmary became) started to be discussed in the 1980s. The draft Strategic Plan of the Health Authority for 1984–94 talked of centralising paediatric services on the Royal Berkshire site. By 1989–90 references began to appear to the centralisation of all services at the Royal Berks, the option long favoured by many clinicians. Alternatives were considered and, while centralisation at Battle (another option) had merits, the cost involved was dauntingly large. 1992 saw an application for the Royal Berks and Battle to become an NHS Trust, based on rationalisation onto the Royal Berkshire site, and in May 1995, Ministerial approval for the £56.3 million development was granted.

Water Supply and Sewerage

> Reading is nothing but an extended cesspool.
>
>   (Dr Southwood Smith – social reformer)

In 1818, at about the same time as the town's water supply system of hollowed-out tree trunks were replaced with cast-iron pipes, the civil engineer William Cubitt advised the town on improvements to the water supply. In line with his advice, an improved pump capable of delivering 250,000 gallons a day was installed, a water tower was erected in Mill Lane and a reservoir built on the site of what is now Spring Gardens Recreation Ground. This extended the area of supply considerably, though the water was still totally unfiltered and was described as 'dark in colour, sometimes contained fish and had a distinct taste' – always assuming one was foolish enough to drink it. Prior to the provision of safe drinking water, beer was the universal beverage for young and old, its mild antiseptic qualities making it safer to drink. The water supply was also intermittent – water was only pumped every other day and repairs could shut the system down for days at a time. Last, and certainly not least, the fish sucked into the pipes used to block them up until they rotted away, further adding to the distinct flavour of the supply.

The water company nonetheless persevered with drawing its supplies from Mill Lane. It obtained the power from Parliament to levy a water rate in 1826 and introduced steam pumps a decade later. The company also installed a large

72   *Mill Lane from the west in about 1898, showing the water tower that was a feature of the town's skyline for many years.*

73   *The sewage pumping station at Blakes Lock on the River Kennet, seen in 1900.*

reservoir near Coley Avenue in 1830. It was designed to hold 200,000 gallons, took two years to build and lasted about two hours – bursting during filling and causing between £1,000 and £2,000 of flood damage to neighbouring property. Small wonder that the Corporation tried to municipalise the water supply from 1846 (finally succeeding in 1868). As late as 1846, almost two thousand of the town's 4,155 houses still had no water supply at all. But the setting up of a rival water company prompted improvements, and a supply of filtered water started to be provided to the entire town from new works at Southcote Mill from 1850. Mill Lane's inferior product was relegated to use for things like street-washing and filling steam locomotives. Prior to this, using the precious water supply for things like street washing was deeply frowned upon. George Palmer tried washing down the filthy gutter in front of his premises in 1846, and had his supply cut off as a consequence. New waterworks at Fobney came into operation from 1878 and were subsequently expanded, along with the town itself.

It will be clear from the above that living in early 19th-century Reading was by no means a guarantee of a long and healthy life. Death rates were between 50 and 100 per cent above the national average – some of the highest in the country – and the average life expectancy of a Reading resident was some five years less than their neighbours in Wokingham. Some of the reasons for this emerged from an 1846 report into sanitary conditions in the town. This revealed that 95 per cent of the borough had no proper drainage of any kind and the town was, in the words of the Royal Commission into the Health of Towns, nothing but an extended cesspool.

Childs describes the state of early 19th-century Reading's sanitation as follows:

> Slaughter houses were found in the heart of the town; pig-sties abounded. There was no arterial drainage. Alongside the drinking wells were cesspools, computed in 1849 at 2,700, some of them so deep that they could only be cleansed at an almost prohibitive cost. There were localities where the subsoil was said to be saturated with drainage. In Silver Street the sewage discharged into a ditch without outlet. Down London Street ran 'a black open gutter' very offensive in hot weather; and Mr George Palmer declared in 1846 that in this respect London Street was not exceptional. The Town Clerk declared that there was 'not a single street in a proper state'. In August of the same year the Reading Mercury affirmed that no-one could pass down a by-street without being offended 'by some stagnant pool of putridity, the insufferable stench of a slaughter-house, or the foul air of a half-choked drain'.
>
> (Childs)

Some prominent citizens saw nothing wrong with this state of affairs. Despite the growth of the national public health movement from the 1840s, economisers on the council fought against it for decades. As late as 1859, one Alderman Brown was arguing that the prevention of fever was impious and that to suggest that a good drainage system would prevent disease was saying more than mortal man ought to do.

Fortunately, a number of local medical professionals were prepared to fight for good sanitation. Outbreaks of typhus and cholera added weight to their arguments. However, the council's first attempt to address the problem was in the form of what Childs describes as an ill-considered and overloaded measure, which contained 327 clauses and involved an outlay of £150,000 and aroused a storm of local opposition even among many of the friends of sanitary reform. The scheme was thrown out, after a government inquiry, in 1847, although the need for sanitary reform was clearly acknowledged. The council's hand was forced when the 1867 Thames Navigation Act (against which the council had lobbied vigorously) prevented local authorities discharging sewage into the Thames or its tributaries.

The council were forced to spend £102,000 on the compulsory purchase of 760 acres of land at Whitley, including Manor Farm. In addition, works costing £228,000 were required to create a sewage farm and the associated network of sewers, and a special Act of Parliament had to be sought in 1870 to give the council the powers needed to do so. A pumping station at Blake's Lock sent the sewage via pipes along the bed of the River Kennet to Manor Farm, where it was simply spread over the land and left to rot down. The land was subsequently farmed, and produced prize-winning vegetables! The scheme came into operation by 1875, but was a major burden on the public purse for years afterwards.

Chapter Thirteen

NINETEENTH-CENTURY IMPROVEMENTS: EDUCATION

Education would result in the plough and the loom standing still; that the spade should be laid aside for the pen ... It might disqualify the laborious classes of society from their duties and set them above their work.

(Opposition to universal education, quoted in North)

Reading School

Reading School was already centuries old by the dawn of the 19th century (as we saw earlier, quite how many centuries old was a matter of some debate). It was at that time entering into one of its finest periods under its most famous headmaster, Richard Valpy. The son of a wealthy Jersey family and a graduate of Pembroke College, Oxford, Valpy was appointed headmaster in 1781. He was only 27 at the time, and the school had been 'in a reduced state'. One of its main problems was its woefully inadequate accommodation, discussed earlier, which became steadily worse. For, at the same meeting of the council that appointed Valpy, they also resolved to build a new town hall (now the Victoria Hall, part of the town hall complex of buildings in Blagrave Street). This was completed in 1786 and further overshadowed the school. Valpy asked the corporation to provide him with a new school building, but they refused. So, in 1790, he built a new schoolhouse at his own expense.

Valpy was a remarkable man – a scholar, actor and poet, who also had interests in politics, agriculture, soldiering, religion and gambling. He was a walking advertisement for life-long learning, studying after his appointment at the school for his Masters degree from Pembroke College (1784) and a Ph.D in Divinity in 1792. He was known as a strict disciplinarian – his nickname was the 'mighty flogger' and the cartoonist George Cruikshank caricatured him as the Revd Duodecimus Wackerback – but the pupils apparently worshipped him. The parents were equally admiring for, under him, the numbers attending the school rose to 119 by 1792 and over two hundred by the time of his retirement. This was despite the high fees, of 50 to 60 guineas a year, an entrance fee of five guineas and extra charges for classics, maths and writing. This was some way removed from the idea of a 'free' school for the town's poorer children, which many saw as the original purpose of the establishment – there were very few free pupils under Valpy.

We know a little of the regime for pupils in Valpy's day. They rose at 5.30a.m., washed outside under the pump in the yard (there was punishment for those who failed to do so) then had lessons until 8.30, followed by a breakfast of bread and (watered) milk. This was followed by more lessons until lunchtime, with sports in the afternoon, more lessons and evening prayers to end the day. Swimming was a major feature of the sporting curriculum, this being one of Valpy's passions. He used to teach them by the unusual method of throwing half crowns, wrapped in white paper, into the river for them to

74 *Dr Valpy, Reading School's most famous master.*

find. His school was also notable for its dramatic productions. Valpy used to supervise every detail of them personally and they were eagerly awaited by the local population – one of their productions of Shakespeare even went on to Covent Garden. Large sums of money were raised by them for charity. Like others of his time, Valpy was not above 'improving' Shakespeare with lines of his own (often patriotic, and with unpleasant references to the French, with whom the nation was then at war). On one occasion, a child actor was having difficulty portraying fear and distress. Valpy solved the problem by giving the child a terrific clout immediately before he went on stage. His performance that night was apparently highly praised!

Valpy also became known as one of the great and the good. He wrote text books that were familiar to generations of schoolchildren nationwide, introduced educational innovations, such as the teaching of Latin in English (if such a thing is not a contradiction in terms), served on the management of a host of charities and twice refused a bishopric. He finally retired after almost fifty years of service, in 1830, dying six years later at the age of eighty-two. His son Francis succeeded him, and presided over an equally dramatic decline of the school. It is suggested that Valpy senior, for all his great qualities, may have been part of the cause of this decline, having stayed on too long and fallen out with the Corporation. Whatever the causes, within five years of his departure the school had lost some of its major funding streams and by 1837 there were only 20 boarders and 17 day pupils (nine of the latter 'free' pupils) left. Francis Valpy resigned in 1839. The decline continued under his successors until, by 1866, numbers had dwindled to two day scholars and one boarder. A devastating report by a school inspector led to its closure.

The charitable works of John Kendrick are detailed elsewhere in the book. When part of his charitable bequest to Reading was lost to Christ's Hospital in 1850, the remainder – the loan charity – was eventually used to rejuvenate the school. The Reading School Act of 1867 laid down arrangements for the funding and administration of a modern grammar school. A 10-acre site at Erleigh Road was bought from the Redlands Estate in 1868 and the Reading-based architect Alfred Waterhouse was engaged to design the new school building. In the absence of additional funding from the council, the Palmer family came to the rescue with a £6,000 loan towards the building costs. The purpose of the school was still in some doubt:

> Was it supposed to be a centre of excellence, serving a fee-paying elite, or was it supposed to be serving purely local needs? People had violently differing views on the matter, and some sought an uneasy compromise between the two. The 1870 prospectus referred to 'a thorough Middle-Class education to be supplemented by a lower school for the benefit of the lower classes'.
>
> (Hylton)

The row continued after the school reopened in 1871, provoking a lively correspondence in the *Times* and attracting the attention of the charity commissioners, who insisted that the trustees draw up a clear plan for the future of the school. But the school was caught on the horns of a dilemma. It needed to maximise the number of boarders to ease its perennial financial problems, but this in turn led to opposition to any form of rate-borne subsidy. As the *Reading Chronicle* put it in 1877: 'Do they mean that the denizens of Silver Street (said to be the poorest street in the town) are to pay for the education of boys who live in the best houses in the town and neighbourhood?'.

75 *Reading School.*

In practice, the council had little say in the matter. Under the terms of the 1867 Act, if the trustees defaulted on their mortgages, the council had to pick up the bill and, in 1886, this is what happened. This unhappy state of affairs rumbled on until 1908 when the school, its land and buildings were handed over in trust to the council. However, the school was still under-used and, in 1916, a decision was made to merge it with the boys' part of Kendrick School.

Kendrick School has its origin in the Kendrick charities, which, in 1877, were used to establish schools for 100 boys (in a building on Kings Road) and 100 girls (in Watlington House). They too had been the subject of some controversy about their role, with the Reading Men's Liberal Association claiming that the Kendrick money was being diverted away from its original purpose of aiding the poor to subsidising the middle classes. During the financial crises of Reading School in the latter part of the 19th century, when the School had controversially increased its fees, Kendrick Boys' School did at least offer to provide a place for any boy who could not afford to go to Reading.

The merger of Reading and Kendrick Boys' Schools solved the problem of under-use, with the number of pupils at Reading School exceeding 500 by 1921. The Kendrick Girls' School was able to move out of its crowded accommodation in Watlington Street, into purpose-built accommodation, next to Mary Russell Mitford's house, on the corner of London Road and Sidmouth Street, in 1927.

Reading's Schools

The history of education in Reading may start with Reading School but, for many Reading children, for most of the town's history, the prospect of any sort of schooling was vanishingly remote. Some earlier efforts had been made to provide free or cheap education. An apothecary called John Hall had founded alms houses and a school in Chain Street in 1696. He had looked to appoint a 'poor, honest, decayed tradesman' to act as its master and saw to it that each child was given a Bible on leaving. However, this was merged with Blue Coat School in 1796. For many at the start of the 19th century, Sunday School was the best chance they had of learning even the rudiments of reading and writing. Some of these were set up in Reading in 1781 by one Robert Raikes, a printer from Gloucester. As at 1809, according to John Man, Reading had just four free schools, run as charitable institutions. One was for boys, one mixed and two for girls (although one of these latter was dismissed by Man as nothing more than a sweatshop for producing cheap needlework).

Between these charitable institutions and the schools for the most privileged (Eton, Harrow – and Reading School in its better years) there were a number of schools for the middle classes, like Baker's Academy in Hosier Lane, off St Mary's Butts, where Man himself had taught. There, for a basic fee of 16 guineas a year (plus quite a number of additional charges), your child could be taught geometry, trigonometry, geography, arithmetic, Latin, Greek, French,

76   *Green Girls' School, Broad Street, c.1883.*

Italian, merchant's accounts, use of the globes, 'natural shorthand', 'every branch of useful and polite literature', dancing, drawing and navigation.

Childs lists a number of the schools operating in Reading in the early 19th century; the Blue Coat School, founded by Richard Aldworth in 1646, stood at the junction of Silver Street and New Street (now London Road); the Green Girls' School had moved to Broad Street in 1790 from St Mary's Butts, where it had been founded eight years earlier with contributions raised by the vicars of the three Reading parishes, and Mrs Cadogan's School of Industry for poor girls was at the west end of Friar Street. The curriculum of the latter was described as follows: 'the girls are clothed and taught to read, knit, and do plain work well; the strictest attention is paid to their moral and religious instruction, the grand object being to make the scholars good servants and useful members of society'.(Childs)

This latter may well have been the sweatshop of which Man complained. Most of these schools were relatively small – Bakers took just 40 pupils, the numbers at Blue Coat fell in 1816 as low as 15, the Green Girls' School had between 20 and 30 and the School of Industry in 1814 had 34 girls.

In the early years of the 19th century there were two major additions to the town's selection of schools – a Christian National School and a Lancastrian or British School both opened in Reading. The latter was a product of the British and Foreign School Society, founded in London in 1808 by a Quaker, Joseph Lancaster, for the education of poor children. The site of the school in Southampton Street was largely paid for by a local benefactor, Edward Simeon.

He was a governor of the Bank of England, whose monument in modern Reading is the obelisk designed by Sir John Soane in the marketplace. Places at the school were sponsored by other local benefactors at the rate of one guinea a year (which is interesting, in that we are told in 1835 that the actual cost of each child's schooling was just six shillings a year).

By 1812, the Reading branch of the school had nearly three hundred boys attending. Their education was frugal; no textbooks were provided – the lessons were painted on boards hung on the classroom walls. Class sizes were huge, and teaching anything at all depended upon the monitorial system, whereby the master maintained some kind of overall order in the class and the older, more able pupils became monitors, who passed their knowledge down to the younger ones. As a Quaker, Lancaster also had his own views about punishment; he rejected the conventional corporal punishment of the day and instead used to place miscreants in a cage, which was then hauled up to the ceiling on a rope. Whilst dangling, they were required to write out the word 'duty' over and over again. The school had intended from the outset to be mixed sex, but initially took only boys until, in 1818, a girls' section was opened. The school survived well beyond the introduction of compulsory education, closing in 1903. At about the same time, in 1819, a national school had also opened in School End, Tilehurst, where it continued to operate until superseded by the Norcot Council School in 1906.

The Beginnings of State Education

The real start of universal education in Reading was the Education Act of 1870, which required every child between the ages of five and 13 to attend school. This was passed in the face of opposition from both ends of the social spectrum. At one end there were the likes of Dame Millicent Fawcett, advancing the rather radical view that any child whose parents could not afford school fees should be left uneducated, in the hope that the process of natural selection would lead to the extinction of this class of person. But many others adhered to a more moderate version of the view that a child's education was the private responsibility of its parents, and that the state should not interfere. At the other end, the poorest parents could not afford even the most modest school fees, or the clothes and shoes in which to dress their children for school, and lived for the day when they could get their offspring into gainful employment.

The Act required the authorities to set up a school board to monitor the educational work of the voluntary and private sectors and to fill any gaps in their provision. It was hoped at first that the Reading Board would have little to do, given that there were by then a wide range of schools in existence. But their initial investigation found that, even by the modest standards of the day, 29 of the town's 62 elementary schools were deficient in teaching skills, apparatus, quality of premises, or some combination of these. The board identified the areas in greatest need and made a start on providing board schools. Coley Street was first, in 1872, closely followed by Silver Street and Katesgrove.

Truancy was a problem from the start. In addition to the clothing problems mentioned earlier, there tended to be a mass exodus by the children to take up summer jobs, or if an attraction like a circus came to town. The generally poor health of the children kept many away and there were some slightly more unexpected reasons for absence. One child, Thomas Gough, was found lying intoxicated in the streets of Reading, while two other absent pupils – J. Prior and J. Huggins – were found to be in prison in Newbury for unspecified crimes. Parents would often conspire in their truancy, forging birth certificates and lying about their ages or the state of their minds or health. A number of children were found to be illegally employed at Huntley and Palmer, but it appears the firm was never prosecuted (George Palmer was on the school board from its inception, though there is no reason to believe that his motives were anything other than philanthropic). Two of the earliest appointments made by the board were therefore a couple of truancy officers, in 1873. In extreme cases, incorrigible truants were sent, under police escort, to special truant schools, some of which were as far away as Poole and Plymouth. Children as young as 11 could be sent there, and their period of detention could run into years.

Even those who made it to school were not always allowed to stay. In some cases, the problem was extreme poverty. Fees for the board schools were a modest 2d. a week for the first child and 1d. for each additional one. But even this was too much for the very poorest and, when children appeared without their school pence on Monday, they would be sent home again. Sometimes they would not return for days, or would return, still without any money. From 1872 a charity, the Destitute Children's Aid Committee, started paying some of the children's fees, and from 1873 it became the guardians' legal duty to ensure that no child missed schooling through an inability to pay – something they had categorically refused to do hitherto.

Other children had to be excluded because their diseased, filthy or verminous condition made them a hazard to the rest of the class. One note from the Silver Street School logbook for 1874 records: 'Sent Charles Garraway home as he came without shoes, and his clothes and person filthy'.

The board decided that children who presented themselves in this state would be washed down by the caretaker, or some other suitable person, who would be paid 4d. for their trouble. Not until 1899 did the need to get the parents' prior consent to this occur to them. Even those children who made it into class sometimes found it difficult to concentrate, due to sheer hunger. The board therefore made arrangements in severe weather for such pupils to receive a breakfast of bread and a pint of soup at the *Rising Sun Coffee Tavern*.

Life for the teachers was not always easy. In addition to the risk of sharing their pupils' infestations, discipline could sometimes be a problem. Again, from the logbook of Silver Street: 'The order of the school broke up on Friday morning 4 December 1874 by Joseph Prior who defied my authority, was very abusive and tried to strike me with a shovel … He was not subdued until well birched'.

One approach to instilling discipline was to bring in ex-army sergeants from Brock Barracks to instruct them in military-type drill. A rather more relaxed approach to physical education, including swimming and football, was introduced from 1899.

The teachers also had to cope with the parsimony of their employers. The board was funded through the rates and, as their statutory responsibilities grew, so the cost also rose – from £1,450 in 1876 to £3,000 three years later. There were claims from the town's economisers that the board was being unduly generous with the public's money. It hardly seemed that way to their long-suffering staff. The schools had inadequate heating and lighting; the teacher at Coley School was still trying to get gas lighting installed in 1881 (It had been generally available in Reading since 1819). His employer's response to his request for improved lighting was to whitewash the classroom walls.

The other pressure on teachers was the ever-increasing number of pupils, which far outstripped any additions to the staff. On one occasion in 1880, a single teacher at the Tilehurst Board School had to cope with 122 pupils. Nor were all of the staff fully qualified. Although the University Extension College took responsibility for the training and vetting of pupil teachers, inexperienced youngsters, including monitors (themselves just pupils of 13 or 14) could find themselves thrown in at the deep end. In one case, a pupil teacher and a monitor were left in charge of a class of 67 and, in another, 'Nellie Hookham, the monitress, was in charge of over fifty children, including several babies'.

By 1902, the town's 12 board schools had an average attendance of over 8,000 pupils. A system which had been set up to fill gaps in the voluntary sector had ended up replacing large parts of it. The Balfour Education Act of 1902 did away with the boards and made their work a responsibility of the council.

Chapter Fourteen

Nineteenth-Century Improvements: More Transport Revolutions

The Railways come to Reading

> … this useless and mischievous project …
> (The considered opinion of the Commissioners of the Thames Navigation
> of the Great Western Railway)

In 1824, before the railway age had even begun, a group of businessmen put forward a proposal to improve the communications between London and what was then the nation's second city, Bristol. A company was formed and John McAdam, best known as a road-builder, was appointed to carry out an initial survey. His proposal was to build a turnpike road, connecting the major town centres between the two cities, and a railway that would skirt round the intervening towns and carry goods only between London and Bristol.

The proposal never got as far as an application to Parliament and, with the 1826 opening of the Stockton and Darlington Railway and, more importantly, the Liverpool and Manchester Railway in 1830, the birth of the modern railway took place elsewhere. The idea was, however, revived in 1832, by which time the promoters could see the striking evidence of the Liverpool and Manchester Railway's success. It was twice as fast as the best stagecoach, halved the cost of transporting goods and had suffered only a single fatality in the course of transporting its first 700,000 passengers. This time, the promoters' choice of chief engineer was rather more adventurous. He was a young man of 27, with no experience of railway building and a local track record based, in part, on a structure – the Clifton Suspension Bridge – that would not be completed in his lifetime. The good news was that he was Isambard Kingdom Brunel.

Advertisements were placed in the *Reading Mercury* and *Berkshire Chronicle* in August 1833, inviting subscriptions to what was to be known as the Great Western Railway. The cost of the scheme was put, rather precisely – and very inaccurately, as it turned out – at £2,805,330 and the shares were £100 each. A dividend of 12 per cent was forecast. Sides soon began to form. The company's prospectus spoke highly of the scheme, promising to:

> multiply the number of travellers, improve the conveyance of goods,
> encourage manufactures, diffuse the advantages of the vicinity of towns over
> the country intersected by the railway, improve the supply of provisions
> to the metropolis and extend the market for agricultural produce, give
> employment to the labouring classes, both during construction and by its
> subsequent effects, and increase the prosperity of the neighbourhood
>
> (Phillips)

They were ambitious claims, but ones that the railway was to fulfil in every
particular. Only in one respect were the early claims of the railway company
inaccurate. They originally claimed a modest reduction in journey times from
Reading to London, from the 4½-5 hours taken by the coaches to 1½-2 hours.
This was done deliberately, to avoid frightening Parliament at the prospect
of unheard-of speeds, which many at the time believed would prove fatal to
passengers. From the start, their services were actually capable of covering the
journey in about an hour.

The mayor and burgesses of Reading supported the scheme and submitted
a petition to Parliament saying so. The *Reading Mercury* also supported the
scheme. Local small landowners and many others opposed the scheme, including
coaching, turnpike and canal interests, the promoters of the rival London and
Southampton Railway, residents who would find themselves living near the
London terminus (then proposed to be at Brompton), the Corporation of
Maidenhead, who feared the loss of tolls on their road bridge and the Provost
of Eton College, who feared that easy access to London might expose his pupils
to the fleshpots of the metropolis and poison their minds. A number of the
opponents met at the *Bear Inn* in Reading in December 1833 to voice their
opposition, though most of the landowners would eventually sell out to the
railway company. Many of the arguments they produced were similar to those
given by opponents of the canal in the previous century, and subsequently proven
wrong. They were led by the Commissioners of the Thames Navigation (who
stood to be a major loser from the scheme). The commissioners claimed that
the scheme would lead to 'the destruction of land, the asseverance of enclosures,
the inundation of foreign labourers and the increased Poor Rate'. They said
that 'no case of public utility had been made out to justify such an uncalled-for
encroachment upon the rights of private property', and their general committee
was 'instructed and empowered to take all such steps as they shall deem advisable
for effectually opposing the progress of this useless and mischievous project'.
The *Reading Chronicle*, at that time the mouthpiece of the local landed gentry,
lined up with the opponents.

One correspondent wrote to the *Reading Mercury* that 'London and Bristol, as
two places of import could have neither community of trade nor reciprocity of
interest'. The railway proposal would, he claimed, merely fill the pockets of the
solicitors, surveyors and contractors. Another claimed that, while it might benefit
Bristol and London by bringing them closer together, Reading was a different
case: 'Here there is no manufacture, nor is it within the range of probability that

any can flourish here; nor can the trade of the place be improved; it now supplies the country around with everything, and more it cannot do'.(Phillips)

Others went in for more spectacular scaremongering – some claiming that the River Thames would silt up from disuse; others that the railway would fail and that no one would take responsibility for the reinstatement of the landscape, removing all the embankments and cuttings.

Subscribers were initially slow to sign up for the scheme, with the result that the first Parliamentary Bill could only propose the London to Reading and Bath to Bristol parts of the route. This was lost in Parliament in July 1834, but a second application, this time for the entire scheme, gained Royal Assent in August 1835. According to the *Reading Mercury* on 31 August 1835 'the glad tidings was received in this town with much rejoicing, and the bells of the three parishes rang right merrily'. Work on the railway began, and it was opened as far as Maidenhead by 4 June 1838 and to Twyford by July. Again, the *Mercury* reported that the 'immense moving houses', travelling at the then unheard-of speed of 28 miles an hour, attracted lively interest.

The stagecoach interests who had originally opposed the scheme missed no opportunity to cash in on it while they could. As the railway had moved westwards towards Reading, a new stagecoach service – 'The Railway' – opened to carry people from Reading, first to Maidenhead and then to Twyford, to connect with the Great Western. From the start, this stagecoach at least was heavily over-subscribed.

Beyond Twyford, Brunel faced what was to rival the Box Tunnel as his greatest engineering challenge on the entire route. His original idea had been to go the north of Sonning and construct a tunnel five-eighths of a mile long at Holme Park. Instead, he opted for a cutting almost two miles long and anything from 20ft to 60ft deep. At its deepest, the contractor, a man named William Ranger, would have to dig out 7,800 cubic feet of heavy clay, sand and gravel for every foot of track they laid. Moreover, every spadeful was dug by hand and – until Brunel later bought in two small locomotives – moved by men and horses. Much of the material removed from the cutting went to make up the embankment on which the railway runs through the centre of Reading. Work began in the autumn of 1836 and the area soon became a quagmire; landslips were commonplace and fatalities disturbingly frequent. The contractor fell hopelessly behind and was dismissed. Three other contractors were bought in, but a particularly wet autumn led to further delays. One of the new contractors – a Mr Knowles – ran out of money and could not pay his staff, leading to a strike. Eventually, Brunel took over direct control of the construction of the Sonning Cutting and had 1,220 men and 196 horses working on it by 1839.

As if the problems of the terrain and the weather were not enough, the nature of the work was intrinsically dangerous. On one occasion in July 1839, a barrel of gunpowder – being used to shift an obstinate vein of clay – blew up at the wrong moment, hurling five of the navvies, including the truck on which one of them was sitting, across the site. Small wonder that the railway felt obliged to make donations to the newly opened Royal Berkshire Hospital. But this was not the navvies' only contact with the town. Many of the townspeople (particularly those who did not profit from them) lived in fear of the navvies' riotous visits – known as randies – after pay-day. The council petitioned the House of Lords for tighter controls over the town's 194 pubs while the railway was being built:

> Every temptation is held out to the men (working on the railways) to spend their evenings in drinking and tippling, and it has frequently happened that several successive days following that on which the men receive their pay have been spent in a state of most degrading intoxication and it has been found impossible on those occasions with the ordinary police force to maintain peace and good order within the Borough.
>
> (Quoted in Wykes)

Local residents' worst nightmares appeared to have been realised when, after the contractor failed and was unable to pay the men, they took matters into their own hands, doing damage to the works and assaulting one of the contractor's clerks. The navvies then took to hanging around the streets of Reading. This so alarmed the authorities that the mayor called for the army to be sent to rescue them, and a squadron of Horse Guards was despatched to Reading. Eventually, the men were reduced to begging on the streets and the generosity with which the people of Reading responded suggested that the navvies may have enhanced their reputation within the town (either that, or the residents feared the consequences of not contributing). A settlement was finally reached with the railway company, which involved the town clerk, Mr J.J. Blandy, advancing the navvies six days' back pay from his own pocket.

The railway opened as far as Reading in March 1840. On the 14th, a group of directors made an inaugural journey from Reading to London, with Brunel himself on the footplate, in one hour 10 minutes. The official opening of services was scheduled for 30 March but, before that, the railway would claim at least one more life. On 24 March, Henry West, a 24-year-old journeyman carpenter from Wiltshire, was working on the final touches to the station roof, when a freak whirlwind hit the town. It drowned two men fishing in a boat on the river, then lifted Henry and a four-ton glazed section of the roof and carried them 200 feet, until they collided with an office chimney and Henry was hurled to his death in a ditch. Colleagues carried his body to the *Boar's Head* on Friar Street, where the coroner carried out an inquest that same evening. A commemorative board to his memory is still to be found in St Laurence's churchyard.

Thousands flocked to Reading to witness the opening of the railway on 30 March. Many of them gathered on the hill in the Forbury Gardens, from where a good view could be had of the 17 trains running that first day. The lucky ones could even go to the station where, according to the *Reading Mercury*:

> Every accommodation was afforded the spectators that could reasonably be expected or desired by them, the extensive platform immediately adjoining the offices having been thrown open to the public, and seats provided.

Stagecoach services at that time tended to be somewhat vague about timetables. Some stagecoach operators advertised that anyone booking all four seats in their coach could depart at what hour they please. For those planning to travel by rail, the Mercury warned the passengers of the new age of strict timekeeping that the railways would usher in:

> The method, so strictly adhered to at every station on the line is, perhaps, one of the most admirable lineaments of railway travelling; and it is highly important that the public should bear in mind the absolute necessity of passengers procuring their tickets at least five minutes before the departure of each train.
>
> (*Reading Mercury* – 4 April 1840)

The initial fares to London, which some local people regarded as excessive, were 8s. first class (whose carriages had eight passengers to a compartment, not only glass windows but also sun blinds, and were 'so capacious and lofty that the tallest person may stand erect in them'), 5s. 6d. second class (with roofs, but open at the sides) and 3s. for the open third-class carriages (in fact, open wagons with seats, described by the *Illustrated London News* as 'a species of horizontal shower bath'). Some local passengers were beyond consideration of class. The Duke of Wellington, when he wanted to travel from London to Reading, en route to his home at nearby Stratfield Saye, simply had his private road-going carriage driven onto its individual railway wagon, enabling him to travel without any possibility of coming into contact with the hoi polloi. The Duke disapproved of railways, on the grounds that they 'encourage the lower classes to travel about'.

Once the railway reached Reading itself, enterprising landlords and coach proprietors got together to provide transport between the station and the main coaching inns, such as the *Crown* and the *Bear*. But in 1844, the railway company opened its own *Great Western Hotel*, immediately opposite the railway station. The building, on the corner of Station Road, still survives and is thought to be the world's oldest railway hotel.

One unusual feature of Brunel's original station at Reading was that it was one-sided or, as Scott put it: 'at once hideous, inconvenient to the public and awkward (not to say dangerous) to work'. Virtually all of the town of Reading at this time lay to the south of the station, so Brunel arranged it that both the up and the down platforms were also on the south side of the tracks, avoiding the need for passengers to cross the railway to get to or from their trains. There were, in effect, two separate up and down stations. While this was supposed to be convenient for the passengers, and kept express services clear of the station, it was a nightmare for the operation of the railway, since it meant that stopping trains on the up line had to cut across the lines used by down express services, in order to enter or leave the station. There were initially no signal boxes to manage the points centrally – each set of points had its own operator – so it depended upon the operators all remembering which of the approaching trains were expresses and which stopping. On one occasion, a pointsman mistakenly sent

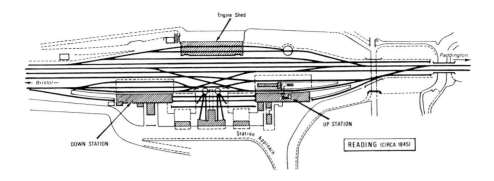

77   A diagram, explaining the working of Reading's one-sided railway station of 1840. (Maggs)

the *Flying Dutchman* express service thundering into the station at 55 miles an hour; it says much for the stability of broad gauge rolling stock that it stayed on the track and the worst that happened was that the luggage on the carriage roofs was flung onto the platforms. As for the pointsman, he was found standing, still clutching his lever, in a dead faint!

The potential shortcomings of this arrangement were apparent to some of the Great Western directors even before the station was built – in March 1839 they asked for plans for a more conventional double-sided station to be drawn up – but Brunel won the day. There were repeated complaints about it once it was in operation, and it was changed to an arrangement of three through platforms and seven bays in 1856. But the station layout was only radically revised to its current 10-platform arrangement in 1897. Even then, this important junction on the network was not given the overall roof its status no doubt deserves – to this day, it has nothing more than the tin umbrellas covering the individual platforms.

Conditions for the earliest third-class passengers on the Great Western were spartan in the extreme. Their open wagons had sides only two feet high, making them extremely dangerous, as well as uncomfortable. Third-class services were only provided in conjunction with goods trains, often travelling at ungodly hours of the day, or at night. Their wagons would also be located immediately behind the locomotive, where they would suffer most from falling hot cinders and smoke. Despite this, Great Western third-class services were the most costly of any of the major railways. This was all part of a company policy to force people to upgrade to the more expensive tickets. On a journey from London to Bristol, a third-class passenger could be exposed to the elements for 10 hours, which in bad weather could be potentially life-threatening. There were recorded cases of second- and third-class passengers on the Great Western being found close to death. On these occasions, railway staff waived the normal company rule, of giving absolutely no assistance to third-class passengers – they would carry the stricken traveller out from the station, leaving them to die in the street, rather than on railway premises.

But the Sonning Cutting was to be the scene of a disaster that changed all this. It was Christmas Eve 1841, and the 4.30a.m. down train from Paddington to Bristol entered the cutting at about 6.40a.m. It was made up of two third-class wagons, followed by 17 goods wagons. The passenger wagons were filled with 38 people (mainly mechanics and labourers – including workers on the new Houses of Parliament – returning home to the west country for Christmas, according to the *Mercury*). There had been recent heavy rain and a landslip had occurred at the cutting's deepest point, covering the track to a depth of about two feet. When the train ran into it, many of the passengers were either thrown out of the wagons, or crushed by the weight of the goods wagons piling in behind them. Eight people were killed and 17 of the injured were taken to the Royal Berkshire Hospital. At the inquest the railway company tried to claim that the landslip had happened while the train was actually in the cutting, and that it could not have been predicted, but witnesses were produced who testified that the bank had been unsafe for several days. The coroners also noted the lack of a nightwatchman in the cutting, and the dangers of putting the passenger wagons between the locomotive and the goods wagons.

The publicity that followed the accident highlighted the appalling conditions in which third-class passengers were expected to travel, and led to William Gladstone's 1844 Railway Regulations Act. This required all railway companies to provide at least one service a day in each direction along their lines, with proper seating and full weather protection, travelling at a minimum of 12 m.p.h. and with fares of no more than 1d. a mile (about half of what the Great Western had been charging). The Great Western's response to the requirement for full weather protection was the equivalent of cattle trucks – windowless wagons with no lighting and precious little ventilation, and with 60 people on plank seats, crammed into a space 20ft 9in x 8ft 6in.

The other unique feature of Brunel's railway through Reading was that it was built to the 7ft broad gauge, while most others used the 4ft 8½in standard gauge introduced by George Stephenson. Reading also got two standard-gauge railways – the South Eastern in 1849 and the London and South Western in 1856. These engaged in a mutually ruinous price war with the Great Western, until the three of them reached an agreement in 1858 for pooling receipts. At about the same time as Gladstone's Railway Regulations Act was going through Parliament, gauge commissioners were meeting, to decide whether the nation's railways should standardise on one or other of these gauges. Despite the technical superiority of Brunel's system, the difficulty of converting the bulk of the network to it proved overwhelming, and its days thereafter were numbered. First, the Great Western started running services on both gauges through Reading, making it necessary to build a further two standard gauge stations and making a complicated layout worse. But it was not until May 1892 that the last broad gauge train passed through Reading.

The railway was an immediate commercial success. As early as 17 April 1840, the 7.40a.m. up train from Reading was so heavily loaded that it required an additional locomotive to haul it. In addition to work-related journeys, it introduced a whole new species of leisure travel:

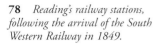

78   *Reading's railway stations, following the arrival of the South Western Railway in 1849.*

79   *The last broad gauge train passes through Reading in 1892.*

> Those who have hitherto been accustomed to spend their holidays in idleness and dissipation, are observed now to crowd the several railways, for the purpose of recreating amidst the woods and fields, far away from their homes, gratifying their tastes with the beauties of nature, and improving their minds by visiting scenes of historic or poetic interest.
>
> (*The Environs of Reading* (1840) quoted in Phillips)

The railways rapidly formed a network that linked Reading with the entire nation. By 1841, the Great Western had reached Bristol. Another branch reached Newbury, en route to the west country, by 1847 and the London and South Western Railway provided a link to Basingstoke and thence to the port of Southampton in 1848. The town became one of the most important railway junctions on the national network, and another chapter in its history as a centre of communications had begun.

Trams and Trolley Buses

As we saw, the coming of the railway in 1840 led some enterprising innkeepers to introduce horse bus services between the station and their establishments. One, the proprietor of the *Peacock Inn* in Broad Street, went further and also established services to Caversham (the *Prince of Wales*), Cemetery Junction and the *Queens Head* in Christchurch Road, Whitley.

But it was the Tramways Act of 1870 that led to the formation of the Reading Tramways Company (a subsidiary of a bigger Imperial Tramways Company).

In 1878 they obtained authority to build a 2¼-mile tramway from Cemetery Junction to the barracks on Oxford Road. These were then about the limits of Reading's built-up area. These horse-drawn trams started operating on 5 April 1879. Their novelty attracted a good deal of early custom, but they soon ran into problems. One of the strangest of these was that the drivers could not at first steer their vehicles through the open points. They ended up going along the wrong track, and coming nose to nose with the tram coming the other way! Nonetheless, demand was soon up to 14,000 passengers a week, and the company had to increase frequencies and introduce double-decker trams to replace the 24-seat single-deckers. These latter were still drawn by a single horse and there were complaints from the outset that it was an excessive load.

The service ran, albeit with many complaints of reckless driving and overloading, until October 1901, when the company was bought out by Reading Corporation for £11,394, as the terms of their licence allowed the council to do. It was immediately apparent that the service was in a ramshackle state. Fifteen of the 85 horses were declared unfit for work immediately, suffering from a 'preponderance of rib', and a total of 50 replacement animals had to be bought during the 18 months the corporation ran the horse-drawn service. During this time, they improved conditions for both the drivers (a pay increase from 3s. 6d. to 4s. a day, for a 70-hour week and one day off in nine) and the horses (an increase in their food allowance from 16 pounds to 20 pounds of corn a day).

At the same time, they set about electrifying the network, and the new service was introduced to a packed town centre on 22 July 1903. The new network

80   *Horse buses preceded the trams and served those parts of the town the trams did not reach. This one, pictured in about 1900, ran between Reading and Tilehurst.*

81   *A horse-drawn tram in Oxford Road c.1890, with one of their horses showing 'a preponderance of rib'.*

retained the original route (slightly extended), with so-called 'side roads' from London Road to Bath Road and a triangular service linking Caversham (in fact, the Reading side of Caversham Bridge) with Whitley and Erleigh Road. Earlier attempts to extend the service into Caversham itself had been thwarted by certain influential residents of Caversham, who objected to paying the cost of the road widening needed to get the trams in. The local press also objected to the cost of the scheme, on top of the 'extravagant expenditure' on the sewerage scheme and the council's other plans for buying the electricity company and incorporating Caversham into the borough.

The new service soon became part of the fabric of the town's life. Workmen's services with cheap fares operated from 5.30a.m. Postmen were carried on them to the start of their rounds and the trams also operated their own parcel delivery service. The libraries used them to move books from one branch to another. Additional services were laid on between London Road and Caversham Bridge on summer Sundays, to carry people to the amenities of the Thameside Promenade. Football crowds would pack onto them on a Saturday – over a hundred crammed into a 48-seater tram, with two conductors trying somehow to gather the fares. Small boys would gather on the upper deck of trams going along Broad Street, for the added pleasure of trying to throw rubbish into the top hat of the statue of George Palmer, which stood in Broad Street until the 1930s.

Unlike other towns, Reading could never enjoy the luxury of closed top trams. This was because the railway bridges on Oxford Road and Caversham Road had very limited clearance and even open-topped vehicles were a tight fit. Signs on the bridges warned passengers to keep your seats (or, presumably, lose your heads). Ironically, the Oxford Road bridge was replaced in 1938, just as the tram network was serving out its final days.

Motor buses began to appear from the 1920s. They were faster and more flexible than the trams that, at their introduction, were capable of no more than 16 miles an hour. These were followed by the phasing in of a network of trolley bus routes from 1936. The first of these ran along Erleigh Road, and served the

82 *An electric tram, parked at its Wokingham Road terminus in about 1930.*

dual purpose of training trolley bus drivers and providing a chance for Reading people to sample (for free) the delights of this new form of transport. The first paid-for trolley bus service opened between Caversham Bridge and Whitley Street in July 1936 and the tramway network was gradually phased out. The Bath Road line had already closed in 1930, with the main line only closing on 20 May 1939, just months before the outbreak of war. Over their 36-year history, the electric trams covered almost 30 million miles and carried an estimated 350 million passengers. The tram cars themselves suffered some ignominious ends, variously becoming a garden shed at a post office near Bucklebury, an office at a gravel pit in Sonning and allotment sheds at School Lane, Caversham (the nearest the trams ever got to going north of the river).

Reading's trolley bus network continued to be expanded right up until 1963, at a time when many other towns were phasing out their services. They even opened a new depot for them in Bennet Road in 1952 (in fact, a second-hand RAF hangar relocated from Cambridgeshire) but it was never fully used and was closed six years later. The debate about scrapping the network in favour of motor buses opened in earnest in 1966 and, despite vocal support for them, their death warrant was signed in July 1966. The last service ran on 3 November 1968; Reading was one of the last six local authorities in the country to scrap its trolley buses.

83 *Reading's No.1 motor bus, in 1926.*

Chapter Fifteen

NINETEENTH-CENTURY IMPROVEMENTS: CIVIC SHAME AND CIVIC PRIDE

The Abbey – Rack, Ruin … and Restoration

The sorry saga of the increasingly ruinous abbey site continued throughout much of the 19th century. A further incursion came with the building of St James's R.C. Church in 1840. It was said that the eminent architect Augustus Welby Pugin built this in the Norman style – his only such work – in order to harmonise with the adjoining abbey ruins. But quite what was left to harmonise with by this stage was debatable, and the fact that the new building destroyed part of the north transept of the abbey church (even using some of the stones of the ruined abbey in its construction) makes his aesthetic sensibilities seem somewhat suspect. St Laurence's Church school followed in 1852.

But public opinion towards the ruins was changing. Public awareness of them was certainly greatly increased in 1828, when a scaffold was built next to the prison for the execution of three poachers who had killed a gamekeeper. This event was said to have attracted between 16 and 20,000 spectators. So, when plans were announced in 1831 to demolish the remaining ruins and use the stone for road-building, the *Berkshire Chronicle* launched a public subscription to buy the ruins and save them for posterity. In the first respect, they were successful but, having bought them, there was no money left to do anything with them. They were simply fenced off.

The council acquired the eastern part of the Forbury for £1,200 in 1854, to provide a pleasure garden. More immediately, it would provide a job creation scheme for distressed workmen at a time of high unemployment. Little expense was evidently incurred in the landscaping, since a public appeal was launched for any surplus plants and shrubs the public could donate. Nonetheless, shortly after its opening in 1856, the pleasure gardens were attracting over 3,600 visitors a day. A new attraction, in the form of a two-ton cannon, captured at Sebastapol in the Crimean War, was installed on top of the Forbury Hill in 1857. The council made the mistake of leaving it in working order, until comedians detonated it during the night on two separate occasions, breaking the windows of nearby houses. By 1859, the pleasure gardens were linked to the abbey ruins, which the council had by then also bought.

84 *While the Corporation debated spending money to restore the abbey Gateway, gravity and old age intervened in 1861.*

Nearby, the abbey gateway's condition was becoming more and more ruinous. After much prevarication, the council brought in the country's leading restorer of historic buildings, George Gilbert Scott. He estimated the cost of restoration at £1,000, which the council scraped together but, when the tender came in at £1,800, there were calls for it to be demolished. Instead, a painfully slow fund-raising effort was launched for the balance. It was punctuated in February 1861 by the collapse of the gateway during a storm. This seems to have galvanised the restoration programme (which had now become a rebuilding programme), and which was completed in 1862. Even then, cost-cutting meant that much of the ornamental stonework on it had to be left uncarved until many years later.

However, the west end of the Forbury continued to be used by travelling fairs and remained in an unkempt state. The council finally bought it in 1860, but there was still some doubt about its final use, which was only resolved in 1869, when the council also purchased 12 acres of Kings Meadows from the Knollys family, for use as recreation grounds. This freed up the west end of the Forbury for use as an extension to the pleasure gardens, and the Forbury Gardens as we know them were opened in 1873.

The Gardens' main feature, the Forbury Lion, came a few years later. It commemorates a desperate rearguard action fought by 300 officers and men of the 66th (Berkshire) Regiment at the Battle of Maiwand, in the Afghan campaign of 1879–80, and was erected six years later. Their sacrifice prevented the army of General Burrow being wiped out by the Afghans. It was paid for by public subscription and designed by George Blackall Simonds, the artistic member of the local brewing family. It is said to be the largest sculpture of an erect lion in the world, and measures 31ft long by 13ft 11ins high. The whole thing weighs some 16 tons and had to be transported from the foundry to the gardens in nine separate pieces, lest it put undue strain on some of the town's rickety bridges. Rumours also abound that the way the lion is standing is in some way anatomically impossible. I can only record that Simonds carried out extensive live drawings of lions on which to base his sculpture. The public were rather more generous to the memory of their dead heroes than they were to their live ones. One of just 13 survivors of Maiwand, a man named Thomas Weston, was expected to live on a pension of 9½ pence a day, until a public subscription was raised to set him up in business as a chimney sweep.

The former dormitory of the old hospitium was occupied until 1871 by Reading School. By then, it was very derelict. It had been used as tenements at one stage and later had its west end sliced off to accommodate the last phase of the town hall. Moves were made in 1878 to demolish it, but it was saved and in 1892 became the home for the forerunner to Reading University. The abbey ruins themselves finally – and belatedly – got some statutory protection in 1914, when the site was designated a scheduled ancient monument. Even so, they still had to fight off a proposal in 1935–7 that part of the Forbury Gardens should be taken as an extension to the town hall and, in 1939, that a network of air raid shelters for nearby school children should be dug in among the archaeology of the abbey ruins. Better late than never (by some people's reckoning, about four and a half centuries late) an appeal fund was launched by the Mayor of Reading in 1985 to stabilise what remained of the ruins.

Burying the Dead

By the early 19th century, the state of the town's burial grounds posed a major threat to the health of the living. Up to 1843, the only places for interring bodies in Reading were the town's three churchyards and a couple of burial grounds attached to non-conformist places of worship. By 1815, St Giles's churchyard was so full that they were having to bury people in the pathways, and it was barely possible to place a spade in the ground in St Mary's and St Laurence's churchyards without disturbing a previous inmate. Horrified early 19th century eyewitnesses reported seeing gravediggers in St Mary's hacking apart the decomposing bodies to make space for new ones. The authorities were left with an average of 600 deaths a year, and nowhere to bury them. One option was for each of the parishes to buy more cemetery land for its own use. But the town's dissenters objected to this, on the grounds that it would increase the church rates they were forced to pay, despite them making no use of the facilities including the graveyard.

The solution was found in the form of a private company, the Reading Cemetery Company, which in 1843 opened a new 10-acre cemetery to the west of the town, just outside the then borough boundary. Strict religious segregation was observed in the cemetery, with church being allocated six of the 10 acres and 'chapel' the rest. They also provided separate places of worship for them, and the dissenters' plots were located nearest the main entrance, so that they did not have to pass over consecrated ground to reach them. The new cemetery remained in private hands until the council took it over in 1887. Despite this new facility, sentiment and tradition meant that many people continued to demand (and get) burials in the old churchyards, until this unhealthy practice was outlawed by the Burial Act of 1852.

Seat of Government

The seat of the government of Reading has travelled around the town over the centuries, but the start of what we now refer to as the old town hall dates back to 1786. It is in fact, four separate buildings, each by a different architect and separated overall by over a hundred years. The first phase, now known as the Victoria Hall, was completed in 1786 at a cost of £1,800. It was designed by a member of the council, Alderman Charles Poulton, who was a cabinet maker rather than an architect. The second phase, including the clock tower, was completed in 1875. Its architect was a local man, in that from 1870 he lived in Foxhill on the Whiteknights estate. But Alfred Waterhouse was an architect with a national reputation. Among his other commissions were London's Natural History Museum and Manchester Town Hall (the latter, in its day, the world's most expensive building). When Waterhouse's designs for the third phase proved to be too costly, an architectural competition was held under the chairmanship of an architect called Thomas Lainson. Lainson somehow managed to award himself the contract, which was completed in 1882. The final phase at the Valpy Street end, housing a library extension and art gallery, was designed by W.R. Howell and opened in 1897. Like so many civic improvements of the day, the last two phases were paid for by public subscription, with the Palmer family prominent among the contributors to the fund. The whole complex was threatened with demolition in the 1970s, but the resultant public outcry saw it restored as an arts and conference centre, the great concert hall opening in the first few weeks of the new millennium.

Let there be Gaslight

As we have seen, early 19th-century Reading was a very dark and dangerous place at night, despite the (rather modest) best efforts of the paving commissioners. But a solution had already been invented, in distant Cornwall. In 1792, William

85   *The town hall, as seen from Friar Street shortly before the outbreak of the First World War.*

Murdoch of Redruth became the first person to light his home and office by gas. The commercial potential of the invention gradually spread across the country. Manchester had its first gas-lit cotton mill by 1805 and five years later a company was set up to illuminate some of the main streets of London. Reading was not far behind, and the *Reading Mercury* reported in November 1817 that the town's subscription billiard room, news room and library were to be lit by gas for the first time. The establishment also provided a lamp outside, 'which throws a brilliant light on the *Bear Inn* and part of the *Seven Bridges*'. This new amenity was welcomed by local people and led to calls for its wider use.

Two years later, the commissioners decided to adopt gas lighting for the town's principal streets, but the budget available to them was only enough to pay for lighting during eight months of the year. In 1821, a public subscription had to be organised to raise the £50 to £60 needed to illuminate the remaining four months of the year.

By 1835, both the cost and the quality of the gas being supplied by the Reading Gas Light Company came under criticism. Local people were outraged when it emerged that the gas that was being sold to the town for 15s. per 1,000 cubic feet actually cost just 3s. to produce, and public opinion forced them to reduce the price to 12s. 6d. But even this was not enough, and calls for more competition led in 1836 to the formation of the Reading Union Gas Company. The upshot was a long-running price war that nearly bankrupted both companies, until they merged in 1862.

Although the gas lights reached as far as Caversham Bridge by 1843, the local authority to the north of the river was as ever economical with its spending, and did not install gas lighting until 1891. When they were incorporated into Reading in 1911, private gas consumers in Caversham had their bills reduced to the same tariff as Reading customers, saving them a total of over £1,000. Gas lighting remained a feature of many Reading streets until well after the Second World War and, when peace was declared in 1945, families brought small children out to see for the first time the magic of gas-lit streets after the years of blackout.

The Royals – the Birth of Reading F.C.

It is appropriate that we include an account of the town's football team in a chapter with 'civic pride' in the title. At the time of writing this, the team is riding high in the Premiership – the first time in its long history that it has reached the top flight of British football. But its beginnings were much less exalted, and there have been occasions when they qualified more for the 'civic shame' part of the chapter title.

The first national rules for football were drawn up and the Football Association was formed as its governing body in 1863. Various clubs were formed in the North of England in the next few years and, in 1871, a group of men met in Reading and decided the town should have its own team. James Simonds,

86   *Reading Football Club in 1906–07 – pictured around the time of their ill-fated fund-raising campaign.*

of the brewing family, was elected as president (and one wonders whether his keen business eye anticipated what a thirsty business playing – or indeed just watching – football would be). The blue and white colours that they play in today were chosen from the outset, but they wore long knickerbockers instead of shorts and a curious variation of the nightcap on their heads.

The game then was very different to the one we know today. If the ball bounced too high, players could pat it down with their hands (this rule got them into trouble in a game with the Old Etonians in 1879, since they – and the officials – played to a rather different code). There was virtually no passing, just solo dribbling, with a team mate running along with the dribbler, shoulder charging anyone who attempted to stop him. Passing only caught on in the 1880s, as did heading the ball, which was introduced to the club by a player from the Royal Engineers. Many of the rules and practices also differed; the referee controlled the game by waving a handkerchief, rather than blowing a whistle; there was a tape for the top of the goal, rather than a crossbar; the teams changed ends after each goal and took single-handed throw-ins, and so on.

The Reading club started out playing at the Recreation Ground at Kings Meadow, but led a very nomadic existence in their early years, moving in turn to Reading Cricket Ground (1879), Coley Park (1882) and Caversham Cricket Ground (in around 1889, where access to the ground was by boat). By 1895 the club was looking for somewhere better to play. They considered Palmer Park, some land behind the *Moderation* public house on Caversham Road and land off the Oxford Road. Then local property developer and councillor Edwin Jesse offered them four acres his company had been using as a gravel pit in west

87 *A match played at the old Elm Park ground during the Second World War.*

Reading for the knockdown price of £100 per annum. This would become Elm Park, the club's home until 1998 (though they did at one stage contemplate moving to a site right in the town centre, opposite the railway station, until opposition from local residents put them off). Jesse attached conditions to the lease, that no alcohol sales or betting should be allowed on the ground.

The club spent £800 draining, levelling and fencing the ground, another £500 on a grandstand, seats, dressing rooms, baths and offices, and the first match was played there on 5 September 1896. The opponents were a scratch team, a 'Mr A. Royston Bourke's XI', and the spectators who had paid their 6d. (for gentlemen – 3d. for ladies and boys) also had the benefit of the Reading Temperance Band for the occasion. It was not an unqualified success; there was a thunderstorm before the match, which had to be abandoned due to the pitch flooding (a foretaste of flooding problems that would affect the ground for the next 30 years). The F.A. then fined Reading for playing against an unregistered team.

Professionalism was legalised by the Football Association in 1885, but Reading was to remain an amateur club until 1895. The first professional club to play them was Burslem Port Vale, who came to Elm Park in 1892. Reading beat them 2-1, but they were less fortunate when they drew the Football League champions, Preston North End, away, in the 1894 F.A. Cup. Ominously, that Preston team were known as 'The Invincibles', and so they proved to be. The match was played in a January gale, on a pitch that anticipated conditions on a First World War battlefield. The Reading team, in smooth-soled footwear, could barely stay on their feet. The cunning men of Preston had studs on the soles of their boots, and had black-leaded them to stop the mud sticking to them. Reading were hammered 18-0, the club's worst ever defeat and believed to be the biggest margin of defeat of any club still in the Football League.

From 1894, the club played in the newly formed Southern League, one of a minority of amateur clubs in the league, but they only waited a season before

88 *One of the team's glory days. Reading played Manchester United in the F.A. Cup in 1955 and came within seven minutes of a famous victory.*

going professional. They remained there until a Third Division of the Football League was formed in 1920. During that period, the club had its ups and downs; in around 1910 an appeal was launched to avert a looming financial crisis – it raised the grand total of 12s. 6d., and the club nearly went under. But soon after, they had a run in the 1911–12 F.A. Cup in which they beat Aston Villa (then the leading team in the First Division) and took Manchester United to a replay. The First World War cost four of the team their lives and saw one, of German origin, briefly interned. For part of the war, another RFC – the Royal Flying Corps – took over Elm Park as a physical fitness training centre.

The club enjoyed four seasons from 1926 in the old Second Division – until their success of recent years, their highest league placing. During the inter-war period, they set the record for the largest crowd at Elm Park (33,042 for a cup tie against Brentford in February 1927) and the lowest for a league game (just 1,785 people saw their 1-0 home win against Bournemouth in April 1939, which coincided with a live radio broadcast of the F.A. Cup final).

The Second World War again brought an end to the normal activities of the club. The war years passed with a variety of ad-hoc competitions and ad-hoc teams, made up of whichever footballing members of the armed forces happened to be stationed nearby. One notable guest was Matt Busby, who would go on to do great things as the manager of Manchester United.

The post-war years continued their record of ups and downs. The club had its record win – 10-2 – against Crystal Palace, in 1946 and came within six minutes of knocking Manchester United's Busby Babes out of the F.A. Cup in 1955. They managed to combine triumph and disaster in a single season in 1988, winning the Simod Cup at Wembley by beating First Division Luton 4-1, at the same time as getting relegated from the old Second Division.

The club completed its move from Elm Park (original construction costs £1,300) to the £37 million 25,000 seat Madejski Stadium in August 1998. This became the scene of the club's greatest triumph in 2006, when they won promotion to the Premiership.

Chapter Sixteen

UNIVERSITY – AND SHOPPING – TOWN: TWENTIETH-CENTURY READING

Shoppers ... can hardly fail to be startled by McIlroy's fantastic building designed at the beginning of this century by Mr Frank Morris, an affair of stepped gables and corbelled balconies in red and yellow glazed bricks and granite all resting, apparently, on two tall storeys of plate glass.

John Betjeman and John Piper (1949)

A new century, and once again the nation was at war. This time it was with the Boers in South Africa and, during the first weeks of 1900, reports came in of four Berkshire men killed and 17 wounded in fighting at Colesburg. Patriotic feeling was running high in the town. The bells of St Laurence's were rung and flags were flown from public and private buildings to mark the relief of Ladysmith. On the darker side, a mob, estimated at up to a thousand people, went on the rampage looking for a meeting of the South African Reconciliation Committee. This body, which existed purely to promote a peaceful ending to the war and accurate reporting of it, was characterised by the mob as a traitorous organisation. Only their failure to find the meeting (they mistakenly interrupted and terrorised a gathering discussing superannuation) prevented something very unpleasant happening.

The next revolution in transport that was to affect Reading revealed itself to the town in 1900, when the Automobile Club of Great Britain undertook a 1,000-mile trial of motor cars around the United Kingdom. Their route took them through the centre of Reading, from Cemetery Junction to Calcot Park, where they were entertained by the newspaper proprietor Alfred Harmsworth. Crowds turned out to watch this unprecedented parade of 84 motor cars, whose drivers 'were all covered in dust and were for the most part clad in thick coats, with peaked caps and a pair of uncoloured glass goggles with leather dustproof flaps, which gave them the appearance of an uncouth-looking highwayman of the olden days'. The motor car would come to dominate the life of the 20th-century town.

By 1903, the novelty of motoring had worn off, at least as far as the police were concerned, for they were out to trap speeding motorists on the Bath Road. In these pre-radar days, their method involved a measured half-mile and a

89   *Balloons from the Royal Balloon Aero Club filling up with a highly inflammable cargo of gas at
Reading gasworks in June 1906.*

concealed police constable with binoculars and a stopwatch. Among their catch
were the chauffeur of the Hon. C.S. Rolls (yet to join Royce and start making
his own cars), a man doing 50 m.p.h. in a racing car, capable – even in 1903 – of
90 m.p.h., and a motorcyclist doing an illegal eight m.p.h. on his motor-cycle
combination. The Hon. C.S. Rolls was to add to the dangers of Reading's traffic
again in 1911, when he piloted a balloon which acted as a 'hare' to a pack of
motorist 'hounds'. Rolls took off from Reading gasworks, pursued by the pack,
and landed some time later near Oxford, where he handed out prizes to the first
three motorists who managed to catch up with him.

The new century saw a new Member of Parliament for Reading elected. He
would turn out to be one of the town's most famous and distinguished citizens.
Rufus Isaacs was born in 1860, the son of a London fruit merchant. He left
school at 14, becoming first a ship's boy and then a stock market jobber. After
being hammered in the stock market slump of 1884, he studied law, was called
to the Bar in 1887 and became a Queen's Council within 11 years. He stood
as a Liberal candidate for Parliament in Reading in 1904 and represented the
town until 1913, when he was appointed Lord Chief Justice. He was sent as an
Ambassador to the United States during the First World War to help promote
the joint war effort, was Viceroy of India from 1921 to 1926 and was made the
first Marquis of Reading. His political career ended as Foreign Secretary to the
National Government in 1931. He lived for many years in Alfred Waterhouse's
old house, Foxhill, on the Whiteknights estate, which he in turn sold to Lord
Hirst, the founder of the General Electric Company. Rufus Isaacs died in 1935.

His statue was repatriated from New Delhi after Indian independence, and since 1971 has stood in the George V Memorial Gardens, just off London Road.

A lecturer from the University College, Arthur Bowley, carried out a survey of poverty in the town in 1912. He found that while there were not huge problems with overcrowding – less than one in seven households were living even at the relatively modest level of more than one person to a room – rents in the town were high, swallowing nearly 25 per cent of the incomes of those living on between £1 and £1 10s. a week. Average wages were correspondingly low, and this he attributed to Huntley and Palmer, who then employed between a fifth and a quarter of the town's manual labour, and therefore dictated local wage rates. An average Huntley and Palmer employee of the day would have been earning £1 4s. 2d. a week. As a result, Bowley estimated that over a quarter of Reading's working class, and a fifth of all Reading households overall, were living in primary poverty – below the level judged necessary just to maintain good health. The poor included nearly half the children of school age and 45 per cent of those below it. Bowley criticised employers like Huntley and Palmer and concluded that 'to raise the wages of the worst-paid workers is the most pressing social task with which the country is confronted today'. Huntley and Palmer were one of the companies at which the Liberal government's threat to introduce a national minimum wage was directed around this time. In this context, news that the Palmer family had donated £150,000 to Reading University College (discussed later in this chapter) was very poorly received indeed by their workforce.

But the workforce at Huntley and Palmer was not going to wait for the government to do something about their wage levels. Agitation over wages and

90 *The Minster Street frontage of Heelas, seen c.1930.*

91 *McIlroy's crystal palace of a department store in 1903, shortly after its opening.*

conditions in the factory had been growing for some time, and a heavy-handed response from the company had resulted in unionisation and public demonstrations. In 1912, the company was forced to grant the first pay rise since 1900 to its workforce.

Bowley's research was borne out by surveys of the early 20th century school population of Reading. These revealed some disturbing statistics about the pupils. Forty per cent of them were found to have defective eyesight, and a high proportion (20 per cent at Central Boys' School and 12 per cent at Newtown, for example) were putting in a substantial working week, over and above attending school. Some were working for 30 or 40 hours a week for as little as one shilling, and were arriving at school having already done three or four hours' work.

But the overall wealth of the area was growing, and with it the importance of Reading as a shopping centre. It was not yet the era when the multiple store made every town centre look identical. Most of the retailers were independent local businesses; Jacksons on the corner of Kings Road is one that survives from that era. But a new type of shopping experience was making its very considerable presence felt – the department store. Heelas was the first. John Heelas opened a small drapers shop on Minster Street in 1854, and his sons John and Daniel joined the business as it diversified into everything from furniture to funerals. They took over the neighbouring Methodist chapel and school in 1866 and, by 1870, they had purchased the *Black Boy Inn*, enabling them to extend into the prime frontage of Broad Street. The shop had a wide client base; Queen Mary shopped there

92 *The Palace Theatre on Cheapside was one of the town's leading entertainment venues, from 1907 until its demolition in 1961.*

93 *The Vaudeville in Broad Street was one of three cinemas to open in Reading in 1909.*

and Reading Prison ordered their inmates' uniforms from them. It remained a family business until 1947, when the millionaire Charles Clore bought them out. From him it passed to the United Drapery Stores Group in 1950 and thence to the John Lewis Partnership in 1953. But only in recent years has the family name of the business been abandoned, in favour of it becoming just another branch of John Lewis.

Other department stores followed. Bulls occupied a prominent position on the north side of Broad Street for over 50 years and William McIlroy opened his store at the junction of Oxford Street and Cheapside in 1903. It was variously known as 'Mac's' and the Crystal Palace, the latter on account of its large expanse of brightly lit shop windows. The building itself was one of the architectural wonders of the town at the time, fantastically decorated beyond the specifications of Walt Disney. It survives to this day, somewhat stripped of its elaborate ornament but still providing a dramatic contrast with its neighbour across the road – that miracle of 1960s brutalism, the Broad Street Mall. Marks and Spencer also opened their first lock-up shop in West Street in 1904. The sign above the door read 'Marks and Spencer. Originators of Penny Bazaars. Admission free'. They opened a further store on Broad Street in 1912, where they chose to concentrate their business, closing the West Street branch in 1936.

Heelas owes its highly visible position in the centre of Reading to the far-sightedness of Councillor J.C. Fidler. He made a fortune building up his father's fruit and vegetable business and diversifying into a range of activities in the City. He was responsible for the rebuilding of the east side of West Street, the Market Arcade, linking Broad Street and Friar Street, the purchase of Prospect Park for the town in 1901 and the building of Queen Victoria Street, the end of which is dominated by the Heelas frontage. Queen Victoria Street was just nearing completion when he died in December 1903. Prior to its completion, the approach to Broad Street for many visitors arriving at the railway station was via the chaos of Smelly Alley (Union Street) or what was then the decidedly seedy Cross Street.

The New Royal County Theatre had opened in Friar Street in 1895, on the site of an older theatre. It was designed by Frank Matcham, a leading theatre architect of the day. From 1907 it had competition in the form of the Palace on Cheapside. They were not direct rivals, in that the Royal County specialised in musicals and dramas, whereas the Palace was known more as a variety theatre, attracting most of the top music hall acts of the day. Any rivalry that did exist between them ceased in 1937, when the Royal County burned down. New-fangled competition was to emerge in 1909, in which year Reading acquired no fewer than three cinemas – Bio-Picture Land in King's Road, the Vaudeville Electric in Broad Street and West's Picture Palace in West Street. West's and Bio-Picture Land lasted only until the First World War, but the Vaudeville survived and flourished, being rebuilt in 1921 as Reading's Temple of Colour and Harmony.

Reading University

> The object of the College is to bring education of a university type within the reach of those who cannot go to the university. Its function is to stimulate the desire for intellectual life, to diffuse both 'liberal' and technical education, to train good citizens, and to erect a ladder by which the chosen intellects of all classes may climb to the universities themselves.
>
> (Preface to the first Reading University Extension College calendar)
> (1892–3)

The origins of the town's modern university lie in art classes, started in 1860 under the auspices of the Department of Science and Art at the museums in South Kensington. The classes were held in whatever spare accommodation could be found in the town, but their popularity grew rapidly. They became involved in the University Extension Colleges movement, which grew up in Oxford, and in particular, Christ Church College, in the 1880s. The general idea was that the established universities like Oxford would send out lecturers, much in the manner of missionaries, to towns without the blessings of such an institution. They would establish a bridgehead, from which it was hoped permanent lecturers, buildings and the basis for establishing a college (and, in the long term, 'a cultivated nation') would spring.

Reading, being close and on the railway line to Oxford, was an ideal target for civilisation in this way. In 1892, Christ Church offered the Reading University Extension College Association the services of one of its alumni, H.J. Mackinder, to help promote the cause. Public subscriptions raised the funds to start it up but, on its launching, the college had no founder, no clear function, no endowment, no capital, no purpose-built buildings and no guarantee of municipal support. But two things worked in its favour. One of Mackinder's first appointments was a young lecturer in history, only two years out of Oxford. Although not a conspicuous success in his first year, William Childs was to stay on at the

94   *Celebrations at the opening of the new University College building by the Prince of Wales in 1898.*

college for 36 years, to become the driving force behind its incorporation as a fully-fledged university and its first vice chancellor (he was also an important local historian). Perhaps even more importantly, the idea won the support of the town's powerful business and propertied interests. Herbert Sutton of the seeds family had bought the hospitium next to St Laurence's Church and in 1893 let it to the college at a nominal rent, to give them a home. Lord Wantage (a former military man, turned Lord Lieutenant of Berkshire) became the president of the college in 1896 and Alfred Palmer (of Huntley and Palmer) became a member of the college council.

The early students were a mixed bag; quite a number were middle-class and middle-aged, more concerned with culture than with qualifications. A larger number were young wage earners, seeking what was often a rudimentary education in science or the arts, with a view to their career advancement. None of the 658 students in the college's first year was full-time, nor were any of the 20 teaching staff. A decision was made early on to specialise in agriculture, based on the town's industrial strengths in biscuits and bulbs. By the turn of the century, the college had just over a thousand pupils and in 1902 was designated as a university college.

The lack of a sound financial basis dogged the college in its early years. They made increasing losses each year and had to be bailed out by benefactors, until

95 *The Committee of the
Women's Students Union
at the University College,
pictured with the Principal
of the College (later its first
Vice-Chancellor) Dr W.M.
Childs in 1908.*

George William Palmer set up a £50,000 trust fund to secure the college's immediate future. They had already outgrown the hospitium site by 1904, and had become bogged down in negotiations with the local authority about an alternative site when another member of the Palmer family, Alfred, agreed to endow it with a further £50,000 building fund and six acres of land at London Road. This included the former Palmer family home. The Sutton family also met part of the cost of the relocation. The new campus was opened by the future Secretary of State for War, Richard Haldane, in 1906, and the Palmer family and the widow of Lord Wantage (after whom Wantage Hall is named) between them endowed the college with another £200,000 for its further development. It was also in this year that the authorities set themselves the target of becoming a fully-fledged university, as a number of university colleges before them had done.

The college included an officer training corps and, with the outbreak of war in 1914, some 80 of them were quickly called up. Many more were to follow, but the loss of male students was offset by a substantial increase in female enrolment, which helped to maintain the college's financial viability. During the war they shared the campus with the Royal Flying Corps and trainee munitions workers. Over 500 of its alumni served in the war and 144 of them lost their lives. Perhaps the best-known of these was the war poet Wilfred Owen, who enrolled with the college in 1912 to study Biology and Latin, but who also went to many of Professor Edith Morley's English lectures. He was killed in action just a week before the armistice was signed. The following year, the composer Gustav Holst joined the teaching staff of the music department.

Several attempts were made from 1911 onwards to win university status. By 1921, the Privy Council had conceded the principle, but withheld the actual award until the college had a slightly larger number of students and an annual income of around £80,000. Their income was then only about £8,000 short of

96   *The White Knights estate, now home to Reading University, as it was in 1791, shortly before passing into the ownership of the Marquess of Blandford.*

that target and their student numbers were up to 1,600 – though only about 700 of these were full-time and just 320 were studying for a degree). The college was finally made a university in its own right in 1926. The final major landmark in its development was its move to the 300-acre Whiteknights campus. This was acquired in 1947, but building did not start until 1954 and the transfer took over 40 years to complete.

If the university itself is a relatively new institution, the Whiteknights estate where it is now based is of great antiquity. The white knight of its name is said to be one Gilbert de Montalieu, the son of a close friend of William the Conqueror. The story goes that he was made Governor of Reading and fell in love with Editha, the daughter of a Saxon King. When Gilbert found her kissing another Saxon, he flew into a rage and killed the man. He later found out that the man was Editha's brother. Editha entered a convent and Gilbert disappeared abroad, sent on a penance to Jerusalem. Many years later, the body of an elderly white knight was found, lying on the grave of Editha's brother. Legend had it that Gilbert had returned, having spent his life atoning for his sin. The site of the grave is said to be somewhere near the Wokingham Road approach to the estate.

The estate subsequently had something of a chequered history. In the 16th century it belonged to the Catholic Englefield family. Sir Francis Englefield's changing fortunes reflect the turbulent nature of the times. He was High Sheriff of Berkshire and Oxfordshire under Henry VIII, imprisoned for his faith in 1551 under the reign of Edward VI, released and made Master of the Court of Wards and Liveries under the Catholic Queen Mary, then forced to flee the country in 1558 when Queen Elizabeth I succeeded her. He eventually died in exile and by 1585 his lands were forfeit to the Crown. But they were bought back by the family in 1606 and remained with them until 1783. Shortly after this, in 1798, the estate passed to George Spencer Churchill, an ancestor of Winston Churchill and Marquess of Blandford. He spent a small fortune, landscaping the grounds and collecting old masters and rare books, among other activities. He succeeded to the title of Duke of Marlborough in 1817, but this did not save him from being bankrupted by his own extravagance two years later. The estate stood unoccupied for a number of years after this, and his house was demolished.

By 1849, the estate was owned by a wealthy bullion broker, Sir Isaac Goldsmid, whose son Francis would later become Member of Parliament for Reading from 1860 until his death in a train accident in 1878. The estate was later broken up into six plots, on one of which the architect Alfred Waterhouse built his home. The Goldsmid family retained overall control of the estate until it was bought by the university.

The Incorporation of Tilehurst and Caversham

One unexpected consequence of Reading acquiring a sewerage network was that, in 1887, the town doubled in size overnight. The administrative area of Reading in the 1880s covered only about a fifth of its present area. The town was expanding rapidly, especially towards the east, where the suburb of New Town had been growing since the 1850s to house Huntley and Palmer's ever-larger workforce. But, being outside the borough, the area could not be linked into its sewerage system. Their sewage was discharged directly into the Kennet, much to the concern of the local health authorities. In 1876, the health authorities renewed the call for this area to be connected to the network but Reading, which had still not yet provided sufficient capacity at Manor Farm to serve even its own population, declined to do so unless Earley, Whitley and Southcote became part of the borough.

By 1884 a case for their incorporation was in preparation. One of the major unanswered questions was whether any expansion should be limited to existing built-up areas, or whether it should seek to anticipate where future expansion would take place. The *Berkshire Chronicle* wrote in 1886 of the council having an 'earth hunger', likening Reading's ambitions for Earley to those of Russia for Bulgaria. In November 1886, a crowded public meeting to present the expansion plans met with a frosty response from most of those present. But energetic lobbying from the borough council meant that a small majority in favour of the extension was obtained from a local ballot in December 1886. The approval of Parliament was obtained in the following year.

The year 1911 saw the borough expand to roughly its present boundaries by the incorporation of 1,800 acres of Tilehurst and 2,504 acres across the river in Caversham. Tilehurst, like Caversham, has a considerable history of its own. The name derives from the Old English 'tigelhurst', a wood where tiles are made, reflecting an industry that continued in the area until recent times. There has been a church on the site of St Michael's since at least 1189. It was an early gift to Reading Abbey and was administered by them right up to the dissolution. The south aisle of the present church dates from the late 13th or early 14th century and the tower from 1737. But most of it was built in 1854–6, and is the work of G.E. Street, a leading church architect of the day.

Many of the place names in modern Tilehurst also have ancient roots. Beansheaf Farm reminds us of the family of John Beansheaf, who held the land from the 13th century. Pincents Farm is an echo of Edmund Pincent, who swapped some land in this area with the Abbot of Reading in 1316. Kentwood was known as Kenetwode (the wood by the Kennet) in the 12th century, but two centuries later it was actually occupied by a family with the name of Kentwood. Many of Reading's leading landowning families, including the Vachells and the Blagraves, later had extensive land-holdings in the area. The Lord of the Manor around the time of the dissolution was Sir Francis Englefield, whose fluctuating fortunes were documented earlier.

As with the 1887 boundary extension, the case for the incorporation of Tilehurst was again built on sewerage. By 1908, the borough had the capacity at Manor Farm to take all the area's sewage, and they were also opposing a proposal by Bradfield Rural District Council to build a sewage works at Scours Lane, just upwind from the newly laid-out riverside recreation area at Thameside Promenade. The council had also carried out some major capital investment in this area. They had bought Prospect Park for public use, built the Park Fever Hospital and expanded the waterworks. For once, the borough's expansion proposals were supported by the neighbouring populations and their local authorities. The same could not be said for Caversham.

The River Thames made a natural division between Reading, a manufacturing town in Berkshire, and Caversham, an attractive residential district in Oxfordshire.
(Part of Caversham's case against incorporation, reported in the *Times*, 16 March 1911)

For centuries, Caversham had existed as a close neighbour of Reading, albeit one separated by a river. Gradually, Reading spread northwards towards Caversham Bridge, bringing the trams with it and integrating the two towns ever more closely. Caversham had grown into a popular residential suburb of its larger neighbour and by 1911 had a population of 9,800. The dependency of Caversham on Reading was obvious. Almost half of its working population had jobs in Reading and many residents enjoyed the use of Reading's amenities, such as libraries, the art gallery and museum, public transport, parks and water supply. Many Caversham children were educated in Reading, at the Swansea Road School and elsewhere. Incorporation into Reading would also give them access to new facilities, like the Park Fever Hospital (particularly relevant, since Lower Caversham suffered an epidemic of scarlet fever in 1908).

Since 1891, Caversham had had its own urban district council. But there had been lobbying from interests in Reading for it to become part of the borough since the 1880s, when Caversham's only democratically elected local government had been the Poor Law Guardians. From about 1908, Reading Borough began to pursue its case in earnest. They were supported by those in Caversham who wanted to see the replacement of the wholly inadequate iron Caversham Bridge that had spanned the Thames since 1869. Many of these realised that the chances of it happening would be greatly increased, if both banks were under the same administrative control.

But they were by no means a majority. There was widespread opposition to the incorporation of Caversham from among the great and the good of the parish. Pro-incorporation members of Oxfordshire County Council were voted off the council and replaced by antis, and a petition was submitted to Parliament from 542 'owners, lessees and occupiers of property in the Parish of Caversham', representing, as they were at pains to point out, over half the rateable value of the district. They argued that they would be 'injuriously affected' by the proposal, which would 'have the effect of depreciating the value of their property and be otherwise injurious to their rights and interests'. Among the arguments they put forward were:

- that they were separated by a river and in a different county;
- that half of the district was rural and that a change of administration made no difference to that part;
- that it would increase local government costs;
- that there was already enough housing land within Reading without it encroaching on Caversham;
- that Caversham would inherit a share of the debts of Reading. They cited as an example the £305,000 cost incurred for Reading's sewerage system. Caversham had its own, independent arrangements, which, they said, served its needs perfectly well. Overall, they claimed, the per-capita debts of Reading Council were three to four times those of Caversham; and perhaps most outrageously they claimed;
- that this was a plot to prevent Caversham becoming a rival to its larger neighbour.

Much of the case against incorporation appears today to be internally inconsistent. On the one hand, they made much of the lower rates paid by the residents of Caversham. At the same time, in an attempt to counter the improved services Reading could offer, they promised all sorts of improvements (to the water supply, the roads, the fire brigade, a new hospital for infectious diseases and a boundary extension into Mapledurham) that would have probably more than wiped out any tax advantage. Other claims included the fact that Reading had not consulted its own residents about the incorporation (this was correct, and a number of those residents apparently thought that Reading would be better off not burdening itself with Caversham).

In the event, Reading was able to demonstrate that Caversham's public services, many of which were administered from Oxford, 28 miles away, were operated inefficiently and to a lower standard than those Reading would provide. Their sewage works were struggling to cope with the growing population, they relied upon the workhouse in Henley, some seven miles away, and paid a disproportionate share of its costs, and its schools performed badly – Caversham even had a lower school leaving age than Reading – 13, as against 14. The case for incorporation was so strong that the *Chronicle* concluded in 1911: 'Incorporation is going inexorably forward and it is time that those ardent but mistaken opponents of the scheme on the Caversham side of the water bow to the inevitable and save the trouble and expense of a prolonged fight in the Houses of Parliament'.

Caversham was incorporated into Reading in that same year. They were promised rates 7d. lower than those payable in Reading for the first 15 years after incorporation. Caversham Urban District Council met for the last time in November 1911 and one of their final acts was to approve all the abortive expenditure incurred on opposing incorporation. The Mayor of Reading told Parliament in March 1911 that this extension would be sufficient for the borough for the next 100 years. This was true to the extent that, from that day to this, the boundaries of Reading have remained virtually unchanged (the one exception being the incorporation of the Caversham Park estate – the estate, which in 1911 was still in the ownership of the Crawshay family, was excluded from that boundary extension on the grounds that it would never be developed). In the meantime, however, the built-up area centred on Reading has extended well beyond the town's administrative boundaries. Further attempts were made, for example in 1947 and 1965, to expand the borough further to reflect this, but they came to nothing. Today, something like a hundred thousand people live within the built-up area centred on Reading, but outside the borough.

One of the other conditions of the boundary review was that, within five years, the Council would build a new bridge, or widen the existing one to at least 45ft, and build a new footbridge to link Lower Caversham and Reading. Caversham Bridge had for centuries been a source of dispute between the two authorities, and had again featured prominently in the boundary negotiations. The bridge had been repaired after a fashion in 1830 and, in the traditional spirit of co-operation between the two sets of authorities, the Caversham half was in stone and the Reading part in timber and iron. It is this bridge that features in the earliest photographs.

As early as 1846, the bridge was deemed to be beyond economic repair, and the wrangles about who would pay for its replacement began all over again. It was also totally inadequate for the amount of traffic wanting to use it, being only wide enough for one wagon to pass at a time and with v-shaped refuges for pedestrians to dodge out of their way. The financial disputes were not resolved until 1868, when a parliamentary Act for a new bridge was approved. The Caversham and Wyfold estates paid the Corporation the sums of £500 and £300, to indemnify anyone north of the river against future claims on them in relation to the bridge. The new iron bridge was completed in 1869, at a cost of £10,154 13s. 9d. One notable feature of its construction was that the ferryman's cottage occupying the island in the centre of the river had to be moved 25ft

97 *The ancient Caversham Bridge was replaced in 1869 by an iron structure that certainly was not picturesque and very soon was again inadequate for the growing traffic using it. It is seen here from Caversham in about 1924, shortly before its demolition.*

to the east. This was no mere shanty, but a three-storey structure measuring 35 ft by 25ft and weighing some 150 tons. It was moved by hydraulic and screw jacks and it is said that not only the ferryman's possessions, but also his family, remained in situ throughout the proceedings. The ferryman was a Mr Piper, who gave his name to the island.

This bridge in its turn proved relatively soon to be totally inadequate for the growing amount of traffic using it (the carriageway was just 20ft wide, with two 5ft pavements). The First World War got in the way of the original timetable for the replacement of the bridge, and the works were not completed until April 1926 – just in time for the General Strike to interrupt the timetable for its official opening. The Prince of Wales – the future King Edward VIII – finally performed the opening ceremony on 25 June 1926.

The same Extension Order that led to the construction of the new Caversham Bridge also required that a new footbridge, 10ft wide, be built over the river near Caversham Lock. Prior to this, the only crossing at this point had been a rickety footbridge known as the Clappers. This had been in existence since at least 1603, at which time it was known as Le Clopper. In the late 19th century, the old bridge had been the scene of some of Reading's most notorious murders, committed by Annie Dyer and discussed earlier.

The Corporation decided that a second road bridge would be of greater benefit to the town. Plans were approved in 1913 and tenders agreed in March 1914 for what was going to be the largest ferro-concrete bridge in the country. Once again, the First World War got in the way and work was not started until 1922. The bridge opened the following year and was tested by parking the largest number of traction engines and heavy lorries the Corporation could assemble on it. One interesting feature of the new structure was the pedestrian path carried under its south side on piles. This was for the benefit of the few remaining horse-drawn barges still using the river at this time.

As we saw, the one part of Caversham that did not transfer to Reading was the estate of Caversham Park. When the Marsack family had sought to dispose of the estate in 1823, they managed to sell the contents of the house, but had great difficulty in finding a purchaser for the estate itself. Repeated attempts failed to reach their reserve price and, meanwhile, it stood vacant and began to decay. Eventually, in 1838, William Crawshay leased it and, six years later, acquired the freehold. Crawshay was known as the 'Iron King'; he was the owner of the Cyfarthfa Ironworks in Merthyr Tydfil, at one time the world's largest, and Caversham Park was conveniently just along the newly built Great Western Railway from his place of work.

By the time of his death, he had made a fortune of nearly £2 million from the growth of the railways. But, in the meantime, the house had once again burned down, uninsured, in 1850 while the family were away. Crawshay rebuilt the house, this time built around a steel frame (one of the first buildings in England to use this construction technique). This new building, by Horace Jones, the architect of Cardiff Town Hall, is the one that we see today. Crawshay also equipped the new building with its own fire engine.

The family retained the house until 1922, when death duties forced its sale to the Roman Catholic Oratory School. Yet again, the building suffered a serious fire in 1926. The Reading Fire Brigade were unable to help, the building then being outside the borough boundary. The Sonning Brigade were at this time voluntary, and took half an hour to assemble, by which time forces from Maidenhead, Wokingham and Henley were also on the way. But the fire was ahead of them all. £30,000 of damage was done, which took two years to repair, although the school continued to function around the restoration works.

Come the Second World War and the building was initially earmarked for a war hospital. But the present owners, the BBC Monitoring Service, took it over in 1941 as an essential war service. While they continued to use the house after the war, the future of the estate land was less certain. Following the 1947 Town and Country Planning Act, Berkshire and Oxfordshire initially agreed not to develop it, to prevent the sprawl of Caversham into Oxfordshire. But by 1959 the borough council was having to look at the possibility of overspill housing. They were close to making a compulsory purchase of 137 acres of the Caversham Park estate, at the knockdown price of £45,000. At the last minute they were caught by a change in the legislation, which now required them to pay the full market value of the land. It would now have cost them around £500,000 – far beyond anything they, or their eventual tenants, could afford. And so it was that the *Times* announced in January 1964 that: 'Homes for between 5,500 and 6,000 people are to be provided in a self-contained village near Reading on which work is due to start early this year. Known as Caversham Park, the site of 180 acres is about 2 ½ miles from Reading'.

Some 1,500 houses were to be built; a complete community, with its own schools, shops, church and community centre. A three-bed house in the village would cost about £4,400. In 1977, local government boundaries finally acknowledged the reality on the ground, and Caversham Park Village finally became part of Reading.

Twentieth-Century Crime and Punishment

The formative years of Reading's police force were documented in an earlier chapter. Over the years that followed, the force has adapted to the changing face of crime. The first record of plain-clothes operations came in 1857, when the watch committee approved the purchase of a plain suit for a Detective Constable Hernaman. In 1897, the Chief Constable had a telephone installed; finger-printing was introduced in 1901 and the photographing of prisoners in 1906. Information technology (in the form of a typewriter costing £20 1s. 4d.) arrived in 1904. Constables on the beat were pretty much on their own until 1928, when the first police telephone box was installed on the Reading side of Caversham Bridge, the first of many to appear across Reading. Unlike *Doctor Who's* version, the technology inside the police box was limited to a telephone linked to headquarters and a one-bar electric fire, to warm the officer as he ate his lunch and sheltered from the rain.

The motor car has become an increasing part of the force's work. In the early 1900s, the Chief Constable's reports simply lumped cars in with steam rollers and traction engines, as locomotives. But, by 1923, the Chief Constable was referring to the use of cars by police forces in New York and Chicago, and lobbying for one of his own in Reading: 'the Kinema is teaching English villains new ways of avoiding arrest; it must also teach us representatives of law and order not to think of these ways as too remote to be dealt with similarly'.(Wykes)

A 12-horsepower Austin was bought for the force the following year, but it appears to have been used more for the Chief Constable's ceremonial duties than for high-speed pursuit. As late as the 1930s, the vehicle fleet of the force consisted of just one car and two motor-cycle combinations, and Reading's police vehicles were not fitted with radios until 1952. The police also had the job of controlling traffic. The use of spot-lit officers on point duty was deemed to be too expensive and, in 1931, a manually operated traffic-light signal box was installed at Cemetery Junction. This system was soon superseded by the automatic variety, which was introduced throughout the borough during the 1930s.

The responsibilities of the police have changed over the years. Until a separate Corporation fire brigade was formed in 1893, it was also the duty of the police to put out fires. On one occasion, in 1862, they had to deal with both a major fire in Market Place and a gang of looters, who were using the fire as cover for their activities in a silversmith's shop. The looters tried to disable the fire engine to keep the blaze going, and 14 constables were injured, either by the flames or the looters. This did not stop one irate property owner in Market Place complaining that the Chief Constable was 'concerning himself with the lives of his constables more than with the property of his masters, the gentlemen of this town'. From 1920, the police also performed the role of film censor, attending showings in the town's cinemas and deciding on their suitability for the people of Reading.

The first women police officers were introduced in 1915 to deal with the problem of prostitution and other crime involving women. It began with one part-time officer, but it soon became clear that her workload was excessive and, by 1917, there were two full-time WPCs in post. However, they were not sworn in like a policeman and had no powers of arrest. Fully empowered WPCs did not appear until 1941, but thereafter their numbers grew rapidly. By 1952 the Women Police Force in Reading had an establishment of 14 and the town could boast the highest proportion of women constables of any force in the country.

After more than 130 years of serving the public of Reading, the town's police were amalgamated into the Thames Valley force in 1968.

Reading Prison had a chequered existence during the 20th century. By 1915, the number of inmates had shrunk to 71, as full employment and an officially-approved outlet for violent tendencies (in the armed forces in France) removed two of the main reasons for people to be locked up. From 1915 to 1919 it was used to house enemy aliens and Irish republican detainees. For almost twenty years after the war it stood empty, and was at one time considered as a site for a new town hall. By 1935, it was being used for a variety of government departments and, during the Second World War, became a detention centre for the Canadian Army. In 1946 it was recommissioned as a prison and in 1949 became a centre for the corrective training of young offenders. It once again became a prison in 1969, at which time it was 'modernised', losing many of its most attractive features in the process. In 1992, it was yet again reclassified as a remand centre.

Chapter Seventeen

The Great War

It was foretold that when the Huns had lost the war by the force of arms they would endeavour to cheat their enemies of victory with tears in their eyes. And so it has come to pass … They think they can play upon our feelings. By appealing to our sentiments and our good nature, they hope to turn aside our past wrath, and from our purpose to exorcise the world from militarism … We must go on until Germany surrenders, and then it will be in our own hands to resettle the world. We do not want to be harsh, but we should be very foolish indeed to listen to the whining Hun, and let him off his punishment and reparation.

(*Berkshire Chronicle* editorial – 8 November 1918)

The first real evidence that war had broken out in 1914 was to be found in the shops. Food prices went through the roof and fears of shortages led to people panic buying. This was despite the fact that nobody at this stage expected it to be a long war – over by Christmas was the prevailing view of people in Reading in August 1914. Nonetheless the troops were rapidly mobilised. Local sailors found themselves being recalled from leave and told to return to their ships, and reservists and time-expired naval men were also called up. Regular soldiers and Territorials both found themselves being prepared to go to the front. Large crowds gathered at the railway station to watch the first detachments depart. The military band played and the mayor made a speech; then the band put down their instruments and boarded the train with them. They were off to the front to act as stretcher bearers.

The armed forces soon found their ranks swelled by hosts of volunteers, whose disappearance off to the front affected the town in all sorts of ways. Simonds' Brewery very quickly lost 35 of its staff to the war, and trained up others by forming their own irregular corps from among their office staff. Reading Football Club lost a centre half and a full-back to the forces in the same week. Men who had deserted from the armed forces years before surrendered themselves to the authorities, asking to have a crack at the new enemy. By September 1914, some 184 Huntley and Palmer staff had answered the call and by the end of the year 515 men – about one in 10 of their labour force – had signed up. The management set up weekly visits to their families to ensure that they suffered no

Right: **98** *Crowds gather
at the town hall in August
1914 to read the notice of
mobilisation at the outbreak
of the First World War.*

Below: **99** *Cheerful
recruits leave Reading station
in July 1915 to begin their
training with the Royal
Engineers. Ahead of them lay
the hell of the First World
War trenches.*

hardship. By the end of the war, some 40 per cent of Huntley and Palmer staff
would do some form of war service and 145 of them would be killed.

Huntley and Palmer promised volunteers from their labour force their jobs
back at the end of the war and made up any shortfall in their army pay to
Huntley and Palmer levels. Suttons undertook to look after the wives and
children of their serving employees and to keep their jobs open until they
returned. The council, too, topped up the salaries of teachers who volunteered
to peacetime levels.

Many of the recruits joined their local regiment – the Royal Berkshires.
First founded as long ago as 1743, the regiment had a long history of battle
honours, starting with St Lucia in 1778 and taking in all the major conflicts of
the 19th century, from the Peninsular Wars against Napoleon, through Crimea
and Afghanistan to the Boer War. Their headquarters was at Brock Barracks

100 *Sergeant W.H. Ridley of the Royal Garrison Artillery is awarded the Distinguished Conduct Medal in Market Place on 27 November 1917.*

on the Oxford Road and they were known, for obvious reasons, as The Biscuit Boys. The regiment soon found itself in the thick of things on the western front, earning themselves a string of battle honours that included Mons, the Marne, Ypres (twice), Neuve Chapelle, Loos, the Somme (twice), Thiepval, Arras (twice), Passchendaele, Cambrai and Baupaume. The regiment also saw action in Italy and Macedonia.

But these battle honours were won at a grievous cost. By the time of the Somme offensive of 1916, jingoism had given way to a more sombre realism, as the nation found itself engaged in a war of attrition of hitherto unimaginable proportions. Every week, the *Chronicle* carried full page lists of the men killed and injured. Further pages were given over to photographs of the dead, wounded and decorated. Local men who had survived the thick of the fighting supplied the paper with detailed accounts of their experiences in the hell that was the trenches, and the paper even published some of the letters from the commanding officers of the war dead to their grieving families. August Bank Holiday in Reading was cancelled in 1916 so that munitions workers could concentrate on turning out more shells.

By the end of the war the regiment had lost a total of 6,688 men. The losses did not discriminate between rich and poor; Major Charles Simonds, of the town's brewing and banking family, died in 1916 along with some of their most junior employees. Some families had most grievous losses to bear. By July 1916, a Mrs Morgan of Kendrick Road had sent five sons to the front, two of whom had already perished, and the Wickens family of Mortimer lost four brothers to the hostilities by 1918.

Back at home, many in the town became obsessed with the idea that Reading was full of German spies. German-born residents, no matter how long they had been resident in Britain, were required to register under the Aliens Restriction Order 1914, and many found their activities minutely observed by their neighbours and their most innocent behaviour reported to the authorities.

The outbreak of war presented major problems for the medical services in Reading. First, a large proportion of their key staff were army reservists, likely to be called up. Second, Reading, conveniently close to the Channel ports and with good rail communications, was always likely to receive some of the wounded returning from the front. In 1914, nobody could have guessed quite how great that flow of patients would become. In the event, many of the reserve staff at the hospitals were transferred, on a part-time basis, to the armed forces' Southern General Hospital at Oxford, leaving the Reading hospitals to fill in as best they could with local G.P.s and retired practitioners. In addition, the hospitals were asked to

101   *Pupils at the George Palmer School making wooden hospital appliances for the Reading War Hospitals Supply Department.*

make beds available to the armed forces; Battle offered 100 beds in the aged and infirm block (which were not at first taken up) and the Royal Berks offered 50 beds. The first convoy of wounded reached the Royal Berks in November 1914. It would be the first of 136 hospital trains to visit Reading over the war years.

By the following February, the scale of demand was far outstripping these initial provisions. The War Office announced that it needed 1,000 extra beds in Reading. The whole of the workhouse and several primary schools were taken over, leaving some 500 workhouse inmates and 3,500 schoolchildren to be rehoused. Many of the workhouse inmates were sent to neighbouring unions; the relatives of some of the others were prevailed upon to take them in; the council's education committee made Grovelands School available and the parks committee donated Prospect Park Mansion House to them. Within a month, the workhouse was converted into a 400-bed war hospital.

In addition, a series of Red Cross Auxiliary Hospitals was created in the Reading area. One of the first of these was at the home of the Lord Lieutenant of Berkshire, Mr J. Benyon, who turned the gallery of his stately home, Englefield House, into a 25-bed hospital. Others were in church halls (such as St Anne's in Caversham and St Luke's in Reading) and, at the time of the Somme offensive, even the West End Free Library was pressed into medical use. Sixteen of these hospitals had been opened in and around Reading by April 1915 and, at their peak, they provided 738 beds. Nursing was not their only preoccupation; none of them was adequately funded by the government, so fund-raising also became a constant necessity. So too did official returns; one thing the government certainly did not keep them short of was paperwork and bureaucracy. The Mayor of Reading organised a care and comforts committee, to provide such things as tobacco, fruit, flowers and books for the patients, and King George and Queen Mary came to Reading to see the town's war work in July of that year.

The first convoy of 120 patients for the war hospital (as the workhouse at Battle was now known) arrived at Reading station on the afternoon of 22 April 1915. So great was the crowd of people who gathered at the station to witness their

102 *Both world wars opened up new career opportunities for women, such as these trainee tram conductresses, pictured c.1914.*

arrival that the police had to put up barriers to hold them back. They were wounded at the battle for Hill 60 in the Gallipoli campaign and, according to contemporary reports their clothes 'still bore traces of the trenches and deep red stains and their wan faces and shattered limbs told their own tale'(Railton and Barr). More would soon follow from the Battle of Ypres.

Reading itself eventually had no less than seven war hospitals, and the casualties flooding into the town made all sorts of demands on its resources. In mid-1915, the Mayor of Reading decided to try to mobilise the business community in support of the war effort. Their first proposal, to manufacture sandbags for the western front on a mammoth scale, was turned down by the War Office. Their alternative proposal was the Reading War Hospitals Supply Department, manufacturing all sorts of medical equipment for the hospitals. Their products ranged from simple bandages and splints through knitted goods and crutches to more complicated items like artificial limbs. They soon outgrew their initial premises in Cross Street, moving to larger accommodation in Duke Street where, at their peak, they directly employed some 60 people. In addition, there were almost sixty separate working parties scattered over the length of Berkshire, also manufacturing goods. These might be schoolchildren, women's groups or a firm's employees, putting in unpaid extra hours. At the Heelas department store, for example, a working group of about 28 staff stayed behind after work to manufacture miles of bandages and other products from raw materials donated by their employers. The local newspapers did their bit by fundraising for the enterprise. At the end of hostilities, it was calculated that up to 1,500 local people had provided over 643,000 items of hospital supplies through the initiative.

One impact of the war on Reading was its effects on the town's largest employer. Previous wars had hardly affected Huntley and Palmer. The Crimean War led to no more than a few shortages of ingredients and the Boer War virtually passed the company by, despite 450,000 men being mobilised throughout the country. This may explain the company's lack of preparedness for the First World War, when it came. They carried very small stocks of raw materials in the factory and found themselves caught out by the price rises in foodstuffs that tend to accompany an outbreak of hostilities. As eggs and sugar doubled in price, and flour went up by 50 per cent, the company was also hit by a massive distortion in its markets. Overseas sales, the area in which the company was traditionally strongest, nosedived, while there was a huge increase in domestic orders – between two and three times anything the factory had the capacity to produce. Once again, the company proved slow to respond to change; despite the domestic demand, some staff had to be put on short time and one floor in the factory was turned over to making clothes, for those called up for the war, and for those dependents of called-up staff left behind in straitened circumstances.

But massive orders from the War Office soon plugged any gaps in the overseas order book. In addition to biscuits (of which the wartime armed forces bought £653,000, almost 6½ per cent of total turnover) they also commissioned the factory to pack tins of basic rations for them. One product that found its way into many a soldier's ration kit was the Number 4 biscuit. This was extremely hard but nutritious and, if soaked in water (or something stronger), apparently made a passable pudding. Unappetising though this may sound, it was apparently much better than some of its rivals, which were said to be usable only as firelighters.

The other big challenge for the company was the drain of manpower into the armed forces. Shortage of manpower and materials meant the company was forced to reconsider its priorities, and the production of tins of biscuits for Christmas, a traditional money-spinner for them, had to be cut to less than half peacetime levels. As the war progressed, rationing of raw materials bit into production ever more deeply. Before the war, about two-thirds of the factory's sugar came from Germany and Austria-Hungary – markets now closed to them. By 1917, sugar supplies were cut to about a third of the pre-war level.

The company was forced to diversify in all sorts of ways. Its extensive marshalling yards were used to load Reading-made munitions for the journey to the ordnance depot in Bristol. Some 60,000 shells were manufactured within Huntley and Palmer's factory itself. Quaker members of the board struggled with their pacifist consciences over this and, in deference to them, non-lethal products were also commissioned – from smoke bombs to steel helmets and parts for aeroplane engines.

The war years saw record levels of output by the company, and market conditions that disguised the underlying weakness of the company. But what the war could not disguise was the poor industrial relations in the company (though it has to be said that Reading's other major biscuit manufacturer, Serpells, also had its industrial relations problems at this time). These re-emerged in July 1916, just as the Battle of the Somme was opening. Picketing staff assaulted people trying to enter the factory (women strikers were apparently particularly violent) and some broke into it, doing about £140 worth of damage. For their part, the strikers complained that it was impossible to live on the £1 1s. a week, plus 2s. war bonus, that they were paid. They were, they said, fighting for their colleagues serving in the forces, so that they might have a civilised standard of living on their return. These differences were patched up, but the company emerged from the war still having an old and uneconomic plant, an excessively wide range of products and having neglected what would become its increasingly important home market.

By the time the war ground to a conclusion in November 1918, many of

103 *A parade along Friar Street, part of the Armistice celebrations in November 1918.*

the British public were in no mood to accommodate the Germans in the peace negotiations. The prevailing mood was more one of 'Hang the Kaiser and make the Germans pay'. But the more immediate priority, when the sounding of factory hooters and the raising of flags signalled an end to hostilities, was celebration. Most of the workforce declared an unofficial holiday and the streets were filled with flag-waving, musical instrument-playing revellers. The street lamps, which had been masked against the threat of the Zeppelins (and later, the first German bombers), were allowed to shine again and the skies were filled with the sight and sound of impromptu firework displays. Even German prisoners of war, engaged in manual work in the town, were seen to join in the celebrations. Only one effigy of the Kaiser was to be seen, and this met its inevitable fiery end in St Mary's Butts.

As if the suffering of the war were not enough, Reading was soon hit by the worldwide influenza epidemic. Queues 70 yards long were reported outside doctors' surgeries a third of the town's Post Office staff and large numbers of railway workers were hit by it and insurance companies reported unprecedented levels of claims on their life policies. One consequence of this was that the work of the war hospital did not end with the hostilities. The epidemic swept through the nation in 1918 and, in Reading, the dead were so numerous that they had to be stored in a marquee on the lawn of the hospital. The war hospital did not finally close until April 1920.

Chapter Eighteen

Reading between the Wars

Reading is more than a prosperous town, it is one of the wealthiest in England, though it seemed surprised when I told it so … Today there are only 2,090 insured workers idle, almost a record low figure in a population of 100,000. Even in the height of the 1931 depression the figure was only 2,520. Perhaps its happy and healthy situation has bred contentment among its inhabitants.

(*Daily Sketch* 18 August 1936)

Homes Fit for Heroes – and Millionaires

Graphic evidence of the hardship under which some Reading people were living came in December 1918, just after the Armistice to the First World War. Without warning, the roofs on three houses in Bosier Square, a slum quarter of Coley, collapsed onto the people sleeping underneath them. Miraculously, no one was killed, but it served as a warning of some of Reading's housing conditions. Nationally, the government had promised homes fit for heroes and the first council estate to be developed in the town after the First World War was at Shinfield Road in 1920. One of Reading's other contributions towards that objective was to be 500 homes for the working classes, built on Ayres' Farm, on the east side of Basingstoke Road. The council spoke highly of the new site: 'The land is pleasing in character, is well situated for draining, is within about ten minutes' walk of the existing tram terminus and is on the bus route'.

The Reading Labour Party (surprisingly, on the face of it) was less enamoured of the scheme, condemning the site as being absolutely unsuited for the purpose. This was possibly due to the fact that it was also downwind of the Manor Farm sewage works and thus subject to the notorious Whitley whiff. Sure enough, this would be an ongoing source of dispute between the residents and the local authority (and their successors in sewage) for the rest of the 20th century. By the latter part of the 1930s, these developments were being complemented by private estates, such as those at Berkeley Avenue, Kentwood and Henley Road, Caversham.

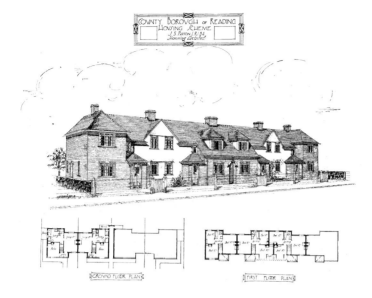

104   *Council homes for servicemen returning from the Great War, planned for Shinfield in 1918.*

105   *The ancient Southcote Manor, shortly before its demolition in 1921.*

At the other end of the social spectrum, a number of the large family estates that ringed Reading were sold off and developed in the inter-war years. Southcote Manor House, home of the Blagrave family, had origins dating back to the 13th century and had been the headquarters of the parliamentary forces during the Civil War siege of Reading. The property still had the medieval trappings of a moat and drawbridge when it was put up for sale in 1918. No buyer was found for the dilapidated property and three years later it was demolished. The site would remain vacant until taken for council housing in the 1960s. By the 1920s, the Blagrave family had relocated to Calcot Park, and a huge estate taking in large parts of Tilehurst, including Beansheaf, Pincents and Turnhams Farms. The last of the Blagrave line, Henry Barry Blagrave, twice failed to find a buyer for Calcot Park, in 1919 and 1926. After he died in 1927, it took two years before Calcot Park House was acquired as the clubhouse to a golf course built in its grounds.

The millionaire Solomon Barnato Joel had owned the estate at Maiden Erleigh since 1903. The future King George VI had visited there when coming to open the Solly Joel Playing Fields in 1927. Joel had donated almost twenty acres of his estate to the National Playing Fields Association, to be used for recreational purposes in perpetuity. He died in 1931 and the rest of the estate was sold off. The house itself was variously used as a home for Maiden Erleigh School, as offices and to house Hungarian refugees until 1960, when the property was sold for housebuilding and Joel's stately home demolished. Erleigh Court off London Road was, for almost a century after 1836, home to former Prime Minister Lord Sidmouth and his descendants, but it too was sold off for development in 1935. Coley Park, between the Kennet and the Bath Road, had been the long-standing home of the Monck family, who had been prominent as Members of Parliament and in other capacities within the town. But after William Berkeley Monck died in 1905, the property was rented out, and in 1937 the whole estate was auctioned.

The General Strike, Recession – and Fascism

After the First World War, Huntley and Palmer announced a new deal for its workers, something that had been put on hold because of the war. The basic working week was cut from 54 to 48 hours and workers with three years' service (towards which war service counted) would be entitled to a week's paid holiday each year. They even announced new wage rates for their employees – males starting at 18s. at age 14 and rising to 45s. at 18; and women's pay ranging from 17s. to 30s. When the unions heard this, they passed a vote of thanks to the company and their union officials. But labour relations generally became rather less happy a few years after the war, with the calling of the General Strike in 1926. Reading did not suffer from post-war unemployment to the same extent as older manufacturing towns. Unemployment peaked in 1921, with some 4,000 people out of work. The response to the call for a general strike was therefore perhaps understandably mixed. The railwaymen and tram staff came out, as did the building industry and workers at Simonds' brewery. But many of the town's other industries, including the gas and electricity companies, carried on as normal.

Many local people volunteered to maintain services (or break the strike, depending upon your point of view) by working as amateur railway porters, special police constables or tram drivers. A nasty incident was narrowly avoided when an angry crowd of strikers, numbering some 4-500, surrounded trams being driven by these volunteers. A brick was thrown and fighting broke out, with police being assaulted. However, only one of those arrested received a custodial sentence, for trying to derail a tram. In another incident, a union official was given a month's hard labour, after threatening violence to an employee of the tram company who returned to work in mid-strike.

106   *Striking workers attend a rally in Market Place during the General Strike in 1926.*

The return to work with the ending of the strike was gradual and, in some cases, painful. The railway company and the tramways did not automatically take back striking staff, arguing that they had broken the terms of their contracts, and the government made it clear that they would not force the employers to do so.

One consequence of the strike for Reading was that it postponed the official opening of the new Caversham Bridge by the Prince of Wales. This did not take place until June of that year when, in a busy day, the Prince also visited many of the town's major employers, the hospital, the university, Reading School and a children's sports day in Palmer Park. Talk of a third Thames bridge for Reading also emerged with the setting up of a town planning committee in South Oxfordshire in 1928, to work with Reading for the orderly expansion of the Greater Reading area. However, the talk proved to be slightly premature – at the latest count, by just over three-quarters of a century.

Although Reading may not have suffered as badly as many towns during the inter-war depression years, its impact was still felt. Many of the town's poorest were driven to seek the help of those Victorian survivors, the Poor Law Guardians. At the height of the depression, the council found itself paying out some £850 a week in outdoor relief, creating a budgetary crisis. The unemployed suffered from poor nutrition and poor health. A voluntary group provided allotments for the unemployed, to enable them to grow vegetables to supplement their meagre diet, and the Reading Tuberculosis Dispensary Care Association reported a substantial increase in the number of tuberculosis cases among the long-term unemployed. An additional wing had to be built at the Park Isolation Hospital to deal with them. Hunger marchers, passing through Reading en route from South Wales to London in February 1934, were a reminder of the even greater

107   *The Prince of Wales, the future Edward VIII, at Huntley and Palmer during his packed visit to Reading in 1926.*

impact the depression was having in other parts of the country. The council, asked to provide them with overnight accommodation, declined them the use of the town hall or the corn exchange and offered them instead the lairage room at the cattle market and straw for bedding – standards of accommodation normally reserved for animals.

Some, in the days before the darker side of fascism was widely understood, looked to Germany and the way the new regime had reduced the number of unemployed by over four million by 1936. Earlier, in 1933, the Reading and District Free Church Council had as its guest speaker a Dr Ernest Deissman, a German academic and passionate advocate of Nazism. He described Hitler as: 'a man of courage and action … [who] … has striven to achieve his ideal of a unified Germany, in which class distinctions would be abolished and all classes would work together for the reconstruction of national life'. (Hylton)

In similar vein, Reading Rotary Club invited Dr Hans Schirmer to address them on some positive aspects of the Nazi movement. The vote of thanks for this presentation was given by local retailer William McIlroy of the department store family, who would serve as Reading's mayor for much of the war. Local Fascist groups were set up. According to one newspaper correspondent, who attended one of the local meetings:

> We listened to an unemployed fascist condemn the Public assistance Committee and the Means Test. He pointed out the ideal state of affairs, but made no attempt whatsoever to tell us how fascism could bring about that state. Indeed, had it not been for a number of youths wearing black shirts, one might have had the impression of being at a meeting of the Labour party.

108 *Empire Air Day at Woodley aerodrome in 1938. The aircraft designer F.G. Miles poses in front of one of his designs.*

But some Reading people were quicker than others to recognise the true nature of Nazism. Rufus Isaacs, the town's former Member of Parliament and the first Marquis of Reading, had been the President of the Anglo-German Association since its formation. In April 1933 he resigned from the association in protest against the German regime's treatment of Jews.

Another development in transport had its impact on the town. In 1929, Charles Powis, a local cycle and motor cycle manufacturer, opened Woodley aerodrome. By 1934, it employed 160 and had a thriving flying club and a successful aircraft-manufacturing concern, headed by the talented young aircraft designer F.G. Miles. Huge crowds gathered there in the 1930s for air displays and light aircraft races. A thriving future was forecast for the airfield.

> It is only recently that internal airlines have been started in England, but during the next three to four years their growth will undoubtedly be rapid. There is in view the formation of a number of central airports to serve sections of the country, and if this materialises, Reading will have a strong claim to selection as an airport serving the south midlands and south of England.
>
> (Quoted in Hylton)

The airport did grow in importance over the next few years, but not for the reason the operators suggested. In January 1939 the Secretary of State for Air, Sir Kingsley Wood, opened a massive £250,000 extension to the Miles aircraft factory to mass-produce the aircraft urgently needed by the Royal Air Force. Once again it was Mr Hitler having an impact on Reading.

Immediately after the end of the First World War, long-standing speculation about a possible merger of leading biscuit manufacturers re-emerged. After some initial fruitless negotiation, this led to the merger of Huntley and Palmer and Peek Frean in 1920, to form the Associated Biscuit Manufacturers Company. But this could not protect them from the post-war recession. They were forced to reduce their labour force from 5,000 in September 1919 to 3,500 two years later, and to reduce the working week of those who remained by a third (to 31 hours a week). The company suffered its first ever annual loss in 1921, leading them to cut wages and shift from the use of male to female labour, which in turn increased the level of poverty in the town. This did not stop them opening prestigious new offices on the Kings Road in 1937 at a cost of £55,000. Belatedly, they also started investing in more up-to-date manufacturing plant, but the first of these production lines came into operation only weeks before everything was turned upside down again, by the outbreak of a new war.

Another major local industry that was turned upside down during 1939 was the CWS Jam factory in Coley. It caught fire one night, and flames 100ft high lit up the skies for miles around. But the real focus of the town's attention now was preparation for the war that was to come. The council announced plans to equip the town's schools with air-raid shelters, at a cost of between £40-50,000, and many major employers did the same. The Air Raid Precautions wardens carried out exercises to test preparedness for bombing raids, and the RAF flew over the town to test the effectiveness of the blackout. Although Reading was only 40 miles from London, it was officially deemed to be a 'safe' area (for the purpose of evacuating people from London and elsewhere). At the same time it was designated as a 'specified area' (in terms of its likelihood of itself being bombed). Both proved to be right, up to a point. Which one applied to you all depended upon whether you were in the wrong place at the wrong time.

Chapter Nineteen

THE SECOND WORLD WAR

Our Guests Arrive

> As a precautionary measure, the Government scheme for evacuating children from parts of London and other vital areas is to commence today. It is an immense scheme and will take several days to complete. Reading will receive some 25,000 evacuees … and they are assured of a very warm welcome. There is bound to be some personal inconvenience during evacuation, as the Corporation transport services will have to be reduced to skeleton extent with the exception of the trolley bus services, but we are all convinced that any hardships will be gladly borne for the sake of the children.
>
> (Quoted in Hylton)

As the signs of impending war became ever more ominous, the people of Reading started to sign up to do their bit. A register of Boy Scouts desirous of rendering national service was opened at the town hall and anyone over the age of 14 was invited to join the ARP, to protect the town from air raids. The borough council had had an Air Raid Precautions scheme in place since early 1937. Air raid trenches were constructed in the town's parks and a scheme to build communal air raid shelters to take 2,500 people was submitted to the Home Office.

Once the outbreak of war was announced, further changes soon followed. Early closing of shops was introduced, along with (temporarily) the total closure of the town's cinemas and its football club. Rationing was introduced, with petrol one of the first commodities to be affected. One consequence was a halving of the town's public transport services, where these relied on petrol buses. The town set up its own Army Comforts Depot, which, by the end of hostilities supplied our fighting forces with 1.25 million wartime comforts, ranging from mouth organs to helmet mufflers. For their part, the council stored all its precious documents, including its ancient charters, in sealed dustbins and concealed them in the chalk caves at Emmer Green.

The war was to have a great impact on Reading, though it was the inhabitants of London, rather than those of the Third Reich, who caused most of it. In 1938, the town's population was estimated at around 100,000; by 1942 it had risen to about 140,000, as roughly equal numbers of evacuees on the official schemes and

109 *The Queen (later the Queen Mother) visits the Reading Army Comforts Centre.*

those making their own private arrangements flooded into the town. The three months preceding the war alone saw an increase of well over 12,000 in the town's population. Those moving to the town were not just fleeing from the bombing; some were transferred war-workers, sent to Reading to help with essential war work in the factories or nearby military installations. Others were civil servants, staffing the various government offices that were relocated to Reading for the duration. Later, as the Blitz destroyed many homes in London and elsewhere, homeless families came to the town in search of shelter. Last, but not least, there were large numbers of the armed forces billeted in or around the town.

The official evacuee schemes alone resulted in nearly nine thousand households being served with billeting notices, requiring them to house incomers. In addition to conventional housing, the National Camps Corporation were building holiday camps at Kennylands, Kidmore End and Bishopswood Farm in Sonning Common, and it was announced that these would also be used for evacuees. The town became so overcrowded that, by October 1941, Reading was declared a 'closed town' – it was officially full. A Lodging Restriction Order was enforced. Under this, the consent of the billeting officer had to be obtained before anyone could move into the borough, and you had to tell the authorities if you moved out.

Not surprisingly, there were all sorts of tensions between the evacuees and their often unwilling hosts. A tribunal met to hear a multitude of more or less ingenious reasons why the appellants should not have evacuees visited upon them. On the other hand, the press also carried reports of the sometimes outrageous, and often comical, behaviour of the inner-city working-class evacuees as they were thrown into close contact with their more privileged hosts.

At the start of the war, Reading had an appalling reputation for failing to observe the blackout, with almost seven hundred prosecutions for breaches in the first year. However, vigilant enforcement by the Air Raid Wardens got the number down to around 250 by 1942. The town's proximity to London, and people's knowledge of what Londoners were going through with the Blitz no doubt also played a great part in the reduction. Many Reading people continued to commute to the city to work, and the anti-aircraft gunfire over London could be seen from Reading. The blackout brought its own problems for the town, with people being run over and motorists crashing as they struggled to navigate the darkened streets.

The two main pressure points caused by the growth in population were housing and schools. There was a relatively high rate of house-building going on in the pre-war years (though, at 351 new homes in 1938, for example, it was scarcely a flea-bite against the scale of the influx of population). There was also already quite a high incidence of overcrowding, particularly on the council estates. However, shortage of materials and manpower meant that house-building effectively ceased by the end of 1940. A national scheme of licensing building work was to come in from January 1942, giving priority to repairing air raid damage and other essential work.

The school situation was worse. There was barely any spare capacity in Reading's schools during the run-up to the war, even before the influx of evacuees began. Reading's own birth-rate had been going up between 1933 and 1938, promising additional pressure on places. The demand for school places increased by about fifty-five per cent in 1939 alone. To address the shortage of accommodation, a double-shift system of part-time education had to be operated by schools until early 1940, when the number of evacuee children declined sufficiently for the authorities to reintroduce full-time teaching. The long-term prospects were not helped by expectant mothers being sent to Reading as a supposedly safe place to have their children and thus further increasing the town's birth-rate. One additional feature of the birth-rate was the incidence in illegitimacy, rising by 1945 to one in seven births – well above the national average.

The first tentative national food rationing scheme was introduced in January 1940, and gradually spread across a wide range of foodstuffs. In Reading, the Local Food Control Committee enforced the government's rationing regulations, and licensed food retailers and catering establishments. Shoppers had to be registered with a specific retailer; the amount of rationed goods a retailer could receive was related to the number of registrations they had. The sensible stockpiling of food, which had been regarded as a virtue before the war, became known as hoarding, and was made subject to fines and confiscation.

In May 1940, with the threat of invasion looming large, the War Secretary Sir Anthony Eden announced the formation of a new volunteer defence force, the Local Defence Volunteers. They were to be drawn from those too old, too young or otherwise unable to serve in the main armed forces. As with other parts of the country, Reading people swamped the authorities with applications to join. There was even a waterborne contingent – the Upper Thames Patrol under the command of retired Rear Admiral Sir Basil Brooke – whose vigilant patrols of the river kept it entirely free of pocket battleships throughout the war. In preparation for the invasion, large-scale mock battles were conducted in the town centre, with Reading and Caversham bridges coming under serious assault

110 *Home Guard exercises were carried out on the streets of the town. Here an armoured car and soldiers patrol the streets during the Battle of Tilehurst in 1942.*

and attacking parties being driven off from the town hall. Other exercises in Tilehurst prompted complaints, when it was felt that some of those posing as 'enemy' soldiers acted with undue brutality to the civilians they 'arrested'.

As the war went on, Reading suffered its share of minor bombing attacks. Reports would appear in the local papers of 'bomb damage in the Home Counties' or 'on the outskirts of a town'. The censor would not allow them to be more specific.

The town's most serious and terrifying encounter with bombing came at about 4.35p.m. on 10 February 1943. A single Dornier bomber flew low over the centre of Reading, dropping a string of bombs that hit the Heelas garage on Minster Street and the Wellsteed department store on Broad Street, before attacking the area around the town hall, machine gunning the streets as they went. By a miracle, it was half-day closing on a Wednesday afternoon, so many of these premises were relatively unoccupied. But the next bomb hit the People's Pantry, a crowded restaurant, where many of the 41 deaths and the 49 serious casualties occurred. In addition, both St Laurence's Church and the town hall suffered serious damage in the attack. Among those taken to the Royal Berkshire Hospital after the attack was a young Michael Bond – the Germans very nearly denied the world the pleasures of Paddington Bear.

It is thought the bomber concerned was itself shot down before reaching the coast. Despite the damage being so extensive that it would be impossible not to notice that Reading had been bombed, the censors still insisted upon the local paper reporting it as happening in a 'Home Counties town'. It was months before the paper could say what everyone knew.

It took even longer for any hint to emerge that this was possibly more than just a random opportunistic attack. The authorities recognised before the war

111 *Bomb damage to St Laurence's church and the Town Hall, after Reading's most serious wartime bombing raid.*

that high-powered radio transmitters could be used as a direction-finding device by enemy bombers. Low-powered transmitters, serving a local catchment, were therefore located instead in many large towns, to transmit BBC programmes more safely. In 1993, it emerged that Reading's transmitter had been located in the People's Pantry, and the theory has been put forward by Brooks that this was the bomber's target. It is known that the Germans had detailed maps of Reading town centre, showing strategic targets – one such is in the possession of Reading Central Library.

112 *Minster Street, following the raid in 1943.*

One group that once again was not universally welcomed in the town were so-called 'enemy aliens', who in fact were often people born in Germany but who had lived in England for much of their lives, or more recent arrivals as refugees from Fascist oppression. They were required to register with the authorities, had their freedom of movement seriously curtailed and in many cases were interned as prisoners for the duration.

With law and order, the incidence of offences to some extent reflected the circumstances of war. Rationing and shortages created a ready market for a whole range of goods. A large increase in population inevitably produced an overall increase in crime, while shop-breaking and larceny (especially of bicycles) were the main growth areas in wartime indictable offences. The dramatic reduction in the numbers of bicycle thefts at the end of the war was put down by the Chief Constable to 'the departure of large numbers of troops from the area'. The fact that there was such a welter of minutely detailed wartime regulations to obey also created some unwitting offenders from among the normally law-abiding population.

One example of this was the 'Blanktown' campaign. By 1940, as the prospect of invasion grew more immediate, the town was told to obliterate anything that might give an enemy invader a clue as to where they were. Road signs were removed, the signs at the station saying 'Reading' were painted over, and even shops whose signs gave some clue as to their location had to remove it. The proprietor of Shinfield Fisheries found himself in court for failing to do so, even though his business was some two miles from the settlement of that name.

Over the war years, the town experienced total war of a kind it had never seen before. Every able-bodied person was recruited for the armed forces or for long hours in war work. Outside that there were the calls of the Home Guard, the Air Raid Precautions staff and a host of other war-related organisations. Food, petrol, clothing and many other daily needs were rationed. Nothing could go to waste; paper, metal, bones and other waste materials had to be recycled. Even people's surplus income was called upon for savings campaigns to fund the war effort. The fact that there was nothing much in the shops to buy made this less of a sacrifice than it might otherwise have been. With most of the nation's beaches barb-wired and mined, holidays were taken at home.

After its initial brief closure, Reading Football Club had a hand-to-mouth existence through the war years. Normal league and cup fixtures were cancelled

113 *A tank visits McIlroys department store on one of the town's many wartime funding drives.*

in favour of events such as the London War Cup (in which the winning team got War Savings Certificates in lieu of medals). Team selection was dictated to a considerable degree by which players were stationed in nearby army camps and had a pass for Saturday afternoon. In one occasion, Reading only got their team up to full strength when their manager spotted a Tottenham Hotspur player in the crowd and persuaded him to take a rather more active part than he had intended in the afternoon's proceedings. At other times it worked to their advantage as well; among their regular players were Frank Swift, the Manchester City and England goalkeeper, and the man who was to become Manchester United's legendary manager, Matt Busby. Despite the ad hoc nature of the matches and the disruptions of war, the club could still attract gates of over twenty thousand.

By the outbreak of the Second World War, Huntley and Palmer's output had shrunk to about half that of the years before 1914. This time, though, they were rather better prepared for war, and an industry-wide committee set them on a war footing; doing everything from ensuring sufficient supplies of biscuits for evacuees to agreeing a fair distribution of essential ingredients between manufacturers. Huntley and Palmer workers were classified as a reserved occupation; staff could not be called up for, or volunteer for, the armed forces. But the company was still forced to shed more labour and, by September 1943, a business that had once employed 5,500 in the factory alone was reduced to a total labour force of just over a thousand. As if with a positive will to lower the corporate spirits further, the Ministry of Food that year delivered its latest contribution to the art of austerity cake baking – 550 tons of potatoes.

Many other Reading companies turned their attention to war production, perhaps the most obvious one being Miles Aircraft Ltd at Woodley. During the war they built over 5,000 aircraft and repaired another three thousand. At the height of the war, over 7,000 people were working there and the airfield was also an important centre for the training of pilots. The flying school there finally closed in March 1955. Miles Aircraft were taken over by Handley Page, who manufactured aircraft there until 1962.

On the front line the local regiment, the Royal Berkshires, was once again at the centre of hostilities. Reading men were among the expeditionary force that was evacuated at Dunkirk; they landed on Juno beach at D-Day and made their way across Europe, helping to secure the crossing of the Rhine. Others landed in Sicily and fought their way up through Italy, or formed part of the 14th Army in Burma. The regiment would survive the war but not the cut-backs of 1959, in which they were merged with the Wiltshire regiment to form the Duke of Edinburgh's Royal Regiment.

As the war turned in our favour, thoughts began to turn to Reading as it would be after the war. One of the topics that was revived was that of a new civic centre. The need for this had been discussed since the turn of the century and the deliberations of the council would rumble on until the current civic offices were opened in 1976. Another topic making a return appearance was

114   *The residents of de Beauvoir Road celebrate the end of the Second World War in Europe with a street party.*

the question of Reading's boundaries. These had remained unchanged since the incorporation of Caversham in 1911, despite the town's subsequent expansion. As an illustration, the absurdity of Whiteknights Park being split between Reading and Wokingham was cited. This would soon become the new home for the university, and they would face the added complication of dealing with two different planning authorities. As we have seen, the boundaries of the borough remain virtually unchanged 60 years later. A general election was held and, as part of the socialist landslide, Reading returned a Labour Member of Parliament, Ian Mikardo, who would represent the town until 1959. He was not Reading's first Labour M.P. – Dr Somerville Hastings was elected as long ago as 1923.

In May 1945 the Germans surrendered. The first place in Britain to hear of it was the monitoring station at Caversham Park. As with the first war, the town celebrated with bonfires, dancing in the streets, fireworks, church bells and street parties, all of it only mildly tempered by the knowledge that there was still unfinished business in the far east.

Chapter Twenty

THE IDEAL ENGLISH TOWN: POST-WAR READING

Reading today, viewed from many standpoints, approaches the ideal English town.
(Reading Official Town Guide, 1947)

Freeze and Floods

The above quotation, somewhat rose-tinted by any standards, must have been written before the events described below. As 1947 opened, Reading – and the nation as a whole – was still struggling to recover from the effects of six years of war. Austerity was the order of the day, with rationing still in place and every effort going to restore the country's pre-war industrial base, rather than on any personal consumption the domestic population might have wanted. Nature chose this moment to visit the country with the bitterest winter for many years. Temperatures of minus 12 degrees centigrade were recorded in Reading, toboggans were out in force in Prospect Park and skaters appeared on Whiteknights Lake, until that, too, became lost beneath the snows.

The government's plans for providing fuel supplies began to break down. There was not enough coal to go round, and what there was could not be delivered because of the weather. Industry faced 50 per cent cuts in their fuel allocations and thousands of jobs were threatened. A local Fuel Allocation Committee sat in daily session to hear pleas from firms, desperate to get additional supplies. The power stations and gasworks were equally short of fuel, so nobody had a dependable source of heating or lighting. Every branch of life in the town was affected. Factories operated their machines by hand and lit their offices with car headlights; shop displays were lit by paraffin lamps and candles; dentists used foot-powered drills; pianos replaced organs in the churches; no alternative could be found to electricity to power the hare at the greyhound track, leading to the cancellation of race meetings; worst of all, a beer shortage was forecast, as Simonds' brewery was reduced by the lack of fuel to making mini-brews, just to keep their yeast alive.

There was a backlash against the Government who, some thought, had mismanaged the crisis. Graffiti began appearing on walls, saying 'socialism = no warmth, no jobs and no hope'. Reading's Labour M.P. Ian Mikardo preferred to lay the blame at the lack of investment in the mines during their long period of private ownership.

The thaw in March came swiftly; too swiftly, not allowing time for the ground to thaw and let the water drain away. The consequences were described by the *Reading Chronicle*:

> The rapid thaw, which followed the recent severe weather, produced the most serious floods experienced in the life of most people in the Thames Valley. All along the river, there are vast areas under water and thousands of people have been forced to live in the top rooms of their houses because the ground floor has been flooded – to a depth of several feet in some cases. From Saturday onwards, the River Thames at Reading has been several feet above normal, though not quite so high as in the record-breaking floods of 1894. The various tributaries have also overflowed their banks, to add to the devastation.

> Practically the whole of lower Caversham has been flooded; many roads are under water and people have had to be evacuated from their homes. At one time the area was threatened with isolation from the remainder of Reading but, fortunately, the level of the floods has not risen, as was feared, during the week …

> … The course of the river has completely disappeared in most parts of Reading district and in its place there is one gigantic stretch of turbulent water bounded on the south by the railway embankment and on the north by the Warren, South View Avenue and Lower Henley Road. De Montfort Island has completely disappeared, the tops of trees being the only indication of its position, while Caversham locks and the Clappers footpath are under water, the lock-keeper's house being approached by a bridge of barges.

> The seriousness of the position was brought home to the people of the town on Saturday, when broadcast instructions were given that all drinking water should be boiled before use … For several days the Fobney and Southcote waterworks has been isolated, the only method of approach being by boat, and the level of the water is now higher than that of the works. In spite of the fact that all available staff have been sandbagging the filter beds to keep out the flood water there has been no means to be sure that the flood water had not by-passed the filters …

> … Some thousands of families are confined to the upper floors of their houses and about two hundred people, mostly the aged and infirm or sick, have been evacuated either to relatives or friends, or to battle Hospital. Altogether 1,600 houses are affected by flood water … in some places the water lies in the ground floor rooms three feet deep.

115 *People are rescued from the floods during the winter of 1947.*

A service of lorries, and boats supplied by the Thames Conservancy, takes workers and shoppers from their flooded homes to a point where they can reach the public transport, and tickets enabling the holders to obtain hot meals at Civic restaurants are issued to residents in the flooded area. Members of the WVS have been touring the district supplying hot meals to those who are unable to leave their homes …

An enormous problem has been that of sanitation and refuse collections have been made twice daily in the Caversham area, while people in the district have been warned by loudspeakers of the danger of throwing refuse and dirty water into the floods because of the danger to health. Only by the strictest attention to cleanliness will disease be averted.

By considerable ingenuity and resourcefulness, the delivery of essential goods such as milk, groceries and bread has been kept going … Between Friday night and Monday morning the postal authorities found it impossible to deliver telegrams, parcels and letters in Lower Caversham, but on Monday morning an Assistant Inspector volunteered to attempt delivery. Driving a large van he succeeded, after several unsuccessful attempts, in delivering almost all his letters and telegrams, some of them having to be offered to the householders at the end of a long pole held by a postman in a punt.

These floods were by no means an unprecedented experience for the people of Reading. Those of 1894 were arguably even more severe than these and in

December 1929 the residents of the Great Knollys Street area awoke to find the ground floors of their houses 18 inches deep in water. Corporation dustcarts had to be used to ferry the local children to school that year.

Coronation

Even without the effects of flooding, the Reading of the early post-war years looked a shabby place. Hardly any money had been spent on its upkeep since the 1930s. Paint was peeling, rusting, disused tramlines still waited to trap unwary cyclists using the potholed roads and there was still the eyesore of the – mercifully few – bombsites, waiting to be redeveloped. The shops had relatively few goods to offer and rationing was still widespread. To meet the food shortages, allotments were popular (especially those where you were allowed to keep pigs) and those householders who had the space were encouraged to keep chickens. The shortage of coal was not so easy to overcome. The threat of another war still hung over peoples' heads; the Reading Battalion of the Home Guard was reformed in 1952 and the town was top of a national league table for civil defence, with 7.4 per thousand of its population enrolled in the organisation.

At the same time, the area was starting to develop its post-war economy, based on leading-edge technology. It had been announced in 1950 that the area was to get its own atomic energy establishment, on the former wartime bomber airfield at Aldermaston. The town was enjoying full employment and the perennial problem of difficulty in recruiting people in a number of occupations, including the railways, hospitals and in local government, was already being complained about. By 1955, it was claimed that there were 185 vacancies for every 100 people unemployed, and difficulty in recruitment was given as a major reason for Huntley and Palmer's eventual decision to relocate its activities to Huyton, near Liverpool.

Life was gradually getting back to normal; petrol rationing ended in 1950, and the growing traffic led to calls for improved traffic management. But what they actually meant by traffic management in those days was the removal of the pedestrian crossings that were an obstacle to the free flow of cars and the erection of railings along the pavements in Broad Street (still at that time an all-purpose road) to stop shoppers getting in the way of traffic. As the *Reading Chronicle* put it:

> One of the most important matters concerning the highways is to keep the traffic moving ... mobility is vital in this hurrying age ... it is equally obvious that the greater the number of crossings, the greater the congestion and delay. This is particularly noticeable in Broad Street, Reading on a busy morning. Each new advance in quickening the life of the community ... brings with it a parallel restriction of right and privilege. Those who find it necessary to cross the highways of busy towns must bow to the inevitable.
>
> (Hylton)

One eccentric on the council's Road Safety Committee came up with the bizarre idea of putting bumps in the road at danger points to slow the traffic down, but the suggestion was quickly dismissed as totally impracticable.

In these days of coal fires, before clean air legislation, Reading suffered from periodic winter smogs so severe that they brought traffic to a halt and threatened the lives and health of many in the town. The provisions of the 1956 Clean Air Act came into force two years after its enactment, and Reading submitted its first pilot scheme for a Smoke Control Area in Coley Park.

Immediately after the war, some 3,750 families in Reading were listed as homeless. Housing was in short supply; so much so that, in the space of four days in 1946, 80 homeless families took over the Ranikhet Army Camp in Tilehurst as squatters. Only a small minority could afford the price of owner occupation (£1,000 for a terrace in West Reading, £2,150 for a typical semi-detached house in Earley or Lower Caversham, through to £4,000 for a four-bedroom house in Emmer Green). The council was just starting to make inroads into the backlog of need for rented accommodation; Reading's 1,000th post-war house was handed over to its occupants in July 1950 and the first post-war flats – at Gosbrook Road in Caversham – were completed in February 1953. The Southcote estate was emerging from a 150-acre site along the Bath Road, and attempts were being made to secure the Coley Park area for housing, but there were still over 4,000 families on the council waiting list at the start of the 1950s. Large parts of the area between Prospect Park and Kentwood Hill were being eyed up by private developers, and Woodley and Earley were already growing fast. To add to the influx, plans were announced in 1953 to relocate 5,000 overspill Londoners 'to the Wokingham area' (which may have been the government's way of describing Bracknell). By 1957, a high-rise solution to the housing shortage was being sought, with proposals to build 15-storey blocks of flats on the Coley Park estate. Many of those who were housed were living without basic amenities and for those without bathrooms the council would open the Jesse Terrace Slipper Baths in May 1954. Despite all this activity, the number of households on the housing waiting list was almost exactly the same in 1959 – 3,700 – as it had been when the war ended.

The appearance of the town centre would have been unfamiliar in many ways to modern eyes. Of the town's four department stores in 1953, Bulls was already closing, McIlroys would be gone within two years, Heelas was in the process of being swallowed up by the John Lewis organisation and Wellsteeds would eventually be taken over by Debenhams. Broad Street could still boast a coaching inn (the *Angel*), a cinema (the Gaumont, originally built as the Vaudeville in 1909 – one of nine cinemas in the town in the 1950s) and tea-shops (the Cadena Café and Lyons). The town also had two theatres – the Everyman (closed 1957) and the Palace (which went in 1960) – and three ballrooms, of which the Majestic claimed to be the most luxurious, offering roller skating nights and 'no jiving on Wednesdays'.

But signs of change were beginning to appear, in the form of the town's first coffee bar (the Palermo in Duke Street), burger bar (the Wimpy on West Street) and supermarket (in the former McIlroy's premises on Oxford Road). Reading was still a low-rise town, though the development plan published by the council in 1953 looked forward to the era of much higher buildings. The first of these to materialise – Reading Bridge House – was not completed until 1963.

1957 saw the latest in a long line of claims to have discovered the solid silver coffin in which Henry I had allegedly been buried in Reading Abbey. This time it was a retired major from Hove who based his claims on investigations with an American electronic gadget. He was denied permission to excavate the site of this ancient monument to prove his claim. The same year also saw the closure of the abbey mills, some 800 years after the monks first harnessed the waters of the Holy Brook to grind corn.

The town – and the nation – needed cheering up, and the Coronation of a young new Queen seemed just the opportunity for doing so. The town also had another reason to celebrate, since July 1953 was the 700th anniversary of Reading's first Royal Charter, granted by Henry III. The council set out to plan a programme of events (mostly ones that would not cost too much, as they were cash-strapped) and they came up with: the floodlighting of key public buildings, concerts, athletics and water sports, dances, a funfair in Hills Meadow, fireworks and a procession. A souvenir teaspoon was to be struck for every primary school child and a £1,000 Queen Elizabeth II Coronation prize fund was set up for which secondary school pupils could compete. A best-decorated street competition was organised and a commemorative tree was planted in the Forbury Gardens.

This Coronation would be remembered as the one that led to a boom in television ownership and many Reading people, rather than brave the bad weather at the outdoor events on the day, found someone with a set and a spare seat for them. In 1946, when the television service resumed, just 46 Reading households held licences. By 1953, the number had grown to around seven thousand, though televisions were still a luxury item, costing around £50 at a time when the starting salary for a scientific assistant at Aldermaston with four G.C.E.s was just £176 a year. For those elderly people without sets, Reading Rotary Club organised massed viewing on sets installed in the town hall. It was said that a thousand people saw the Coronation by this means, though how they all got to see it on the small screens of the day is difficult to imagine. Thereafter, the ownership of televisions spread like wildfire and, by 1955, television audiences began to outstrip those for radio programmes. Three years later and 26,777 Reading households had television sets (or at least had television licences).

April 1954 saw one of the town's greatest post-war tragedies. Fire broke out at the Dellwood Nursery Home, where 15 infants, the youngest a day old, were asleep in the main ward. Thanks to the courage of the nursing staff, some of whom suffered serious burns, most of the babies were got out alive, but many had suffered smoke inhalation and a total of 13 died.

The cult of violence that had for so long been an unwelcome element of the Reading man's leisure activity found a new form of expression. Young men

116   *Newtown crowns its own Coronation Queen in 1953.*

117   *The tiny victims of the Dellwood fire are laid to rest in 1954.*

'dressed in the Edwardian style' (or as we would say, Teddy Boys) took to gathering outside dance-halls like the Olympia and picking fights with servicemen or anyone else who was interested. On one occasion in 1954 this escalated into a near riot, with an estimated 500 people taking part. They extended their repertoire to seat slashing in cinemas and the film featuring the first great rock and roll hit *Rock Around the Clock* was banned throughout Berkshire. The Chief Constable of Reading, speaking at a school speech day, advised that the best thing to do with teddy boys was to ignore them, while groups of evangelists went into the town centre with their soap boxes on Saturday nights in an effort to convert them to Christianity.

The ownership of the Kennet and Avon Canal passed to British Transport Waterways in 1955, following the nationalisation of the railways (it had been owned by the Great Western Railway since 1852). That same year, a parliamentary bill sought to abandon the now largely derelict canal. This in turn led to the formation of the Kennet and Avon Canal Association. As long ago as 1906, the amount of commercial traffic using the Reading end of the canal was estimated to have fallen below one boat a day, but people were still arguing for its preservation for business rather than leisure use. Claims were made that a restored canal would attract 100,000, 200,000 or even a million tons of goods traffic a year, all for a cost (£320,000) that was said to be about equivalent to a mile and a half of new trunk road. A canoe was sent to paddle the length of the canal for publicity purposes (this being the only craft that could now navigate it, and even this had to be carried for two miles of its length). As they proceeded, they gathered signatures on a petition for its preservation, which had swelled to 21,000 names by the time they reached the Houses of Parliament.

Despite the problems encountered by the canoe, a flotilla of cabin cruisers attempted the following year to navigate the canal, as a further means of drawing attention to its condition. The last pleasure boat to have successfully made the journey was thought to have been in 1951 (and that with a good deal of help) and, 20 years before that, one user suggested that it 'might have been deliberately laid out to create the maximum difficulty for the navigator'. Departing from Reading, the flotilla got precisely five miles before coming up against the impenetrable dereliction that was Burghfield Lock. Parliament refused to allow the closure of the canal, but a Committee of Inquiry into British Inland

118 *Leisure craft make a vain attempt to navigate the derelict Kennet and Avon Canal during the early 1950s.*

119 *Anti Nuclear demonstrators pass through Reading in about 1960, on their protest march between the Atomic Weapons Research Establishment at Aldermaston and Trafalgar Square.*

Waterways in 1958 ruled that there was no case for reopening it for commercial traffic. Any case for its survival would have to be based on its amenity and leisure value. After a long campaign and much hard work by the conservationists, the canal was reopened by the Queen in August 1990.

Still on a water-related topic, another ancient Reading (or rather Caversham) landmark disappeared in 1956. For 300 years the firm of Freebody had built boats on a site next to Caversham Bridge, but now its 72-year-old owner announced its closure.

In the 1930s, marchers through Reading tended to be unemployed workers, delivering their petitions to Parliament. By the 1950s, and for many Easter weekends afterwards, it was nuclear disarmament demonstrators, going between the atomic weapons establishment at Aldermaston and Trafalgar Square. The 1958 march numbered only about a thousand, some of whom were put up in private homes, but most of whom slept in local schools. Within a couple of years, the numbers of marchers were exceeding 10,000 and a dozen schools were needed to house them.

The 1960s and Beyond

By the start of the 1960s, the face of modern Reading was beginning to emerge. The Palace Theatre in Cheapside, a fine example of the Edwardian music hall, had been going downhill for years, a victim of competition from the cinemas and television. Despite attempts to diversify, it finally closed its doors in 1960 and was redeveloped the following year. At about the same time, Reading's first high-rise office building, the 10-storey Reading Bridge House, was making its appearance. Although it replaced a long-standing eyesore on this prominent riverside site – an ironworks – critics feared it would add to local traffic congestion. Another piece of Reading's history – albeit a dilapidated one – was disappearing from Hosier Street. Finches Court dated back to the late 16th or early 17th century, incorporated stones reclaimed from Reading Abbey, and it was claimed that Lady Vachell, the daughter of Sir Francis Knollys and wife of John Hampden (see chapter five), watched the progress of the Civil War siege of Reading from its roof.

The ethnic mix of the town was also starting to change. An estimate in 1956 put the West Indian population of the town at just 250, but their numbers were forecast to double within the year. The Asian population was also beginning to increase rapidly. By 1968, the number of non-English speaking school pupils was large enough for the council to set up a special reception unit for them in the Alfred Sutton Boys' School.

Retailing habits were also being transformed. If the 1900s were the heyday of the department store, then this was the age of the mall. 1968 saw the departure of Baylis' supermarket from its prime site at the junction of Broad Street and St Mary's Butts. They said it was partly due to the lack of car parking in the town centre and that, in future, they would concentrate on more suburban locations for food shopping. As they left the town centre, across the road from their premises a very different retail experience was coming out of the ground. The original idea of the Butts Centre (now known as the Broad Street Mall) had been conceived in 1959, and the council had compulsorily purchased the four-acre site in 1964. The Broad Street Mall opened in 1972, providing large quantities of town centre car parking and, two years later, the rival Friars Walk mall opened on the north side of Friar Street. The prototype of all of Reading's shopping malls – J.C. Fidler's Market Arcade, dating from the 1890s, had been largely destroyed during the war and was replaced between 1957 and 1965. Meanwhile down at Chatham Street, a thousand-space multi-storey car park – at the time, one of the largest and most advanced in the country – was opening.

The downside of all this modernisation was the wholesale destruction of Reading's architectural heritage. At one time, it was said that one listed building a week was being demolished, somewhere in the town. This led to a protest movement and, in 1961, to the formation of the Reading Civic Society. As a result, many important buildings were saved, including the old town hall and what remained of Market Place after the vandalism of the 1960s.

It was by now emphatically the age of the car and traffic congestion was a major problem, with long-distance east-west traffic still having to come along the A4 through the centre of the town. During peak holiday periods, the traffic jams could stretch from the Wee Waif in Twyford in one direction to Theale in the other, and motorists could take an hour and a half to get through the town.

120   *Broad Street during the University Rag Day celebrations of 1963, showing an extreme example of the uncomfortable relationship between people and traffic existing in the street at that time.*

Proposals to address this problem first saw the light of day in 1958, but relief was a long time coming. The original scheme took the road to the north of Reading, crossing the Thames twice and carving a swathe through the Berkshire Downs. But by 1965 a combination of environmental protests and traffic considerations led to it being rerouted to the south of the town.

What locals saw as the Reading by-pass and the authorities originally called the 'London–South Wales Motor Road', finally became the M4 motorway and carried its first traffic in 1971. Its opening saw a reduction of 60 per cent in the traffic on some of the town's roads. At about the same time, the town made its first faltering attempts to tame the car, removing non-essential traffic from Broad Street, though it would still remain the town's central bus depot – and thus a dangerous and unpleasant place for pedestrians – for many years to come. Traffic on other roads was eased by the opening in 1969 of the first phase of the inner distribution road between Caversham Road and Castle Street. For many years the scheme ended with the ski-jump that was supposed to be the Southampton Street flyover, until construction was completed in the 1980s.

The Reading Rock Festival has been part of the town's life for over 30 years and has made the town internationally famous in circles where it might otherwise have remained unknown. It started life as a jazz festival in Richmond in 1961 and, after a brief sojourn at Windsor Race Course, came to Reading a decade later. It was not universally welcomed; the local press questioned the public order implications of holding it, and incandescent local residents warned of the legions of 'layabouts, anarchists, drug-pushers, sexual perverts and other trouble-makers' it would attract. The arrangements for the first festival now seem quaintly amateurish, with just a 3ft perimeter fence with 200 guards along it to keep trespassers out, and weekend tickets costing a modest £2. The first year it poured with rain and the revellers were up to their knees in mud. The Police were taking no chances, and the 550 officers present took 144 fans to a specially convened court, sitting throughout the weekend. Predictably, there were complaints of heavy-handed policing. Local traders, who saw their takings go through the roof, suddenly learned to welcome the idea, and the festival has now become an established, if not universally loved, part of the town's life, one that transforms its appearance over the August Bank Holiday weekend.

1974 saw at least the temporary end of centuries of self-contained local government for Reading, when local government review saw a number of the borough council's powers being handed over to Berkshire County Council. Forecasts that this would affect local people for a century to come proved to be wide of the mark; Berkshire County Council was itself abolished in 1998 and Reading Borough Council's lost powers were restored to it. One thing that did not change was the borough's local government boundaries.

The 1970s saw the three B's, the industries that had been the bedrock of the town's economic growth in the 19th century and beyond, start to sever their links with Reading. For a time, it had looked as if the seed firm Suttons were going to strengthen, rather than break, their association with Reading. In 1961 they announced plans to build the country's most modern seed establishment on four acres of their trial grounds at London Road. But, by 1974, news came that they were to leave the town entirely for Torquay. One of the reasons they gave for the move was the encroachment of the soon-to-be-completed A329(M) motorway link onto their trial grounds. But more major considerations were the greater ease of recruiting the casual labour they needed in Torquay and the fact that their trial grounds, now linked to the M4 motorway, had now become hugely valuable for industrial development. Six hundred jobs were lost to Reading by the move, though the industrial park that replaced it helped offset the losses.

The second of the town's core industries to leave was the biscuit-maker, Huntley and Palmer. In 1955, the company built an automated biscuit-making factory at Huyton, near Liverpool. Many assumed that the Reading factory would be similarly automated but, in the early 1970s, it was announced that all production was to be concentrated in the North-West. The Reading factory baked its last biscuit in 1977, ending a tradition going back 150 years. The administrative offices of the company remained on the Kings Road for a few years after this.

The last 'B' – Simonds' Brewery – was the longest-established of the three, dating back to 1790. Courage took it over in 1960, and itself became part of the Imperial Tobacco Group in 1972. In the following year they announced plans to redevelop their site in Reading's town centre and the prospect of the town losing another 1,100 jobs seemed imminent. But then the option was raised of developing the new brewery on a 70-acre site at Worton Grange to the south of the town and close to the M4. It would become one of the biggest in Europe, producing 1.5 million barrels a year, and the old Bridge Street premises produced their last ale in 1980.

By the latter part of the 1980s, Reading town centre faced a serious challenge. Encouraged by the then government looking favourably on such schemes, developers came forward with proposals for a major out-of-town shopping centre at Great Lea, just south of the M4 at junction 11. It would have had a seriously damaging effect on the central shopping area. The Great Lea proposals eventually came to nothing, but they gave the town the warning it needed. The response was the transformation of the town centre seen in recent years.

Although general traffic had been removed from Broad Street some years previously, it still remained the town's main bus interchange, and was a dangerous and unpleasant place for the large numbers of shoppers using the town centre. Plans were drawn up for a phased pedestrianisation of Broad Street and Queen Victoria Street. They were controversial at the time, not least for the impact it was claimed they would have on the bus services, but the town could not have accommodated the growth in retail trade that it has seen in recent years without pedestrianisation. The second, less visible, development was the introduction of town centre management. Reading became one of the first towns in the country to appoint a town centre manager and move towards the kind of integrated management seen in out-of-town shopping developments.

But the most dramatic transformation of the town centre took place on the banks of the Kennet. We left the story of the Oracle in the mid-19th century, as the cleared site was being bought back from Christ's Hospital by the Corporation. It later became part of the Simonds brewery that occupied the Bridge Street site until 1980. What little was left of the Oracle itself next saw the light of day in August 1997, when archaeologists excavated the remaining foundations as the site was being prepared for a new shopping and leisure centre.

The new centre took its name from the old workhouse, but where had the original name come from? The first mention of it appears in 1649, some years after the workhouse opened. Many suggestions have been made. One was that the name was a corruption of the words 'work hall'. Another was that it derives from orchal or oricello, a yellow dye from Orchal in the Canary Islands used in the cloth industry. A third explanation is that it refers to an oriel, an architectural feature in the form of a recess built out at upper-storey level. The Fox-Talbot photograph of the entrance shows something like an oriel above the door. It could be a reference to an oracle itself. This was a place where the gods were supposed to speak to mortals – the Greeks and Egyptians had them at Delphi and Thebes. The term was not always used respectfully – one usage of the word implied manoeuvring behind the scenes that enabled you to obtain whatever response you required. So maybe it was an early satirical reference, now lost in the mists of time, to the Corporation's mismanagement of Kendrick's ill-fated bequest?

After being vacated by the brewery, the site was originally earmarked for office development, but the planning permission was never taken up. Plans for a shopping centre on the site were first put forward in 1989, but they were very different to the Oracle as it finally materialised. They included housing, a supermarket and a floating restaurant. These plans were abandoned during a recession in the 1990s and were later replaced by the present scheme. The 22-acre, £250 million development was opened in September 1999. Extra police had to be drafted in to prevent gridlock, as it was forecast that a quarter of a million people would visit the centre in the first three days. The Oracle helped to propel Reading into the top 10 shopping locations in the country, and the centre itself won an award as European shopping centre of the year.

One of the features of the development was that it brought this important stretch of riverside back into public use. The council had sold it off to the brewery a century before. Over a long period, the town had turned its back on its waterways, taking away public access and lining many stretches of the river banks with unsightly industrial uses. But, for the last quarter of a century and more, the council has pursued a steady policy of reversing this process, and has achieved a transformation in areas such as this and on the south bank of the Thames, between the bridges.

The process of transforming the town centre continues. As this is being written, the Chatham Street area is undergoing large-scale redevelopment, there are controversial plans in preparation to turn the inner distribution road into a one-way system and plans are also being made to reconfigure the central railway station. The station is currently one of the most serious bottlenecks on the national rail network, and the revised layout will create the potential for many more rail services to and from Reading. Large parts of the town centre adjoining the station are planned to be redeveloped in conjunction with it.

The Past and the Future

Reading is presently in the seventh year of the new millennium. What does the town's past tell us about its future prospects? First, we have seen that, from its very earliest days, the town's position as a centre of communications has been vital to its prospects, both in a negative way (such as the unwelcome occupations by the 10th-century Danes and by both sides in the Civil War) and in a positive one (such as the way they brought business to the town and helped the town's 19th-century industries to grow). In relation to that, we have seen how historic developments in transport (such as the canals and the railways) have been feared and resisted by important interests within the town. But their predictions of the doom and gloom that would follow from these innovations have proved to be false, and have led to a step-change in the town's prosperity.

In recent years, the two biggest transport issues for Reading have been trying to cope with the phenomenal growth in the ownership and use of the car, and the impact on our economy of the equally dramatic growth in air travel. Both have benefited the town, which is on the M4 motorway and close to the world's busiest international airport, Heathrow. But today the issue is not (as in the 18th or 19th century) whether some new innovation in transport poses a threat or the promise of new prosperity. Rather, the problem is that we have been living for the past 30 years or so off the back of investments made in the 1960s and 1970s (such as the building of the motorway and the last major upgrade of the Great Western railway line). The scope for continuing to do so looks very limited. The forecasts are that, over the next 20 years, if nothing else changes, the motorway and other key roads will go from being at, or slightly above, capacity, to being hugely overloaded. At current levels of investment the railways, already overloaded in peak hours, will not be able to accommodate the large numbers of people being forced off the roads by congestion. There is no consensus about how the problem should be addressed, even if the necessary money were available. One camp says we should go with the flow of human desires and expand the road network to permit more journeys by car. The other looks at the problem of global warming and the more local consequences of air pollution, and says we have to change people's habits – getting them to make fewer journeys, and more of these by means other than the private car.

No magic new transport solutions are waiting in the wings. The boom in personal helicopter travel, forecast after the war, still looks as much of a science fiction dream as it ever did! The answer may therefore lie in a mixture of making the roads and railways we have got work more efficiently (just as they did, say, with the Kennet and Avon Canal in the 18th century), some building of new capacity (road-widening, or the removal of bottlenecks on the rail network, such as the current Reading station, though the number of schemes like these is likely to be limited by their cost) and some radical changing of our travelling habits.

But the very existence of an efficient road and rail network in the area has created a new problem for us. It is that Reading is no longer a self-contained centre for business, as it has been in the past. It is now just one – albeit the most important – centre in a very complex multi-centred Thames Valley. The labour force has, over the last 30 years or more, relied upon this good network of communications to develop hugely complicated patterns of (mainly car-borne) commuting across the area. People change jobs much more often than they change houses and rely on being able to commute in this way. As the roads and trains fill up, these journeys become ever-more time consuming and more difficult. But, unlike a simple pattern of commuting where, for example, everyone heads off to London in the morning and comes back in the evening, such a multitude of different trips is almost impossible to replicate with good-quality high-capacity public transport.

Another problem that affects Reading today, but has also beset the town in the past, is labour shortages. As we saw, there were periods in the 1950s when Reading had 185 job vacancies for every 100 unemployed workers. Some economic forecasts see us heading towards an equally serious shortage of skilled labour over the next 20 years. In the 1950s, one of the responses to the problem was to allow a much higher rate of housebuilding to expand the workforce. Some would argue for a similar response today, but others believe the pressures this would bring to bear on local services and infrastructure would be intolerable. Many of the latter would favour the approach known as 'smart growth' – that is, trying to grow the economy through increased productivity without having to take more land for offices and factories, without having to draw in additional population as a means of swelling the local labour force and without overwhelming the area's transport. But the potential for this depends upon a whole series of unknowns, such as:

- How far can we use relatively cheap investment in new technology to make expensive human beings more efficient?
- How successful will be in getting those local people who are not currently working into the labour market and in getting employers to take them on?
- To what extent can we find new ways of working, to avoid people having to join the ever-longer queues of commuters sitting in traffic jams or standing in overcrowded trains and buses?

One threat that is presented as a new phenomenon is globalisation, and the threat it poses of local jobs being exported to where labour costs are cheaper. But this is no more than a global version of something that has been going on throughout Reading's history, from the loss of the woollen cloth industry in the 17th century to the decision to decant Huntley and Palmer's biscuit manufacturing to Liverpool in the 1950s and Suttons to Torquay in the 1970s. If we learn anything from this aspect of the town's history, it should be to avoid complacency. The Elizabethan clothiers and 1950s workers at Huntley and Palmer may well have thought their long-established businesses were immune to competition, just as world-leading businesses in other parts of Britain thought they were invulnerable. In this respect, the information technology sector on which the town is now heavily dependent is no different from the mining, steel-making or the making of ships or cars, on which other communities across Britain have relied in the past. Reading's jobs could disappear just as easily to competitors who are cheaper or more efficient. The Reading citizens of the future will need all the vision and determination shown by the best of their forebears if they are to continue to prosper in an increasingly competitive world.

BIBLIOGRAPHY

Aburrow, F. Leslie, *St. Mary's Thousand Years 979 – 1979* (1988)

Adams, William (ed.), *Encyclopedia of the Great Western Railway* (1993)

Alexander, Alan, *Borough Government and Politics: Reading 1835-1985* (1985)

Allsop, Niall, The Kennet and Avon Canal (1987)

Aspinall, A., Dodwell, B., Lambert, M.D., Slade, C.F., and Smith E.A., *Parliament through Seven centuries – Reading and its M.P.s* (1962)

Babbage, Terry, *Tylehurst Described* (1976)

Barres-Baker, M.C., *The siege of Reading, April 1843*

Beckinsdale, R.P., *Companion into Berkshire* (1972)

Beecroft, Joseph A., *A Handy Guide to Reading* (1882)

Betjeman, John and Piper, John, *Murray's Architectural Guide (Berkshire)* (1949)

Bray, R.S., *Reading's Forgotten Children – The Start of Schooling in the Town* (2003)

Brooks, Robin J., *Thames Valley Airfields in the Second World War* (2000)

Burton, K.G., *The Early Newspaper Press in Berkshire*,(1954)

Cameron, Kenneth, *English Place Names* (1961)

Childs, W.M., *The Town of Reading During the Early Part of the Nineteenth Century* (1910)

Childs, W.M., *Making a University* (1933)

Clew, Kenneth R., *The Kennet and Avon Canal* (1968)

Coates, Charles, *The History and Antiquities of Reading* (1802)

Cooper, Mike, *The Wyvern and the Raven* (1984)

Corley, T.A.B., *Quaker Enterprise in Biscuits* (1972)

Corley, T.A.B., *The Road to Worton Grange: Simond's and Courage's Brewery at Reading 1785 – 1980* (1980)

Cunliffe, Barry, *Wessex to AD 1000* (1993)

Darter, William Silver, *Reminiscences of Reading by an Octogenarian* (1888)

Dils, Joan (ed.), *Reading Turnpikes* (1977)

Ditchfield, P.H. (ed.), *Reading Seventy Years Ago – A Record of Events from 1813 – 1819* (1887)

Dormer, Ernest W., *John Kendrick of Reading* (1927)

Downs, David, *Biscuits and Royals: A History of Reading Football Club* (1984)

Dowsett, G.R., *The Municipal and Parish Church of St. Laurence in Reading* (1933)

Gaute, J.H.H. and Odell, Robin, *Ladykillers* (1980)

Griffin, Sarah, *The Siege of Reading* (1996)

Guilding, J.M., *Notable Events in the Municipal History of Reading* (1895)

Hall, David, *Reading Trolley Buses* (1997)

Harper, Charles G., *The Bath Road* (1899)

Helps, Douglas A., *The Reading Gas Company – A Retrospect* (1912)

Hinton, Michael, *A History of the Town of Reading* (1954)

Homer-Wooff, G.H.R. and Jones, Peter J., *The Postal History of Reading* (Two
   volumes, 1981, 1982)

Howard, John, *The State of the Prisons in England and Wales* (1777)

Humphreys, A.L., *Caversham Bridge 1231 – 1926* (1926)

Hurry, Jamieson B., *The Rise and Fall of Reading Abbey* (1906)

Hylton, Stuart, *Reading Places, Reading People* (1992)

Hylton, Stuart, Reading, *A Pictorial History* (1994)

Hylton, Stuart, *Reading at War* (1996)

Hylton, Stuart, *Reading: The 1950s* (1997)

Hylton, Stuart, *A Reading Century* (1999)

Hylton, Stuart, *Reading Past and Present* (2000)

Hylton, Stuart, *A History of Manchester* (2003)

Hylton, Stuart, *The Grand Experiment* (2007)

Jackson, Robert, *Dark Age Britain* (1984)

Jordan, Edgar, *Reading Tramways* (1996)

Jordan, H.E., *The Tramways of Reading* (1957)

Kean, O., *A Brief History of the Development of Reading Waterworks* (1950)

Kift, Mary, *Life in Old Caversham* (1980)

KIND, *A Brief History of the Reading British School* (2000)

Lassam, Robert, *Fox-Talbot – Photographer* (1979)

Leaver, Revd Robin A., *A Short History of St Mary's Chapel, Castle Street, Reading*
   (1973)

Long, Roger, *Ancient Berkshire Inns and their Stories* (1996)

Longmate, Norman, *The Workhouse* (1974)

MacDermott, E.T., *The history of the Great Western Railway (Volume 1)* (1927, 1964)

Maggs, Colin G., *Great Western Railways Principal Stations* (1987)

Malpas, John, *Caversham Park and its Owners* (1997)

Man, John, *The Stranger in Reading* (1810, republished 2005)

Mathers, S.J. and Smith, N.J.P., *The Geology of the Reading District* (2000)

McIntyre, Martin, *The Royal Berkshire Regiment 1914 – 1959* (2005)

Morgan, Kenneth O. (ed.) *The Oxford History of Britain* (1999)

Myatt, Frederick, *The Royal Berkshire Regiment* (1968)

Naxton, Michael, *The History of Reading School* (1986)

North, Leslie, *Royal Reading's Colourful Past* (1979)

Paget-Tomlinson, Edward, *The Illustrated History of Canal and River Navigations*
   (1993)

Pearman, M.T., *Historical Notices of Caversham* (1894)

Petre, F. Loraine, *The Royal Berkshire Regiment Volume II – 1914-1918* (1925)

Petyt, Malcolm (ed.), *The Growth of Reading* (1993)

Phillips, Daphne, *How the Great Western Came to Berkshire* (1975)

Phillips, Daphne, *Coronation Reading* (1977)

Phillips, Daphne, *The Story of Reading* (1980, 1999)

Phillips, Daphne, *The Great Road to Bath* (1983)

Phillips, Geoffrey, *Thames Crossings* (1981)

Platt, Colin, *Mediaeval England* (1978)

Railton, Margaret and Barr, Marshall, *The Royal Berkshire Hospital 1839 – 1989* (1989)

Railton, Margaret and Barr, Marshall, *Battle Workhouse and Hospital 1867 – 2005* (2005)

Read, Sue, *Reading in the News* (1998)

Reading Corporation, *Charters of the Borough of Reading 1253 – 1953* (1953)

Reading Museum and Art Gallery, *Reading Abbey* (1988)

Reading University Extra-Mural Department, *Redding 1540 – 1640* (1980)

Room, Adrian, *The Street Names of England* (1992)

Slade, Cecil, *The Town of Reading and its Abbey* (2001)

Southerton, Peter, *Reading Gaol by Reading Town* (1993)

Spriggs, F. Gordon, *History of the Church of Greyfriars of Reading* (1963)

University of London Institute of Historical Research, *The Victoria History of the County of Berkshire* (volumes, 1906 – 1924)

Verey, Anthony, Sampson, Stuart, French, Andrew and Frost, Simon, *The Berkshire Yeomanry* (1994)

Waters, Laurence, *Rail Centres, Reading* (1990)

Wilson, Patrick, *Murderess* (1971)

Wood, Peter, *Poverty and the Workhouse in Victorian Britain* (1991)

Wykes, Alan, *The Queen's Peace – A History of the Reading Borough Police 1836 – 1968* (1968)

Articles

Brossler, Adam, Early, Robert and Allen, Carol, 'Green Park Phase II Excavations 1995 – Neolithic and Bronze Age Sites', *Oxford Archaeology* (2004)

Burton, K.G., 'A Reception Town in War and Peace – Some Aspects of Life in Reading 1938 – 50', *Planning Outlook*, vol.3 no.3

Childs, W.M., 'Notes on the town of Reading in the seventeenth century', *Reading University College Review*, vol.7 no.19 (1914)

Dils, Joan A., 'A suburban trio – Earley, Tilehurst and Caversham 1851 – 1911', *Berkshire Old and New*, vol.17 (2000)

Fellgett, Mary, 'Daily and Domestic Life in seventeenth century Reading', *Berkshire Old and New*, vol.3 (1986)

Goose, N.R., 'Decay and regeneration in seventeenth century Reading', *Southern History*, vol.6 (1984).

Hodder, T.K., 'Suttons in Reading', *Journal of the Royal Horticultural Society*, vol.81 no.5 (1956)

Hunter, Judith and Rip, 'The Press Gang during the Seven Years' War 1756 – 1763', *Berkshire Old and New*, vol.20 (2003)

Nixon, John, 'The Gentlemen Danes – the story of Danish/ Norwegian prisoners of war in Reading 1807 – 14', *Berkshire Old and New*, vol.11 (1994)

Preston, Arthur E., 'The demolition of Reading Abbey', *Berkshire Archaeological Journal*, vol.39 no.2 (1935)

Scott, W.J., 'Reading new station – Great Western Railway', *Railway* magazine, (1899)

Smart, Patricia, 'Reading Cemetery: a private enterprise', *Berkshire Old and New*, vol.5, (1988)

Newspapers and Primary Sources

Berkshire Chronicle
Great Western Railway magazine, vol.47 No.9 (1935)
Petition opposing the incorporation of Caversham into Reading – submitted to the
    House of Commons (1910)
Reading Chronicle
Reading Mercury
Reading Official Town Guide 1947

Other Sources

Reading Borough Council – Reading's literary heritage
Reading Chamber of Commerce – Friends of the wounded
Rixon, Peter, 'The town of Reading c.1200 – 1542' (Unpublished Ph.D. thesis, 1998)
Suttons seeds – Suttons at Reading

Index

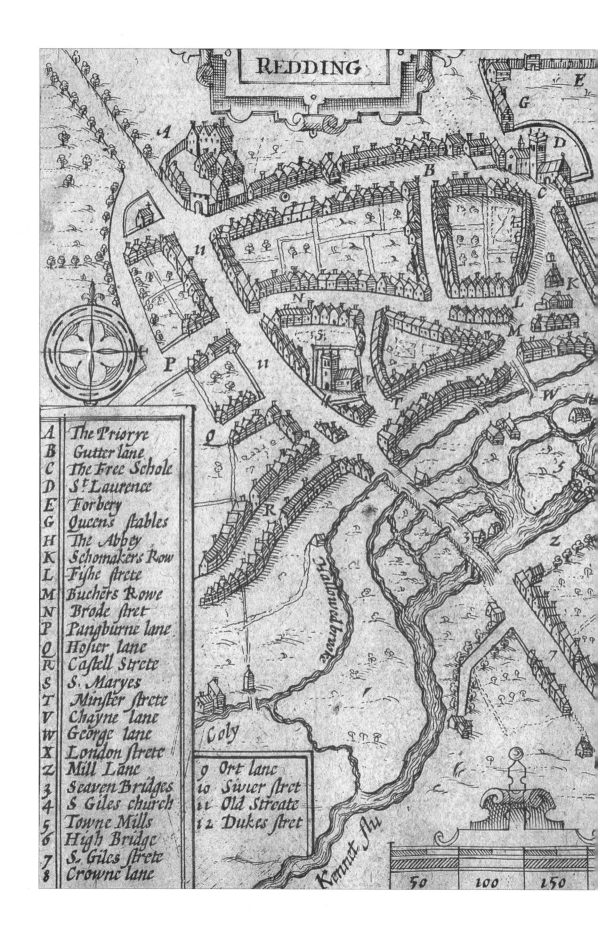

REDDING

A	The Priorye
B	Gutter lane
C	The Free Schole
D	S.t Laurence
E	Forbery
G	Queens stables
H	The Abbey
K	Schomakers Row
L	Fyshe strete
M	Buchers Rowe
N	Brode stret
P	Pangburne lane
Q	Hosier lane
R	Castell Strete
S	S. Maryes
T	Minster strete
V	Chayne lane
W	George lane
X	London strete
Z	Mill Lane
3	Seaven Bridges
4	S. Giles church
5	Towne Mills
6	High Bridge
7	S. Giles strete
8	Crowne lane

9	Ort lane
10	Sivier stret
11	Old Streate
12	Dukes stret

Coly

Kennet flu

50   100   150